Likud Leaders

ALSO BY THOMAS G. MITCHELL
AND McFARLAND

Israel's Security Men: The Arab-Fighting Political Careers of Moshe Dayan, Yitzhak Rabin, Ariel Sharon and Ehud Barak (2015)

Israel/Palestine and the Politics of a Two-State Solution (2013)

When Peace Fails: Lessons from Belfast for the Middle East (2010)

Likud Leaders

The Lives and Careers of
Menahem Begin, Yitzhak Shamir,
Benjamin Netanyahu and Ariel Sharon

THOMAS G. MITCHELL

McFarland & Company, Inc., Publishers
Jefferson, North Carolina

LIBRARY OF CONGRESS CATALOGUING-IN-PUBLICATION DATA

Mitchell, Thomas G., 1957– author.
    Likud leaders : the lives and careers of Menahem Begin, Yitzhak Shamir, Benjamin Netanyahu, and Ariel Sharon / Thomas G. Mitchell.
        p.   cm.
    Includes bibliographical references and index.

    ISBN 978-0-7864-9713-3 (softcover : acid free paper) ∞
    ISBN 978-1-4766-1985-9 (ebook)

    1. Likud (Political party : Israel) 2. Statesmen—Israel—Biography.
    3. Prime ministers—Israel—Biography. 4. Israel—History. I. Title.
JQ1830.A98L55566 2015
956.9405′40922—dc23   2015000541

BRITISH LIBRARY CATALOGUING DATA ARE AVAILABLE

© 2015 Thomas G. Mitchell. All rights reserved

No part of this book may be reproduced or transmitted in any form or by any means, electronic or mechanical, including photocopying or recording, or by any information storage and retrieval system, without permission in writing from the publisher.

On the cover: *from top left clockwise* Menahem Begin, 1974 (Milner Moshe/Israel National Photo Collection/Government Press Office); Yitzhak Shamir, 1988 (Harnik Nati/Israel National Photo Collection/Government Press Office); Ariel Sharon, 2001, and Benjamin Netanyahu, 2011 (Israel Department of Defense)

Printed in the United States of America

McFarland & Company, Inc., Publishers
  Box 611, Jefferson, North Carolina 28640
    www.mcfarlandpub.com

Table of Contents

Preface and Acknowledgments 1

One. The Founder—Vladimir "Zeev" Jabotinsky— and the Creation of Revisionist Zionism 5

Two. Menahem Begin, Underground Commander 26

Three. A Party Is Born and Grows: From Herut to the Likud 48

Four. Begin in Power, 1977–1983 60

Five. Yitzhak Shamir's Preparation 84

Six. Prime Minister Shamir: The Great Procrastinator 105

Seven. Sharon: A General for the Likud 124

Eight. Netanyahu: King of the Princes 147

Nine. "You will get him as prime minister": Sharon as Prime Minister 168

Ten. Bibi Melekh Israel (King of Israel) 185

Eleven. The Future of the Likud 200

Chapter Notes 207

Bibliography 219

Index 223

Preface and Acknowledgments

I decided to write this book for a number of reasons. First, even though I am no longer financially able to write full-time, I am unable to give up the intellectual stimulation of research and writing. Second, in 2013 my book *Israel/Palestine and the Politics of a Two-State Solution* was published with a chapter on the history and ideology of the Revisionist Zionist movement. I wanted to do a proper job of addressing the subject as the Likud Party has been the dominant party in Israeli politics since 2001 and one of two important parties since its creation in 1973. Other books have been written on both Revisionist Zionism and the Likud, most notably Colin Shindler's *The Land Beyond Promise,* published originally in 1995 with a new paperback edition in 2002. But it focuses on the organizational aspects of the party as a party. I want to focus on how the party's Arab policy—that is, its policy on the Arab question of the territories and what form a final settlement with the Palestinians will take—has changed from one leader to the next.

I intend to frame that enquiry in the form of a series of minibiographies of the ideological founder of Revisionist Zionism, Vladimir Ze'ev Jabotinsky, and the four leaders of the Likud Party to date: Menahem Begin, Yitzhak Shamir, Benjamin Netanyahu, and Ariel Sharon. This is the format I used for my previous book on military politicians in Israel. I intend, however, to only devote two chapter per person instead of three, except for Begin who gets three chapters with the second devoted to the creation of the Herut and Likud parties, and Jabotinsky, who gets a single chapter covering both his life and his ideology, as I do not have to devote a chapter to the military career of each politician. Because Sharon's political career predated that of Netanyahu, I write about his career before dealing with Netanyahu. I then have a chapter covering Netanyahu's second and third governments followed by a chapter dealing with Sharon as prime minister. The book then has a conclusion examining the possible future of the party based on a comparison with the Fianna Fail party in Ireland, the qualities that Likud leaders have in common, and a few thoughts on the Likud's territorial policy.

Third, when I arrived in Israel in 1975 to work as a volunteer on an Israeli kibbutz and subsequently to study at an Israeli university, Israel was still controlled by the Labor Party. As a result my education in Zionism was on the heroes of the Labor Zionist trend: David Ben-Gurion, A. D. Gordon, Berl Katznelson, Yitzhak Tabenkin, et al. Then much was not taught about diaspora Zionist figures like the political Zionists: Theodore Herzl, Max Nordau, Haim Weizmann, and Jabotinsky. For me writing the chapter on Jabotinsky is a matter of self-education. And finally, I have always felt that Yitzhak Shamir deserves a proper biography in English; at present his only biography is in French and it deals mostly with his career and life prior to becoming prime minister. Having grown up in a country where every president—even if he is only in office for a month—is entitled to numerous children's and juvenile biographies not to mention proper historical biographies, I think that Shamir is sorely entitled to a proper biography in both English and Hebrew.[1] I'm not able to undertake such a task, but at least my two chapters should, hopefully, fill a gap until a future Israeli historian does write a proper biography of the third longest serving prime minister and the operational commander of *Lohemei Herut Israel*.

By concentrating on the party through its leaders I hope to shed light on what qualities are necessary to become a leader of the Likud and the Israeli Right. I also hope to illustrate the focuses of policy at the leadership level. And here it is where the continuity or discontinuity of policy will be most readily revealed rather than by an analysis of party election publications or educational material for the party's youth wing. I take upon myself this task not out of great sympathy with Revisionist Zionism or the Likud, but because the party represents a major actor. If I wrote a book about Hamas this would not mean that I am in sympathy with its ideology. The Likud is as important an actor in the Israeli-Palestinian conflict as Hamas is.

Now comes the part where I get to thank everyone who helped me write this book. First, I would like to thank the outer-library loan staff at the Madison Public Library for getting me all the books on Jabotinsky, Stern and Lehi without which it would have been impossible to write the first and fifth chapters, the reference librarians at the Meadowood Branch

Library through whom I placed orders for the books, and all the libraries that loaned me books from their collections. I would also like to thank my niece, Jessie Mitchell, who assisted me with research by answering questions I put to her in reading Charles Erlinger's biography of Yitzhak Shamir, which is in French. This was a big help. I would also like to thank my Ameriprise Financial advisor, Leslie J. Niemeyer, whose wise investing of my money enabled me to write this book.

One

The Founder—Vladimir "Zeev" Jabotinsky—and the Creation of Revisionist Zionism

Vladimir Jabotinsky was born into a middle-class Jewish family in the Russian Black Sea port of Odessa on October 5, 1880. Odessa was then a cosmopolitan manufacturing and trading center with a population of just over 300,000 during the time of Jabotinsky's youth when he lived in the city on a regular basis. Odessa was comparable to many Mediterranean cities with a cosmopolitan character consisting of Russian bureaucrats and administrators, Greek, Italian, and Armenian merchants, and Jews fleeing anti–Semitism in other parts of Russia. After the Russians the Jews were the largest ethnic group. Jabotinsky was an acculturated Jew with no knowledge of Yiddish and none of Hebrew beyond the minimal amount that was required for his bar mitzvah ceremony. Jabotinsky had no interest in anything Jewish—either from a religious or cultural standpoint—until he became a Zionist in 1903.[1]

Young Jabotinsky showed early on an aptitude for languages and as a youth in addition to learning very polished Russian he also acquired French, English, Italian, and German. This saw him well through the remainder of his life as having learned one or more languages of each of the three primary European language families (Slavic, Germanic, Romance) he as an adult could learn others. He eventually became fluent in ten languages. He first added Yiddish and Hebrew soon after becoming a Zionist through self-study and tutoring. He also added several other Slavic languages: Ukrainian, Polish, and Czech. Later in life when he became a Revisionist Zionist leader he would demonstrate the ability to study language grammars and mem-

Zeev Jabotinsky as young man, September 1, 1903.

orize vocabulary so that he could give short addresses in various other languages. He also made a living translating literary works in other languages into both Russian and Hebrew.

When Jabotinsky was seventeen and had finished high school he went to Switzerland and Italy to attend university. He registered at the law school in Bern but rarely attended classes as he became more caught up in the student life of a vagabond. He then went to Rome where he was a student at the university for three years. There he studied history and literature. He became caught up in the *fin de siècle* artistic and philosophical currents that were then considered to be cutting edge. While there he began writing a series of literary articles on Italian politics and life that were published in the *Odesskie Novosti* (Odessa News), the Russian language newspaper for which he became the literary critic upon his return to Odessa and for which he would write off and on for the next decade or more—into the First World War.

In 1901 Jabotinsky at age 21 returned to Odessa from Rome. He became the literary and theater critic of the *Odesskie Novosti* writing reviews of plays appearing in the city as well as books, interviewing authors, and writing the occasional short play of *feuilleton* himself as Herzl did in Budapest and Paris.[2]

In 1903 Russia experienced a wave of anti–Semitic pogroms or race riots in which Russian and Ukranian peasant mobs attacked local Jewish communities. Jabotinsky became caught up in organizing a self-defense movement for the Jewish community in Odessa, which probably contributed considerably towards the city not experiencing its own pogrom. This became the start of Jabotinsky's Zionist career, which would last until the end of his life some 37 years later. This forming of military units would also become a feature of Jabotinsky's career repeated periodically: the formation of the Jewish Legion in 1917–18, the formation of the Hagana in Palestine in 1920, and of the Irgun Zvai Leumi in the 1930s. From this Jabotinsky then went on to visit Kishinev, a town that had suffered a devastating pogrom and wrote about it as a journalist. That year he covered the Sixth Zionist Congress in Basel, Switzerland where he witnessed the big fight between Zionist leader Theodor Herzl on one hand the Russian Zionists on the other over whether or not the Zionist movement should send a group to explore the possibility of establishing a temporary Zionist colony within what is today Kenya, but was then Uganda. Herzl won a pyrrhic victory but the Russians made clear that they would withdraw from the movement if Palestine was not made the movement's final aim.

Jabotinsky seems to have suffered the same type of personal crisis that Theodor Herzl and his partner Max Nordau had experienced about eight years earlier. Jabotinksy, like Herzl and Nordau before him, felt unfulfilled personally and intellectually by his job as a literary critic and play write and possibly had experienced anti–Semitism first hand. He wanted to fulfill himself by getting involved in nationalist politics, which was then the rage in Europe. He logically had three possible options: Ukrainian nationalism because he lived in what was geographically a Ukrainian city; Russian nationalism because he was culturally a Russian; or Jewish nationalism, i.e., Zionism, because he was a Jew. Anti–Semitism limited Jabotinsky's future in either Ukrainian or Russian politics. Possibly because of what he saw and experienced in Kishinev or Basel or both he picked the third option. The first evidence that we have that Jabotinsky showed any interest in the Jewish question and Zionism was a series of columns he wrote in 1902–03 defending Zionism against the charge that it was a return to the ghetto made by a bourgeois Russian Jewish intellectual, Joseph Bikerman, in the Russian journal *Russkoe Bogatsvo* (Russian Wealth). Jabotinksy mostly used straw-man arguments to weakly parry those advanced by Bikerman.[3]

While still continuing to make a professional living as a journalist, Jabotinsky became actively involved in the Zionist movement as a supporter of Haim Weizmann, the leader of Russia's Zionists and the head of his own Democratic Faction, that served as an opposition to Herzl within the movement, who would later become Jabotinsky's chief political rival in the Zionist movement. Jabotinsky played a major role in doing the basic organizing for the Helsingfors Conference held in Helsinki, Finland in December 1906. At this conference the compromise formula of "synthetic Zionism" was arrived at under which the movement would support practical measures to facilitate Zionist settlement in Ottoman Palestine while continuing the political work of trying to secure a national charter for Palestine. Jabotinsky would work on other conferences and in 1909 was appointed the editor of a Zionist newspaper in Constantinople (Istanbul).[4]

During this same time period Jabotinsky was busy learning both Hebrew and Yiddish. It took him about a year to learn Hebrew well enough that he could began writing in the language and he soon began translating Hebrew poetry into Russian. Eventually his Hebrew translations of famous poems from other languages would be highly regarded. Yiddish took a bit longer, but Jabotinsky was aided by the fact that he already knew German and Hebrew, the two languages that provide the vocabulary for Yiddish, and he knew a Slavic language, Russian, which is similar enough to the Polish that provides the grammar for Yiddish.[5]

At the outbreak of the First World War Jabotinsky was on assignment in North Africa for a Russian newspaper in Moscow, *Russkiya Vedomost,* seeing if the Muslim Arabs in North Africa would follow the Sultan's call for jihad against the Allies. Jabotinsky went and spoke to Jews in the major cities in the Ottoman provinces of North Africa and concluded that the Arabs would not rise up and he reported this back to his paper. While in Alexandria, Egypt, Jabotinsky came into contact with several hundred Russian Jews who had been Zionist pioneers in Palestine and had been expelled from the territory by the Ottomans as enemy aliens. Djemal Pasha, the Turkish military commander in Palestine had begun expelling foreign Jews of military age in Palestine by the thousands. One of these was Joseph Trumpeldor, a one-armed Jewish war hero from the 1904–05 Russo-Japanese war. The two came up with the idea of offering the services of the expelled Jews to Britain to fight against the Ottomans in Palestine as a Jewish unit in the British army. The British general in Egypt said that the Jews could serve as a support unit but not as an infantry unit and they had to be willing to fight anywhere against the Ottomans and not just in Palestine. In 1915 Britain was preparing to invade Turkey at Gallipoli and wanted to form a unit of mule herders to bring ammunition from the rear to the front lines. Jabotinsky rejected this as undignified for the first organized Jewish military unit in centuries. But Trumpeldor, who had actual military experience, recognized the importance of the task to the war effort and agreed to it. A battalion, known as the Zion Mule Corps, was formed and commanded by Lieutenant Colonel John Henry Patterson, an Anglo-Irish bastard, probably from Ulster, who had worked his way up through the ranks of the British army and became famous by killing a pair of man-eating lions at Tsavo, Uganda, while building a railroad across East Africa.[6]

The Zion Mule Corps served with distinction throughout the Gallipoli campaign of 1915 and at the end part of the unit returned to civilian life and Egypt and a core agreed to enlist in the British army as the core of a future Jewish Legion to fight in Palestine. It was disbanded a little over a year after it was founded on March 26, 1916. Jabotinsky had headed to London from Alexandria to begin making the case at the War Office for a Jewish Legion. There he allied himself with Haim Weizmann who had moved to England from Germany before the war and established himself as a chemistry professor at the University of Manchester. While Jabotinsky lobbied the War Office for a Jewish Legion, Weizmann lobbied the Foreign Office and the British establishment on behalf of a Jewish national charter for the Zionist movement for Palestine. Weizmann was the only Zionist leader in Britain who supported Jabotinsky's goal of forming a Jewish military unit in the British army. When Lt. Col. Patterson returned to London from Egypt he immediately got in touch with Jabotinsky—the two had begun corresponding in November 1915—and the two began plotting strategy to lobby the War Office more effectively. The two became fast friends and for the remainder of his life Jabotinsky would periodically call upon Patterson to perform political missions for him and Revisionist Zionism. Jabotinsky enlisted in the British army in the autumn of 1916 and joined the 120 remaining members of the Zion Mule Corps in their London barracks.[7]

Lord Kitchener, the head of the British general staff, was opposed to the creation of a Jewish combat unit but he drowned on June 5, 1916, when the ship he was traveling on hit a German mine and was sunk. Leopold Amery, a Conservative MP and British intelligence officer who was a secret Jew, supported the creation of a Jewish unit and worked with Patterson. The concept of a Jewish Legion was opposed by both upper-class assimilated Jews and lower-class Jews from Russia that did not want to see Jews fighting on behalf of Russia.[8]

David Lloyd George, the Welsh politician who became prime minister of Britain halfway through the war, decided to encourage the Zionists after the United States entered the war in April 1917 as a means of winning more active participation of America in the war effort. Lloyd George was one of those politicians who although not personally anti–Jewish, nevertheless believed the propaganda of the anti–Semites regarding the power and influence of the Jews. Thus, he supported Foreign Minister Arthur Balfour in issuing the Balfour Declaration in November 1917 in support of establishing a Jewish homeland in Palestine.

Vladimir Jabotinsky wearing the uniform of the Judean Battalion Kadima in the Jewish Legion of the British Royal Fusiliers, September 1, 1918.

Months before on July 17, Weizmann had met with British Foreign Secretary Balfour and stressed the importance of issuing a public declaration of British support for a Jewish homeland in Palestine partly as a recruiting tool to get British and American Jews to enlist to fight for Britain in Palestine. That same day Patterson was appointed the commander of a Jewish regiment yet to be raised. He had the solid support of both Jabotinsky and Trumpeldor. Trumpeldor was prevented from enlisting in the British army because of his missing arm.[9]

When the Balfour Declaration was issued, Jabotinsky helped celebrate the victory at Weizmann's home in Kensington. Three months later Jabotinsky was commissioned a lieutenant in the British army. That month the Legion was given the honor of marching through the streets of London. Later that year Jabotinsky's future bitter rival, David Ben-Gurion, a Russian Jew and Zionist pioneer in Palestine expelled by the Ottomans, wrote to Patterson from New York City to inform him that the Zionist movement had established recruiting offices for the Jewish Legion in New York, Greece and Argentina.[10]

In August 1918 the first battalion of the Jewish Legion, commanded by Patterson, was deployed to the Jordan Valley fifteen miles north of the Dead Sea. The unit suffered from harsh conditions due to the great heat and the swarming mosquitos. Jabotinsky commanded a machine gun platoon in the fighting in the Jordan Valley the following month in what was a diversionary attack for General Allenby's advance up the coast of Palestine. On October 1, 1918, Allenby captured Damascus. At the end of the war there were 6,000 Jewish Legionnaires in Palestine and another 2,000 American and Canadian Jews who had enlisted but not deployed were swiftly demobilized in Britain.[11]

Patterson was given command of the Sinai peninsula and southern Palestine in early 1919. In April he was ordered to demobilize Lieutenant Jabotinsky. Patterson protested but was overruled and Jabotinsky began his civilian career once more as a Zionist organizer. Jabotinsky spent the summer of 1919 in Tel Aviv and then moved his family, his wife and young son Eri, to Jerusalem in the autumn.

Jabotinsky's home became a meeting place for prominent Zionists in Palestine including Eliyahu Golomb, the future commander of the Hagana along with Jabotinsky, and Itamar Ben-Avi, the son of the father of modern Hebrew, Eliezer Ben-Yehuda. Jabotinsky and Golomb founded the Hagana as a self-defense force in the Jewish Yishuv (colony or settlement) in Palestine.

In January 1920 Patterson retired from the British army at age 53 after 35 years of service. He was the only British officer to start the war as a lieutenant colonel and end it at the same rank, which Jabotinsky took as proof of anti–Semitism working against him.[12]

In April 1920 anti–Jewish riots took place in Jerusalem. Six Jews were killed and 211 wounded in the pogrom. After the riots Jabotinsky was arrested along with 19 other Hagana members and sentenced to fifteen years in prison for illegal possession of firearms. Jabotinsky had earlier informed Governor Ronald Storrs that he was forming a self-defense force. Storrs was instructed by London to treat Jabotinsky as a political prisoner and not a criminal and he allowed Jabotinsky's wife to furnish his cell with furniture from his home. Jabotinsky was transferred along with nineteen other Zionist prisoners to Acre Fortress, the most secure prison in Palestine. Some 2500 Jews signed a petition demanding the release of Jabotinsky and the other prisoners and presented it to the mandatory authorities. Allenby then commuted Jabotinsky's sentence to one year and freed him from hard labor and reduced the sentences of the others from one year to six months.[13]

The following year when an Arab pogrom broke out in Jaffa against the Jews, Patterson's successor as commander of the Jewish Legion, Colonel Eliezer Margolin, allowed members of the Legion to go to Jaffa with their weapons to help end the rioting. The Legionnaires killed 16 and drove off hundreds of rioting Arabs. The Arabs killed 27 Jews and wounded 106.[14]

Upon his release from prison in 1921 Jabotinsky became a member of the Zionist Executive in Jerusalem. But only some eighteen months later he resigned in January 1923 in protest at the Executive's weak reaction to the British decision in late 1922 to partition the Palestine mandate that the League of Nations had awarded to Britain in 1920 and remove Transjordan from the territory to be considered part of the mandate.[15]

Nineteen twenty-three could be looked upon as the year in which Revisionist Zionism as an ideology was founded. In Riga, Latvia, the Order of Trumpeldor was founded as a Zionist youth movement, named after Jabotinsky's old collaborator who had perished in a border skirmish with Arabs at Tel Hai near today's Kiryat Shemonah on March 1, 1920. Jabotinsky had earlier pleaded with the Zionist Executive to evacuate the settlement because it was indefensible, but his pleading was ignored. After its fall, Trumpeldor was turned into Zionism's first martyr.[16] Jabotinsky found out about the Riga group and rechristened it Betar, which is both the name of the last Jewish stronghold to fall during the Bar Kokhba Revolt in 135 A.D. and an acronym for Brit Trumpeldor—the union of Trumpeldor. The movement would eventually spread across Eastern Europe and to the United States, Canada, Argentina, Australia, and North Africa. Betar would eventually supply the leaders of and many of the rank and file members of the two Revisionist underground organizations in the 1940s, the Etzel and Lehi. Betar was founded as a paramilitary unit, with ranks and saluting and pseudo-military ceremonies. The recruits were taught the importance of *hadar* a Hebrew word that can be variously translated as glory, majesty, or pride. Jabotinsky basically adopted European gentile notions of what makes a gentleman in terms both of manners and personal etiquette and values and trained the youth of the Eastern European ghettoes in it under the label of *hadar*.[17]

In 1923 and 1924 Jabotinsky also penned two essays, "The Iron Wall" and "The Morality of the Iron Wall," in the Parisian Russian Zionist journal *Razsvet* in which he outlined his view of the Arab question. He argued that the Arabs would only give up struggling against Zionism when the Zionists had repeatedly demonstrated to them that resistance was futile through the development of an "iron wall" or irresistible force that protected the Zionist Yishuv. He had expounded on this belief in a meeting of the Executive on July 12, 1921. Eventually this was to be adopted by Labor Zionism as well and was the basis of the philosophy of people like David Ben-Gurion, Yigal Allon, Moshe Dayan, Yitzhak Rabin, and Ehud Barak.[18]

In April 1925 in Paris Jabotinsky founded the Revisionist Party, known in Hebrew as haTzohar for haTzionim haRevisionistim. The term Revisionist Zionism comes from the idea that it was necessary to revise the existing labor Zionism in favor of the original political Zionism of Theodor Herzl, Max Nordau, Israel Zangwill et al. who believed that the chief aim of Zionism was the founding of a Jewish state in Palestine through the acquisition of a public charter that would have the force of law. Another key tenet of Revisionist Zionism was a prohibition against mixing Zionism with another political ideology such as socialism, fascism, liberalism, etc. To illustrate this principle Jabotinsky atypically took a Talmudic principle called *sha'anetz* that one should not mix two separate materials in a fabric. In practice Jabotinsky made his own personal political beliefs of nineteenth-century liberalism (twentieth-century American conservatism) and imperialism as a default. Jabotinsky did not think that he was mixing liberalism and Zionism.[19]

The movement was founded based on two groups: one based around the Zionist journal *Razsvet* (Dawn), which had been published in Berlin but in December 1924 moved to Paris, and a group of Jewish students from Riga who were critical of the leadership of the Zionist movement provided by Weizmann. These two groups soon evolved into the party, haTzohar, and the Betar youth movement. The movement's first generation leadership consisted largely of Russian Jews who following the Russian

Revolution emigrated from Russia to either Palestine or Western Europe. The second generation consisted of Polish Jews who spoke either Yiddish or Hebrew or both and were educated in Poland.[20]

In time the Revisionist movement would consist of three separate main entities: haTzohar, Betar, and the Irgun Zvai Leumi (National Military Organization, the Etzel), which was founded in 1937. Jabotinsky served to symbolically unite the three separate components in his role as symbolic head of each: the leader of the Revisionist Party, *Rosh Betar* (head of Betar) and commander of the Etzel. But in the last fifteen years of his life most of his time and energy was devoted to the Revisionist Party followed by Betar. In the 1930s two additional minor organizations were founded: an organization for Jewish Polish war veterans and a labor exchange.[21] In 1935 Jabotinsky acquiesced to the radicals in his party and quit the World Zionist Organization to form his own New Zionist Organization along with some Orthodox religious Zionists. In 1946 the NZO was abolished with the remaining Revisionist Zionists returning to the World Zionist Organization. Betar members and member of the Etzel who were not Revisionists used the term Jabotinsky's movement to refer to the overall movement. In 1930 about a quarter of Betar members were also Revisionists. By 1930 the formative period of Betar was over with and Jabotinsky increasingly viewed it as the youth wing of his party and as a strategic reserve for future party members.[22]

Throughout his career Jabotinsky made a series of temporary ideological alliances with major Zionist figures only to abandon them when they disagreed with him. In the first phase from 1903 to 1923 he allied himself with Weizmann against Max Nordau and the other Zionists who wanted the Zionists to be flexible as regards their final destination and strategy. The World Zionist Organization was neutral during the First World War because it had important assets in both camps: Russian Jewry and British and American Jewry in the Allied camp, and German and Austro-Hungarian Jewry in the Central Powers camp and with the Ottomans in control of Palestine. Jabotinsky and Weizmann rolled the dice on their belief that the Allies would be victorious and received a big payoff.[23] Then from 1923 to 1938 Jabotinsky allied himself to the British while putting pressure on them and pushing for fulfillment of the Balfour Declaration and the terms of the mandate through independence.

Jabotinsky saw Britain as the Zionists natural strategic ally for two main reasons. First, it was the first and only great power to recognize the Zionists and ally itself with them both in Herzl's time and afterwards. Secondly, Britain as a democracy was open to public pressures in a way that non-democratic powers like Russia, Germany, and Poland were not.

Whereas Haim Weizmann behaved like a classic court Jew or shetl Jew in appealing to the British establishment and flattering them, Jabotinsky believed in using public pressure through petition campaigns and diplomatically pressuring London through other powers and the League of Nations in Geneva. But in the final analysis Jabotinsky formed a sentimental attachment to Britain as a young adult and like Weizmann was unable to abandon that allegiance later on.[24]

Jabotinsky did flirt with two other powers. In the mid–1930s he met with Benito Mussolini in Rome and hinted about the possibility of taking the mandate for Palestine and giving it to Rome. But this was only talk designed to demonstrate that the Zionists had other options and thereby increase their leverage in London. In 1939 with war fast approaching, Jabotinsky spoke with Polish diplomats about the possibility of Warsaw receiving the mandate from London and then opening up Palestine to a mass exodus of Polish Jewry. But this was desperation rather than calculated strategy. Revisionist historiography also claims that Jabotinsky supported a plan for an invasion of Palestine by the Etzel in late 1939 that was only abandoned by the outbreak of the Second World War. But there is no real evidence that Jabotinsky supported such a plan. The previous year in Warsaw at the Third World Conference of Betar Jabotinsky argued publicly with Menahem Begin that the balance-of-power in Palestine was unfavorable to such sorts of schemes.[25]

Jabotinsky faced fundamental political obstacles to coming to power and implementing his ideas. First, most of his following was in Eastern Europe especially in Poland and the Baltic States. His party was very weak in Palestine and his opponents had control over the distribution of legal immigration certificates so that his followers received fewer than did the labor Zionists or the General Zionists. Second, due to a demonstration by some Revisionist Zionists at the Western Wall in Jerusalem that started the August 1929 riots that roiled the Yishuv, Jabotinsky was banned from entering Palestine and the last time he set foot there was in 1928. Third, his party was headquartered initially in Paris and then from 1936 onwards in London, away from his followers. Jabotinsky was a bit of a *bon vivant* with a taste for fine restaurants, good wine, art museums and literary saloons that Palestine simply could not support in the 1920s and 1930s. Even if Jabotinsky could have called in political favors to get the ban on his presence in Palestine lifted, he did not really want to live there. He wanted to live where the political action was and where he could enjoy himself intellectually. So he spent his time during his final decade traveling back and forth from London to Paris to Warsaw and touring Betar camps throughout Europe (especially Poland and the Baltics) and the United

States. Jabotinsky made major visits to the United States in 1926 (5.5 months), 1935, and in 1940 (six months) where he finally died in August 1940. Fourth, most of the colonial administrators in Palestine were pro–Arab in a vague romantic fashion, even if they were not anti–Semitic, and Britain had to take into account the sentiments of the Arabs both in Palestine and in its other colonies in the Middle East and of Muslims in India.[26]

In August 1929 Jabotinsky made a fiery speech to the Sixteenth Zionist Congress in Zurich. He called for Jewish sovereignty to be applied over the entire original territory of the Palestine mandate—on both banks of the Jordan River. This may have encouraged his maximalist followers in Palestine who staged—without Jabotinsky's knowledge—a demonstration involving the blowing of a ram's horn at the Western Wall. Haj Amin al–Hussein, the Mufti of Jerusalem, used this to start a rumor that the Jews were out to destroy the al–Aksa Mosque and rebuild the Jewish temple on top of the ruins. On August 16 a young Jew was stabbed to death in Jerusalem and soon a countrywide pogrom was taking place against the Jews.[27]

After the deaths of over 130 Jews and hundreds of Arabs the British authorities restored order. As a result of the riots the British government came into conflict with the Zionist movement and in October 1930 the Passfield White Paper was published calling for restrictions on Jewish immigration and land purchase. Weizmann resigned from the presidency of the Zionist movement in protest. Ben-Gurion called for a rebellion against Britain until wiser heads in his party calmed him down. Weizmann lobbied the British government and Jabotinsky started a petition drive to put pressure on London. In February 1931 Prime Minister Ramsey MacDonald, the first Labour Party prime minister, abrogated the Passfield White Paper. He declared that immigration would be decided upon objective economic criteria rather than political considerations.[28]

Jabotinsky's most sustained attempts at power were at the Zionist Congresses of 1931 and 1933. From 1930 onwards Mapai and the Revisionists were in competition for control of the Zionist movement both in Palestine and in Europe. In 1931 Jabotinsky stormed out of the Zionist Congress saying, "This is not a Zionist Congress," and tore up his delegate's card after Weizmann refused to confirm that a Jewish state in Palestine was the movement's goal. Weizmann had earlier declared that a Jewish majority in Palestine was not his goal. By storming out, Jabotinsky allowed Nahum Sokolow, Weizmann's publicist, to be elected as president of the Zionist movement instead of Jabotinsky. Before the Congress the Revisionists won 21 percent of the vote compared to 29 percent for Mapai.[29]

From August 1929 to 1934 a trio of Revisionists in Palestine known as the maximalists formulated a radical ideological alternative to Jabotinsky's liberal-influenced Revisionism. The three were: Uri Zvi Greenburg, the poet of the messianic Zionist camp in the 1930s and 1940s; Abba Ahimeir, a former Marxist and admirer of Mussolini; and Yehoshua H. Levin, who was influenced by the Social Revolutionaries and Bolsheviks in Russia. All three originally came from the labor Zionist camp. Ahimeir became the leading figure of the three. They founded a group called *Brit haBiryonim* or the union of thugs. The group was only in existence for two years, 1930–32, and used demonstrative violence against property but also publicly supported fascism and Hitler. Ahimeir praised Hitler as late as April 1933 and the following month Jabotinsky publicly disowned him. After Jabotinsky disowned them they began to lose influence. But their actions served to exacerbate the conflict between the Revisionists and the labor Zionists.[30]

In a November 1932 article Jabotinsky sanctioned strike breaking in Palestine. On November 27, 1932, Ben-Gurion held a three-hour press conference in which he spent much of it attacking Jabotinsky and the Revisionists. Later in February 1933 at a large mass meeting in Tel Aviv Ben-Gurion referred to Jabotinsky as "Vladimir Hitler." And at other times he referred to him as "Il Duce."[31]

In 1931–33 there were two main issues in contention between the two camps: incorporation of non–Zionist Jews—usually prominent celebrities—into the Zionist organization and the allocation of immigration certificates for Palestine. In 1931 after Mapai beat out the Revisionists for control of the Zionist movement after Weizmann lost temporary control, Jabotinsky made a major push campaigning across Poland in the summer of 1933. But David Ben-Gurion, the leader of Mapai and future prime minister, also made a major push across Poland. In the midst of this, Haim Arlosoroff, a promising young labor Zionist leader was murdered on a beach in Tel Aviv where he had been walking with his wife on June 16, 1933. Ahimeir had been advocating murder as a means of solving disputes with his opponents. Sima Arlosoroff, his widow, identified Avram "Abrasha" Stavsky, who had been Menahem Begin's bodyguard in Poland before immigrating to Palestine, as one of her husband's murderers. Arlosoroff had just returned from conducting delicate negotiations in Germany with the Nazis to allow German Jews to emigrate from Germany to Palestine while forfeiting most of their property. The Revisionists had objected to this agreement, which violated the boycott of Germany that they had organized. Both Ben-Gurion and the future Golda Meir publicly stated that they thought that Stavsky was the murderer. Ben-Gurion wrote to one correspondent,

> I'm afraid [the Revisionists] absolutely are capable [of murder]. They're not only capable, they did it. Obviously not every Revisionist would do such a

thing. The great majority would leave the party if they knew the full truth. But ... the leaders, Jabotinsky, Abba Ahimeir, and others, educate their youth to kill.³²

But the 1933 election to the World Zionist Congress took place in the shadow of the murder accusation and Mapai and its allies ended up defeating the Revisionists 44 percent to 16 percent. During Jabotinsky's campaign visits to Warsaw he was accompanied by a young Betar leader named Menahem Begin.³³

Stavsky went on trial in Jerusalem and the Palestine Police were quick to prove that they were capable of solving the sensational murder and the mandatory authorities of conducting a fair trial. Jabotinsky raised funds for Stavsky's defense from a wealthy South African Jew, Michael Haskell, and hired Horace Samuel, a cousin of Sir Herbert Samuel, the first head of the mandate and a former Legionnaire, as Stavsky's defense attorney. Jabotinsky also asked Patterson to observe the trial for him. The trial began on April 23, 1934, and six weeks later on June 8 Stavsky was convicted of murder. Five weeks after that on July 19 the Court of Appeals overturned the conviction on a technicality. Stavsky was spared from the gallows. Patterson was convinced that he was innocent because Mrs. Arlosoroff was a confused witness who initially claimed that her husband's murderers were Arabs before changing her mind and deciding that they were Jews.³⁴

In 2004 a biography of Magda Goebbels, the wife of Nazi propaganda minister Josef Goebbels, was published. The author claimed that Magda had been a Zionist in the 1920s and the lover of Arlosoroff before he immigrated to Palestine. Author Anja Klabunde claimed that when Arlosoroff and Magda met in Germany in 1933 she warned him that he was in grave danger and must leave Germany immediately. Klabunde claimed that Josef Goebbels hired two hit men who followed Arlosoroff to Palestine. Whether one wants to believe such a sensationalist theory, or merely that ordinary Arab thieves murdered Arlosoroff in a robbery attempt—two had confessed to the murder to the Palestine Police and later told Lehi prisoner Ya'akov Kotik in prison that they had killed Arlosoroff, the case against Stavsky was weak.³⁵

Between October 10 and November 11, 1934, Ben-Gurion and Jabotinsky held a dozen meetings in London to try to work out their differences. The mediator who got them together, Pinhas Rutenberg, was a former official in Alexander Kerensky's short-lived democratic government in Russia and then head of the Palestine Electric Company. He was a friend of Jabotinsky and an admirer of Ben-Gurion. Surprisingly they found themselves in agreement on many different things regarding Zionist activity. On October 27 they signed two agreements: a non-violence pact between their two movements and a labor accord. In their final meeting they signed a third agreement—an agreement on discipline within the Zionist movement. The two leaders addressed each other as friend in their correspondence and came to respect each other. After one meeting Ben-Gurion wrote to Jabotinsky, "Whatever happens, I grasp your hand in esteem." Jabotinsky replied, "I grasp your hand in genuine friendship." In March 1935 the Histadrut, the labor federation for Palestine, reacting to the earlier invective between the two movements voted to reject the agreements reached with Jabotinsky. The gap between the two movements then widened further with the split of the Revisionists from the World Zionist Organizations in mid–1935 and the creation of the New Zionist Organization a few months later. It widened again after the Etzel was formed in 1937.[36]

In April 1936 the Arab Revolt began with a general strike enforced by strong-arm tactics and attacks on vulnerable Jews traveling on the roads. The revolt was to last on-and-off for the next three years. Initially Jabotinsky did not regard the Arab Revolt to be dangerous. Jabotinsky supported retaliatory measures against the Arabs for two reasons. First, he thought that they would demonstrate the vigor and military capacity of the Yishuv. Second, he thought they demonstrated that the Yishuv was no longer prepared to tolerate anti–Zionist measures by the mandatory power and that if London insisted on imposing them it would have to do so by force of arms. In 1937 an uneasy peace settled over Palestine as the Peel Commission arrived to investigate the political situation after having earlier held hearings in London. Jabotinsky testified to the Commission in London in February 1937 and then again later to parliament in July 1937. Both times he used humanitarian arguments in opposition to partition. But in reality Jabotinsky opposed partition for more real politik reasons. First, he estimated that in Britain the opponents of partition outnumbered the supporters and he felt it would be bad politics to be on the losing side. Second, he felt that the Jewish state within the partition boundaries would be too weak to defend itself and would be subject to endless Arab irredentism that would eventually result in its destruction. And finally, he felt that the Jewish state would be too small to absorb the Jews of Poland and Eastern Europe who were in danger from Hitler. He felt that an annual immigration rate of 150,000 would be impossible without Transjordan.

The Revisionists formed the spearhead of the opposition in the Yishuv to partition in the public campaign from 1937 to 1939. The Revisionist slogan was "cursed be he who pronounces the word." He was joined by some labor Zionists like those that would eventually become Faction B within Mapai and then Mapam and Ahdut ha'Avoda led by Yitzhak Tabenkin. Supporting partition were Ben-Gurion, Berl Katznelson and their supporters and Weizmann.[37]

Zionism in general and Revisionist Zionism especially was taking a more militant turn in the late 1930s as the Hagana developed an offensive capacity under the instruction of Orde Wingate and the Etzel began reprisal bombings in November 1937. On June 28, 1938, Shlomo Ben-Yosef, a new immigrant to Palestine was hanged for firing on an Arab bus in retaliation for an Arab attack on a Jewish car on the Rosh Pina-Safed road. He became the first of many Zionist martyrs who would die over the next decade at the hands of the British.[38]

In addition to writing plays, numerous journalistic articles and doing translations of other writers' works into Hebrew and Russian, Jabotinsky also found time in the 1920s to write two novels. The first, *Samson the Nazarene*, published in 1927 is a standard historical novel with a twist. Using the story from the Bible as his starting point, Jabotinsky wrote a novel about a man, Samson, who was torn between two cultures—the Irsraelite and the Philistine—and was not sure of his true parentage. The book portrays Samson as a pagan hedonist with no religious belief. The main message that Revisionists took from it is Samson's supposed dying utterance of "get iron," i.e., arm yourselves. This was obviously partly autobiographical as Jabotinsky was completely secular and torn between the Russian and Jewish cultures.[39] The second novel, *Piatero/The Five*, was published in 1930, and was more openly autobiographical in nature with the narrator sharing several biographical details in common with Jabotinsky such as involvement in the self-defense effort of 1903. The story revolves around a Russian middle-class family in Odessa with five children. The children suffer from horrible fates one after another. It could easily have ended with a simplistic Zionist argument with one sibling being saved by Zionism. But it does not—Jabotinsky was possibly hedging his bets and wanted to be remembered as a successful writer if he was forgotten as a Zionist activist and politician. The novel reeks with despair and impending doom within the Jewish diaspora of Eastern Europe as well as with nostalgia for the prerevolutionary Odessa. It is not as famous as *Samson*, but may well be the superior novel.[40]

In 1931 a group of about 2,000 Hagana members led by Avraham Tehomi, the leader of the Jerusalem branch of the Hagana, split from the main Hagana organization to form Hagana B, sometimes referred to as Irgun B (the second organization), over a difference in policy. Tehomi was born in Odessa in 1903 and organized civil defense for the Jews there during the Russian Civil War. In a 1936 meeting with Jabotinsky in Vienna he offered to form a small (50-man) anti–Arab terrorist force but Jabotinsky turned down the offer. These were eventually joined by a number of Orthodox Jews and Revisionists. The Revisionist Betarim functioned as "an underground within an underground" inside the Etzel. Tehomi spent most of his time as Hagana commander in acquiring weapons because the organization was always short. In July 1937, following the publication of the Peel Partition Plan, Tehomi negotiated a solution to his differences with the Hagana and returned to it with his men leaving only the Orthodox and the Revisionists behind. Although Lehi historian Zev Golan claims that an unauthorized reprisal action in Jerusalem precipitated the split. Each member of the Hagana B was asked individually if he wanted to return to the Hagana or remain in the Irgun. The organization's arsenal of weapons was then divided proportionately among the two groups.

Those remaining then became the Irgun Zvai Leumi (National Military Organization), a name influenced by Josef Pilsudski's revolutionary organization in Poland. Jabotinsky quickly lost control of the Etzel (the Hebrew pronunciation of the acronym). The Etzel was headed by David Raziel, an Orthodox youth, and by Avraham Stern, a classicist romantic at the Hebrew University who spoke fluent Italian and German and read Latin, and who ironically enough was a protégé of Hebrew University President Judah Magnes, founder of Brit Shalom, which advocated a bi-national state with the Arabs. Stern was tall, elegant, polite, somewhat resembled the Hollywood actor Tyrone Power, was usually serious but with a sense of humor given to practical jokes.[41]

Stern was recruited into the Etzel in 1932 by his friend and future rival David Raziel. He had been a member of the Hagana and spent August 1929 as an unarmed guard in Jerusalem and in the southern Galilee. Stern participated in the Etzel's second officers course and then graduated from Hebrew University in 1933, from whence he went to Florence, Italy to live briefly. In 1934 Stern began shipping firearms from Poland to the Etzel including the organization's first submachine guns. Stern was married in January 1936 to his fiancé Roni, whom he had met eight years before. When the Arab Revolt began in 1936 he was Avraham Tehomi's assistant and when Tehomi returned to the Hagana, Stern was co-opted on to the High Command of Etzel.[42]

Stern, who emigrated from Poland in 1925, returned to Poland as the Etzel's representative in November 1937 and with the help of militants there like Natan Friedmann-Yellin, and Israel Scheib, and others negotiated agreements with the military regime in Warsaw for it to train Betar members who were secret Etzel members in Poland and arm them. Neither Jabotinsky nor Begin were aware of this, but Begin did support the militants against Jabotinsky. Twenty-six Etzel members underwent a four-month course in military training and guerrilla warfare at Andrikhov in the Carpathian Mountains in the late winter and early spring of 1939. These officers then served as the backbone of the Etzel's and later Lehi's combat arm.[43]

At the Third World Conference of Betar in Warsaw in September 1938—against the backdrop of the Munich crisis—Begin openly revolted against his idol and was supported by many senior Betarim including Scheib and Friedmann-Yellin. Jabotinsky used realism against Begin's romanticism and did not stand a chance. Jabotinsky rejected comparisons with other European national liberation movements, such as those in Italy, Ireland, and Poland, as irrelevant and groundless. In his final two years Jabotinsky was living on borrowed time as he suffered from a weak heart and an international situation that was totally beyond his capability to deal with.[44]

Jabotinsky had a low opinion of Poland during its short democratic phase from 1918 to 1926, when it suffered from anti–Semitism until Josef Pilsudski took power in a coup in that year. Under the military regime following Pilsudski's death in 1935, Poland was actively promoting the emigration of its Jews to other countries. In a letter to his top aide, Josef Schechtman, Jabotinsky wrote on February 28, 1939, that although Britain regarded Poland as an important power, Warsaw was dependent on London and not the reverse. So that it would likely have little leverage over British policy on Palestine, which proved to be the case. In the late 1930s Jabotinsky hoped to use Polish pressure on Britain but Warsaw was afraid of upsetting London.[45]

In September 1939 Jabotinsky wrote a confidential letter to all of the movement's branches saying that there was no longer room for "big gestures," i.e., an invasion of Palestine by Etzel members from Poland, and that the movement had to support Britain in the war. For Jabotinsky this invasion was a passing fancy in the late summer of 1939; for Avraham Stern it was a practical possibility. But when the Etzel High Command discussed Stern's plan of bringing 40,000 trained Etzel/Betarim from Poland along with Jabotinsky it concluded that the organization would not be ready to execute the plan until 1940 at the earliest. This was at a meeting on August 31, 1939, that was raided by the police and resulted in the arrest and imprisonment of most of the High Command.[46]

The meaning of World War II for the Etzel and Zionism was the main topic of discussion among the High Command in prison. It was while in prison that Stern developed a theory that the British were through and that the Etzel should help their enemies—the Axis powers—just as the

Nili spy organization had helped the British against the Ottomans during World War I. "If not, if the Axis loses, people will say I was insane. I'll have to chance that," argued Stern in a prophetic prediction of how he was viewed during and after the Holocaust.[47]

The British had turned the Russian Compound, a Russian Orthodox Church property in central Jerusalem into the Jerusalem Central Prison in order to house the Etzel High Command and later used it for other high profile prisoners during the Revolt. Former prisoners said that Arab terrorist prisoners in Israel today have it much better than either Jews or Arabs had it during the last decade of the British mandate.[48]

From the end of the partition debate in July 1938 until the outbreak of World War II in September 1939, Jabotinsky was obsessed with the coming catastrophe to Polish Jewry in particular and European Jewry in general. Although Jabotinsky probably did not anticipate the Wehrmacht and Luftwaffe overwhelming France as quickly as they did, he was well aware of the military weakness of Poland. Former Jabotinsky aide Benzion Netanyahu credited Jabotinsky with correctly foreseeing the Holocaust, one of three correct predictions that he made about the future.[49] In January 1939 Jabotinsky wrote,

> To be frank I sometimes fear that the time has already passed eleven o'clock; perhaps twelve o'clock has already rung. That means midnight. That means the end. However, it is best that we shake off this fear. Let it be only eleven o'clock. This is therefore, the last hour.... Perhaps it is still possible to find some place on the enflamed horizon, where the flames have not yet reached. And perhaps we will still try to be saved.[50]

Earlier in September 1938 during the Third World Betar Conference in Warsaw, Jabotinsky spoke at one of the main synagogues in Warsaw on Tisha B'Av, the feast that commemorates a number of major catastrophes in Jewish history. He predicted,

> The catastrophe is coming closer. My hair has turned white and I have aged in these three years because my heart is bleeding, for you, dear brothers and sisters, do not see the volcano that will soon begin to spurt out the fire of destruction. And I want to say one more thing to you on this Ninth of Av: Those who will succeed to escape from the catastrophe will merit a moment of great Jewish joy: the rebirth and rise of a Jewish state. I do not know whether I will earn that.[51]

Jabotinsky predicted that war would not come in the late summer of 1939 largely because he knew that the Jews as a people who unprepared for the war. In the late 1930s Jabotinsky simultaneously predicted war—the rational action to the evidence—and hoped that it would not come—the emotional reaction.[52]

Jabotinsky spent the final year of his life writing his final book, *The War and the Jews* (published in America as *The Jewish War Front*) and attempting to revive his scheme of a Jewish Legion from two decades before except this time in the guise of an entire Jewish army. Jabotinsky soon decided that the United States would have to be the base for this scheme. The United States boasted the largest Jewish community outside of the war zone and it already had a Revisionist movement in place. On March 13, 1940, Jabotinsky arrived in New York accompanied by two senior aides. Benzion Netanyahu, the editor of the Revisionist newspaper in Palestine *HaYarden* and the father of a future Israeli war hero and a Likud leader, left Palestine to meet up with Jabotinsky in New York.[53]

Within days of arriving in America Jabotinsky packed the Manhattan Center with a call for a call for mass migration of at least 300,000 annually to Palestine from Europe. At least 5,000 attended the rally and members of other Zionist movements were receptive to his message. On March 31 he spoke to 1500 Betarim at their annual assembly in New York. Jabotinsky's American constituency consisted largely of religious Zionists, Jewish military veterans, and the lower socioeconomic strata of secular Jews who were attracted to Jewish tradition, ethnicity and Zionist assertiveness. This describes the constituency of the Herut Party and later the Likud Party in Israel following independence. Revisionist pursuit of major Jewish philanthropists was largely unsuccessful. But in late 1939 a Revisionist envoy did get American Supreme Court Justice Louis Brandeis to issue a statement in support of the right of Jews to immigrate freely to Palestine and that the notion of illegal Jewish immigration to Palestine was nonsense.[54]

Jabotinsky was depressed for much of his time in America as his wife was stuck in England unable to get a visa and his son Eri was in a British prison in Palestine for his Aliya B (illegal immigration) activities. Under these circumstances most of his aides dismissed the Jewish army scheme as impractical.

But at Jabotinsky's urging Professor Benjamin Azkin and Lt. Col. Patterson lobbied the British ambassador in Washington, Lord Lothian, to form a Jewish unit in the British army. Lord Lothian promised to lobby members of the cabinet on behalf of the scheme. Over 5,000 attended a second rally at the Manhattan Center on June 19 where Jabotinsky spoke in favor of his Jewish army scheme.[55]

Jabotinsky visited a Betar camp in upstate New York on August 3, 1940, to rest and attend a ceremony. Upon arriving he went immediately to his room where he suffered a massive heart attack that was fatal. A few days later a huge funeral was held in New York City with tens of thousands attending. His pallbearers included Col. Patterson, author John Gunther, future American ambassador to Israel James McDonald, publisher William Ziff (who was Jabotinsky's American publisher), and Prof. Benjamin Azkin of the City College of New York who eventually headed Hebrew University's law school. Jabotinsky's body would rest in New York until 1964 when Prime Minister Levi Eshkol permitted him to be reinterred on Mount Zion in Jerusalem. Ben-Gurion had adamantly refused the requests of Menahem Begin that Jabotinsky be allowed to be reburied in Israel. He did this on principle because he only allowed the reburial of two individuals from the diaspora: Herzl and the Baron Rothschild, who had financed the early Zionist settlements.[56]

Jabotinsky's legacy for the Israeli Right and eventually for the Likud Party is great. He established the importance of oratory and writing skills for the leader of the movement. This is seen in the coming to power of both Menahem Begin and Benjamin Netanyahu. Second, Jabotinsky started the tradition of militant Zionism and of reliance on military force as a solution to Zionist problems. This can be seen in the mythology of the Jewish Legion and the paramilitary nature of Betar. Third, and most important, Jabotinsky gave the Zionist secular Right an ideology: conservatism mixed with territorial maximalism. Begin later pragmatically adapted "both banks of the Jordan" to "the complete land of Israel" meaning Western Palestine from the sea to the river. Fourth, he gave the future Herut Party and the Likud the major institutions that it relied on: Betar and the Etzel (and indirectly Lehi as well).

For Israel Jabotinsky's legacy is three-fold. First, he spoke about the importance of a military and military training. Ironically, it was the Left that would develop the militia, the Hagana-Palmakh, that would defend the country from Arab invasion in 1948 and serve as the basis of today's Israel Defense Forces. But in 1944 the Jewish Brigade was created by the British army and fought in Italy. Many of its officers went on to serve in the Hagana and IDF during the War of Independence. The Jewish Brigade was the child of the Jewish Legion. Second, he developed a realistic policy on the Arab question, the "iron wall," that posited that the Palestinian Arabs would behave like a nation and not sell their national identity and culture for a few economic benefits. This was adopted by Ben-Gurion privately and after independence publicly by Ben-Gurion and the labor Zionists. And finally, he developed a set of pressure tactics and the strategy of pressure politics that have proven so useful with the United States even if they at the time failed with Britain.[57]

Two

Menahem Begin, Underground Commander

Menahem Begin was born the youngest child in a well-off Jewish family in the town of Brest-Litovsk, known to the Yiddish-speaking Jews as Brisk, on August 16, 1913. Brisk had for centuries moved back and forth between Poland and the Russian Empire. Before World War I it was part of Russia, but after the Versailles settlement it became part of the newly-independent Poland. Begin's family was wealthy until World War I when Russian Cossacks entered the town and burned down many of the Jewish homes including that belonging to Begin's father, Ze'ev Dov. During the war Ze'ev Begin moved his family eastwards to Kobrin and they initially lived in an abandoned country house before renting a house in Kobrin.

Ze'ev Dov Begin was a wool merchant, like his father before him, and good at his business. Ze'ev Begin was a Zionist activist and journalist who supplemented his income with Zionist activities. He named his eldest son Herzl after the founder of political Zionism. His youngest son was named after a minor figure in the Bible and the name means "comforter" in Hebrew. When Theodor Herzl died in 1904, Ze'ev Begin took an axe and with a few friends broke into the local synagogue to hold a memorial service for the Zionist founder. One of those breaking in was the grandfather of Ariel Scheinerman. In the 1920s Ze'ev Begin worked as a journalist and in 1923 he was chairman of the local haShomer haTzair, the Marxist Zionist youth movement, which was the first Zionist youth movement to establish a chapter in Brisk. In 1927 Jabotinsky's Betar youth movement established a chapter in Brisk. At first Menahem missed the uniforms of haShomer haTzair, but in 1929 when at age 16 he heard Jabotinsky speak in Brisk for the first time he decided that his future was with Betar. Begin later rationalized why he switched youth movements, but the simple truth was that his father thought that it would be easier to get him into university if he belonged to a youth movement that was conservative and nationalistic rather than Marxist.[1]

Ze'ev Dov was an admirer of German culture who despised both the Russians and the Poles as anti–Semites. By the time his son was growing up things had changed somewhat and Menahem developed a life-long hatred of Germany because of the Holocaust. And although he suffered from anti–Semitism he respected and even admired Polish nationalistic culture with its romantic poets and writers.[2]

Begin grew up speaking several languages, like Jabotinsky. He spoke Yiddish at home, and both Polish and Hebrew at school. He went to a Mizrakhi or religious Zionist movement school for primary school and developed a love of Jewish religious ritual that he retained for his entire life and which helped him in politics later in Israel. His favorite subject in school was Latin, although he once received a failing mark because he refused to sit for an exam on the Jewish Sabbath and the teacher refused to reschedule it for him.[3] Because of his admiration for Jabotinsky, Begin later learned Italian, which is close to Latin, and French. He also studied

Menahem Begin (right) with Vladimir Zabotinsky (center) in Pinsk, December 12, 1933.

English in school and perfected it living in Palestine under the British mandate. And during the early part of World War II Begin was a prisoner in the Gulag where he had an opportunity to learn Russian, refreshing what he had picked up as a child in Korbin. So by the time Begin became a politician he had some degree of fluency in seven languages. This was down from Jabotinsky's ten languages, but an improvement on Yitzhak Shamir's five languages. Begin wrote propaganda articles for Betar in three langauges: Polish, Yiddish, and Hebrew.[4] As commander of the Etzel he wrote proclamations in English and Hebrew. And as an opposition politician and prime minister he used the other languages he knew when meeting with foreign leaders.

In 1931 Begin graduated from high school and that fall he left Brisk and moved to Warsaw to study law at the university. Upon arriving in Warsaw the first thing he did was to telephone the office of Betar and ask for a meeting with Polish Betar leader Aharon Propes. Propes was nine years older than Begin and had helped Jabotinsky to establish the youth movement in Poland in the mid–1920s. Propes was impressed by Begin and he offered him a position as organizer for the rural areas. The job paid only about ten dollars a month, but Begin threw himself into the work and studied just hard enough to get C's at law school. He supplemented his income by giving private lessons to Jewish students in law and Jewish history.[5]

With the job came a position on the Polish High Council of Betar—the policy-making body of the movement. Begin slept on park benches as he traveled around Poland lecturing for Betar. His dedication earned him a promotion to deputy commissioner for Betar in Czechoslovakia in 1935, the year Jabotinsky pulled out of the World Zionist Organization. In 1937 Begin returned to Poland as a member of the commission that ran Betar. Begin made a habit of attaching himself to his idol Jabotinsky whenever the Rosh Betar traveled to a city that Begin was present in or near. About this time Jabotinsky used his influence to have Begin freed from prison for some minor offense. Begin also became friendly with the radicals who were close to the Etzel. Begin as deputy commissioner had a habit of personally seeing off all Betar members who made Aliyah (immigrated) to Palestine. This is how he first met Yitzhak Yezernitsky in 1935.[6]

Begin's big moment of fame came at the Third World Conference of Betar in Warsaw in September 1938 when he openly challenged his idol, Jabotinsky, over policy towards Palestine. Begin championed the idea of an armed revolt to see control of Palestine from the British that Avraham Stern was supporting in Palestine. Although Betar had paramilitary features, its members did not receive military training when Begin was a teenager in the 1920s. Begin had never handled a firearm, let alone developed any expertise in tactics. But he grew up on Polish romantic poetry and reading about Giusseppe Garibaldi and the Italian Risorgimento.[7] Begin took a leave of absence to practice law in a small town in eastern Poland during 1938, but he spent much of his time preparing for the conference.[8]

On the first day of the conference Begin gave a fiery speech. "Everything has changed—both in Israel and in the world. We must draw conclusions. Most of all, the conscience of the world has ceased to respond. The British send the best of our young men to the gallows," a reference to Shlomo Ben-Yosef, who was at that point the only Jew hanged by the British. "We must face the truth: They must first and foremost consider the Arabs." He claimed that this was because the Arabs weren't afraid to kill the British and to die for what they believed in. "We have had enough of surrender," shouted Begin. "We want to fight, either to win or to die!" ended Begin. "Italy would not have been liberated without Garibaldi," Begin added playing on Jabotinsky's admiration for Garibaldi.

At this point Jabotinsky broke in with a series of logical questions. "Sir, you may want to recollect the ratio of Italians to non–Italians in the country at the time," urged Jabotinsky. Begin then shifted to an argument about the Irish in 1916. Jabotinsky again cut in, "How do you propose to

Zeev Jabotinsky (bottom right) meeting with Betar leaders in Warsaw, January 1, 1939. Menahem Begin is at bottom left.

get Betar soldiers into the country without foreign assistance?" Begin made a remark about moral force. "Have you taken note, sir, of the proportion between Hebrew forces and Arabs in Israel?"

In the end, although Jabotinsky demonstrated the impracticability of Begin's argument, the conference went along with Begin in voting to modify the Betar oath. The old version said, "I will raise my arm only in defense." The new version read, "I will raise my arm only in defense and the conquest of my Homeland." A young radical rabbi named Israel Scheib spoke in defense of Begin at the conference. Scheib would go on to become Lehi's chief propagandist during the Revolt against the British. Jabotinsky compared Begin's speech to a squeaking door—a totally useless sound.[9]

After the conference Begin and the radicals reconciled with Jabotinsky by forming a mock suicide pact in response to a remark by Jabotinsky. The next year in March 1939 after Hitler swallowed up the rest of Czechoslovakia, Begin was appointed the Betar commissioner for Poland—the most senior position in the country that was the most important by far of Betar's realm. Begin seemed to be oblivious to the upcoming war. He spent the summer getting married to Aliza Arnold, the nineteen-year-old daughter of a successful lawyer and the leading Revisionist in the town of Drohobych, the town where Begin practiced law in 1938–39. Jabotinsky attended the wedding.[10]

Natan Friedman-Yellin, who was a Betar member close to Begin, obtained exit visas for Begin and his wife as well as for himself and his wife. Begin had attended Friedman-Yellin's wedding on September 5, as the Germans were in the process of defeating the Polish armies. The next day the two couples met in the courtyard of the house of Begin's sister and with a few belongings prepared to leave the country. Friedman-Yellin tried to buy four train tickets for Lvov in Ukraine, but there was no train for Lvov. So instead they got tickets for Vilna in eastern Poland, soon to be the capital of Lithuania. They boarded the train at dusk, but the train did not pull out of the station until after midnight. After a few hours the train stopped because the Germans were bombing. The four decided that it would probably be just as fast and much safer to travel by foot to the east. They began walking to the east sleeping in barns at night. By October 28, 1939, they finally made it to Vilna (Vilnius) and moved into a small Catholic village outside the city in a house rented by Rabbi Scheib and his wife Batya, then part of the Soviet occupation zone. Scheib had abandoned his position as a propagandist for Betar in Warsaw at the start of the war after the building that housed the newspaper he worked for was hit by a bomb and destroyed.[11]

The group decided to wait there until they could get exit visas to safety. On September 1, 1940, Begin received an official letter requesting him to report to the city hall for questioning. Begin ignored the letter. A few days later he noticed that the house was under surveillance. Suddenly one day there was a knock on the door and three men demanded Begin's presence at city hall for questioning. After getting them to show identification Begin gathered up a suit, polished his shoes, conceded the chess game he had been playing to Scheib and left.

Begin soon found himself being accused of anti–Soviet activities by the NKVD Soviet secret police. After spending weeks undergoing interrogation where Begin debated with his Jewish interrogators about the nature of Zionism, he was thrown into Lukishki Prison, a prison for political prisoners on the outskirts of Vilna. Finally on March 8, 1941, Begin was informed that the Soviet judges had sentenced him in absentia to eight years in the corrective labor camps—the infamous Gulag—dated from the date of his arrest on September 20, 1940. He was sentenced under Article 58 of the Soviet penal code as a socially-dangerous element.[12]

Begin had begun to sink into depression following Jabotinsky's death in August 1940. The task of arguing with his interrogators pulled him out of the depression. Begin again went into depression in prison and stopped paying attention to personal hygiene.[13] This was the start of a life-long pattern of sinking into depression when things went badly and then reviving and coming out when faced with a new challenge or opportunity. It would continue until 1983 when Begin slipped into depression for the last time and never came out of it.

The inhabitants of the initial cell that Begin spent time in were regularly changed to keep the prisoners off guard. Twenty people were kept in an unfurnished cell with only a small window for light. The inmates were given spittoons to eat and drink out of, and these were only replaced when they refused to use them. In transport nearly seventy men were forced into military transport railroad cars designed to carry 40 men. During the entire train journey the prisoners were only given bread and salted fish to eat—so they were constantly thirsty, but the only water to drink was polluted. During the journey to the camp along the Pechora River in the Soviet arctic region, Germany invaded the Soviet Union. Begin traveled in the car with Lithuanians and Poles. The Lithuanians cheered at the news of Soviet defeats and the Poles were sad. When they entered the arctic region there was no night as the sun rose again as soon as it set. This phenomenon is known as white nights and gave the name to Begin's prison memoir. "What a paradox! Our days are black and are nights are white," exclaimed one prisoner.[14]

Begin based through two transit camps on his way to the main Pechora

Camp. At the first Begin and the other prisoners had to walk for hours before reaching the camp from the railroad station. They then boarded barges for the journey up the river to the camp. At the second camp Begin was in hospital with a fever for about two weeks. At the Pechora Camp there was nine months of winter and three months of summer a year. Fortunately Begin arrived during the summer. The prisoners worked twelve-hour days and spent sixteen hours a day in the open with meal breaks and roll calls. The prisoners were always hungry due to the meager food rations that they received each day, which were tied to their fulfillment of the assigned work norm. Begin was once sick with a fever for four days and then returned immediately to work. Those authorizing sick time for the prisoners themselves faced additional prison time if they were too lenient in allowing prisoners time to recover in the eyes of the authorities.[15]

One day all Poles working in the various Pechora sub-camps were called together for a meeting by the camp director. He announced that it had been mentioned in Pravda that the Soviet and Polish governments had signed a political accord. The Soviet government had decided to amnesty all Polish citizens in the Gulag, but before he could do this he needed to receive a directive to do so from the NKVD. As soon as he had all the Polish prisoners would be released and transported to recruitment centers where they could join the army of Wladyslaw Anders who was recruiting an army within the Soviet Union to fight on the Western front with the allies. In the meantime they were all expected to work as usual and fulfill their work quotas.

When the directive finally came the Polish prisoners spent three days and nights sleeping in the open because their transport to freedom was not ready yet. Finally they were let back into some huts for their final night in the camp and thieves stole Begin's final possessions while he was asleep. When he went into the Gulag he was warned by other prisoners that "they" would steal everything from him.[16]

While he was in the Gulag, Begin heard many stories about the caprices of Soviet officialdom. One Jewish prisoner who had been in Dachau in the 1930s thought that before the war the Jews were treated better by Hitler in the concentration camps than were prisoners treated in the Soviet Gulag in the 1930s and 1940s. It was only when the decision to embark on the final solution was made by the Nazis that this changed with the creation of the death camps.[17]

Begin would later claim that he spent two years in a Soviet prison, presumably counting 1940 and 1941. But in reality it was just one year: September 1940 to September 1941 and two-thirds of that was spent in Vilna. Begin spent another six weeks on the train and another three weeks on the barge. He only spent a month in the camp working, and half of that was spent in the hospital in the transit camp. The one month at the camp was a summer month. Begin was released just before one of the coldest Russian winters in years in which 40,000 men—80 percent of the prisoners—would die from exposure and starvation.[18]

Begin spent months working his way south hitching rides on trains after he was amnestied. Anders's army was anti–Semitic and did not really want Jews enlisting because they considered them to be poor fighters. Begin had his initial physical for Anders's army in Margilan in Central Asia. He was initially rejected because of a poor heart and his poor eyesight. But after he wrote to the army's chief of staff he was granted an interview. Begin spoke of his fear of being rearrested by the Soviets if he was not allowed to enlist. The senior officer took pity on him and he was allowed to enlist as a private to serve as a clerk.[19]

When Begin was still waiting to go into the Gulag a young female Betar member visited him in prison posing as his wife. By coded language she passed some news of his real wife—that she had immigrated to Palestine. She also informed him that there was a note for him in the bar of soap that she brought him. Aliza had sent Begin in prison a handkerchief with the word "ola" (Hebrew for female immigrant) stitched into it in Latin letters. One of Begin's cellmates helped him to decipher the hidden message. Aliza had had herself smuggled across Europe to Palestine where she was interned for several months in a camp. Upon her release she moved into a very small apartment in Jerusalem.[20]

Begin arrived in Palestine in April 1942 with a detachment from Anders's army. In late 1942 the entire army of some 70,000 men left the Soviet Union for the Middle East where they fought in the Western desert against the Afrika Korps and then in Italy. Once Begin arrived in Palestine it only took him a few hours to get word to Aliza that he had arrived. He also learned that Friedman-Yellin and Scheib had also arrived. Begin moved into the apartment with his wife and began working as an army clerk in Jerusalem. In late 1942 he was appointed head of Betar in Palestine, giving him a senior position in the Revisionist hierarchy.[21]

Following the split within the Etzel in September 1940, Stern tried to fashion an alliance with the two European Axis powers by sending envoys to meet with Italian and German officials in the Balkans and in Beirut in the spring of 1941. His overtures were rejected because the Italians had thrown in their lot with the Arabs and the Nazis did not want any kind of alliance with Jews.[22] In the autumn of 1941 Stern declared a revolt against the British in Palestine and by the spring his organization was nearly destroyed with most members in British detention camps. On February

17, 1942, High Commissioner Harold MacMichael reported that some eighty members of the Stern Gang, as the British referred to Stern's organization, were in prison, mostly in the Misra and Latrun detention camps.[23]

Stern himself was shot while hiding in a closet in a Tel Aviv apartment by a British detective (or after coming out of the closet and surrendering).[24] In the spring of 1942 the organization was reborn under the name *Lohemei Herut Israel* (Fighters for the Freedom of Israel) or Lehi for short. The new leadership consisted of a triumvirate of three known as the Merkaz or Center: Yitzhak Yezernitsky, Israel Scheib, and Natan Friedman-Yellin. All three were former Polish Betarim and Begin knew two of them quite well. When Begin arrived in Palestine the three speculated on whether Begin would join the Etzel or Lehi. Scheib correctly predicted that Begin would eventually join the Etzel because his actions did not match his rhetoric.[25]

David Raziel, one of the founders and commander of the Etzel Underground Organization, May 1, 1941. He was killed in action during World War II serving with British.

Scheib met with Begin and accused him of being a deserter from the Revisionist struggle in Palestine because he refused to desert from Anders's army. Begin was obsessed with both legality and honor. He did not want to conform to the traditional anti–Semitic image of Jews as cowards. He initially felt that the Betarim should enlist in the Polish army and fight against the Germans when Poland was invaded rather than flee and make their way to Palestine. Throughout 1943 Begin resisted pressure to desert and join the struggle in Palestine.[26]

In 1941 David Raziel had been killed by a German aircraft that attacked the vehicle he was in on a mission for the British army in Iraq. Raziel, loyal to Jabotinsky, had been willing to carry out the secret mission against the pro–Axis Arab government in Iraq. His successor was Ya'akov Meridor, who was a skilled operator but not much of a leader. In 1942 Arieh Ben-Eliezer returned from America where he had spent the initial part of World

War II. Ben-Eliezer and Meridor both agreed that the Etzel needed a new commander and both figured that Begin would make a good commander. This was for three reasons. First, Begin was already the head of Betar in Palestine and was known as an activist. Second, Begin was unknown to the British and so could operate more easily than more well-known Etzel members. Third, Begin had not been involved in the split and so possibly had the potential to bring the Etzel and Lehi back together again.[27]

Eventually a deal was worked out with the Polish army where Begin was given a year's leave from the army in exchange for Revisionist Jews in the United States using their political influence on behalf of the army. Begin was supposed to go to America as part of the Revisionist delegation but because the British objected, the delegation never went. Begin kept from them that he intended to start a revolt against the British government in Palestine in the near future. So Begin was given his leave and the army never asked for him back and Begin never volunteered to go back. But Begin's sense of honor was satisfied.[28]

Begin began as the new Etzel commander on October 17, 1943. The first thing he did was cut off ties to the Revisionist Party for security reasons. Begin wanted to open the Revolt in the autumn of 1943, but the Etzel was not ready and Begin had to delay until the winter of 1944. Begin lived in Jerusalem but commuted to Tel Aviv during the week to run the Etzel. Begin eventually moved to the Savoy Hotel in Tel Aviv, which was owned by a Revisionist. But Begin ended up moving several times during his first few months in Tel Aviv in order to find a secure location.[29]

Begin began work on writing the Etzel's declaration of Revolt on January 28, 1944. It was pasted up on the walls of the main cities of Palestine in the morning of February 1, 1944. Begin launched the

Avraham Stern (Yair), one of the founders of the Etzel Underground Organization and later founder and head of the "Lehi" underground movement, January 9, 1942. He was murdered by the British.

actual revolt with attacks on British immigration offices later that month. Next were attacks on tax offices and finally on police stations. The idea behind all of these symbolic attacks was to provoke a British overreaction that would then alienate the Yishuv and Britain's diplomatic allies. Begin agreed not to attack any British military facilities in Palestine as long as the war against Germany continued in Europe.[30]

By the end of 1943 the Etzel had effectively about 600 members. When the split occurred in 1940, about a third remained in the Etzel, a third went with Stern, and almost a third took advantage of the situation to drop out completely. Over a thousand members had with the organization's permission enlisted in the British forces—a way of dropping out of the internal struggle and also gaining combat experience and weapons training. For weapons the Etzel had a grand total of four sub-machine guns, thirty rifles and some sixty pistols of various makes. It had less than a ton of explosives, no printing press, no radio, and no communications equipment. It also had very little money.[31]

The first few months were spent raising funds, and when necessary carrying out expropriation raids on merchants in order to get money. Begin probably did not question too closely where money came from as long as no one got hurt or killed. In August 1944 Lehi carried out an assassination attempt against British High Commissioner Sir Harold MacMichaael that left him wounded in the leg. This led to pressure by the mandatory authorities on the Jewish Agency for greater cooperation in apprehending the dissident Zionists. In October 1944 the Hagana decided on a new policy of tracking, capturing and interrogating members of the two underground organizations. Hagana leader Moshe Sneh, who knew Begin from Poland, met with Begin secretly on October 8 and tried to convince him to call off the Revolt on the grounds that he lacked both a democratic mandate and the inside information to make decisions for the Yishuv. Begin refused. On October 15, 1944, the Etzel and Lehi launched a joint pamphlet calling on the Jewish population to ignore British requests for information. On October 26 the labor Zionist newspaper *Davar* announced that the organized Yishuv would take action against dissident terror. On October 31 Sneh and Eliahu Golomb from the Hagana and Begin and Eliahu Lankin from the Etzel met. Golomb appealed to Begin on the grounds that a new British partition plan that was more favorable than the Peel Plan was in the works. Begin replied, "The Homeland is a unity and cannot be cut up."[32]

The Hagana's new anti-dissident policy, which has gone down in Israeli historiography as the *saison or sezon* (French for season meaning hunting season), was to be carried out by the Palmakh and Hagana intelligence. Some 170 people went through a special training course on October 20 in preparation for this role.

On November 6, two Lehi assassins killed Lord Moyne aka Edward Guinness, the senior British official in the Middle East, outside his home in Cairo. This was then used by the Hagana as a pretense to launch the saison. But paradoxically it was not launched mainly against the Lehi but rather against the Etzel. This was for several reasons. First, the Etzel with its former connection to the Revisionist Party was seen as a real political threat to the ruling Mapai—General Zionist alliance in a way that Lehi was not. Secondly, the Hagana was able to convince Friedman-Yellin to call a truce and cease operations as long as the war continued. Begin would not agree to any pause in operations. Finally, Lehi had promised that if any of its men were lifted it would retaliate by killing Hagana personnel. It was the combination of the pause in operations and the threat of retaliation that left Lehi virtually unscathed except for the arrest of one person and the capture of the movement's archives in February 1945.[33]

Meanwhile from November 1944 to the spring of 1945, the Palmakh captured hundreds of Etzel members—300 to 500—and deposited them at kibbutzim for interrogation. The Hagana found it was running out of space to hold the prisoners and most were released after a few days and eventually any names of comrades that they gave up during questioning were simply released straight to the British—over a thousand in total. The British then deported the most wanted prisoners, like Ya'akov Meridor and Arieh Ben-Eliezer to camps in Africa for detention until the insurgency was crushed. In early December the British complained to Hagana liaison officer Reuven Shiloah that they were only getting the unimportant terrorists and that the Hagana was only providing information on the Etzel and not on Lehi as well. They also complained that the Hagana was only passing along extracts from captured Etzel documents while the Hagana was keeping the originals. Remember, this was in the age before mechanical copying machines.[34]

Eliahu Tavin, head of Etzel intelligence, was captured by the Hagana on February 27, 1945, and not released until late August 1945. He was taken to Kibbutz Givat haShlosha near Petah Tikva and interrogated. When he refused to give up Begin or anyone else he was subjected to a fake execution. For days he was beaten and kept chained in a cave. Although Hagana intelligence finally called off the saison in June, the Hagana-Palmakh called off the saison both because it was unpopular with its members and because Britain had failed to reward the Jewish Agency politically for its cooperation. Tavin remained in captivity. He was finally released as a favor to Begin during negotiations leading to the Hebrew Resistance Movement.[35]

During the saison most of the Etzel High Command wanted to retaliate against the Hagana. Begin refused as he knew that this would result in a civil war that he could not possibly win. The Palmakh was much better armed and trained in guerrilla warfare than was the Etzel. The Palmakh was able to operate in company-size units whereas the Etzel could operate only in squad-sized units on special operations such as sabotage missions or arms raids. Begin knew that public opinion in the Yishuv favored the mainstream Hagana. Reality and command had tempered Begin in the six years since he challenged Jabotinsky at the Third World Betar Conference. He limited himself to attacking the Hagana-Palmakh in wall posters as Cain—the Biblical slayer of his brother. This was Begin's finest hour as Etzel commander. The Etzel was able to resume operations in May 1945 and with the war over it felt free to conduct arms raids against British military camps.[36]

Begin was very angry with Lehi for having given the Left an excuse to launch the saison. Begin attempted to negotiate a reconciliation with the Lehi Center, but by 1944 Friedman-Yellin was over on the Left having become pro–Soviet in a bid to attract support from the Soviet Union. But Begin was able to negotiate a degree of cooperation between the two movements. Because Begin knew both Friedman-Yellin and Scheib well from Poland there was a certain amount of trust. They agreed to notify each other of operations so that their operations would not compromise each other—an operation by one organization could lead to a heightened security level that could compromise an operation by the other underground. This in turn was preparation for a united resistance front with the Hagana-Palmakh against the British.[37]

World Zionist Organization head Haim Weizmann trusted in his personal relationship with Prime Minister Winston Churchill to accomplish his mission. On November 4, 1944—two days before Lord Moyne's assassination—Weizmann was informed by Churchill that a new partition plan was in preparation that was more favorable to the Zionists than the 1937 Peel Plan. Churchill personally favored the Jews getting the Negev Desert as part of their state.[38] The labor Zionists of Mapai put their trust in their relationship with members of the British Labour Party. In July 1945 while Churchill was attending the Potsdam Conference in Germany, the British electorate voted the Conservatives out of office and voted Labour into power. This meant that soon Ben-Gurion would see if Labour would deliver on the promises that Labour backbenchers made to him and other Zionists.

British Middle East policy under Foreign Secretary Ernest Bevin soon reverted to that urged by the Foreign Office for many years: a pro–Arab

Two. Menahem Begin, Underground Commander 39

policy that meant appeasing the Arabs at the expense of the Zionists. On July 13, 1945, the Etzel hijacked a truck full of explosives and on July 25 they used part of this haul to blow up a bridge on the Haifa-Kantara railroad. Shortly after this Begin began to receive peace overtures from the Hagana about forming a united resistance. Mapai leader David Ben-Gurion had since 1942 been in the process of shifting the reliance of the Zionist movement from Great Britain to the United States. Unlike both Jabotinsky and Weizmann, Ben-Gurion was not afraid to challenge London with armed force if necessary with this tied to a diplomatic strategy. Lehi under Scheib and Friedman-Yellin lived in an anti-imperialist fantasy world in which first the Axis powers and then the Soviets would help to liberate a Hebrew state from the Nile to the Euphrates. Begin wanted by comparison merely control of the original Palestine mandate and was willing to entrust policy to Ben-Gurion if he were willing to lead a revolt against Britain.[39]

By late September 1945 the Hagana was in serious talks with both the Etzel and Lehi. The British had broken the Hagana's code so that when Moshe Sneh informed the group's London office of the talks he was inadvertently informing the British as well. On October 8, 1945, the General Zionist Council passed a resolution encouraging illegal immigration. This led to the Hagana concluding an agreement with the Etzel and Lehi on October 25, 1945, creating the Hebrew Resistance Movement (usually referred to in English as the United Resistance Movement). Under the agreement all three movements would be free to carry out arms acquisition operations, but all other operations would have to be approved by a committee controlled by the Jewish Agency and known as the X Committee. The Hagana-Palmakh carried out activities during this period, which lasted until the end of July 1946, in three areas: arms acquisition, illegal immigration, and against British communication infrastructure. On October 31, 1945, the Palmakh blew up two British police boats in Haifa harbor and one in Jaffa harbor and sabotaged railroad lines around the country. On the night of June 16–17, 1946 the Palmakh destroyed eight bridges around the country cutting off Palestine from the outside except for a single bridge, which the Palmakh failed to destroy when the saboteurs were spotted by British sentries and killed.[40]

It was really only with the end of World War II that the Revolt began in earnest. Begin is really remembered, and often reviled, outside of Israel for four main actions carried out by the Etzel between 1946 and 1948: the bombing of the King David Hotel in July 1946, the hanging of two British sergeants in reprisal for the execution of three Etzel members captured in an operation in July 1947, the Deir Yassin massacre on April 9, 1948,

Menahem Begin during his "Rabbi Sassover" period with wife Aliza and son Benyamin-Zeev in Tel-Aviv, December 12, 1946. Courtesy Jabotinsky Institute.

and the importation of arms on the *Altalena* in July 1948. Due to the limited nature of this biography, I will now review these four incidents in turn.

When Begin took over as Etzel commander he made the former commander Ya'akov Meridor his military or operations commander. When Meridor was captured and deported, Amihai "Gidi" Paglin, an activist from a Hagana family who got in touch with Meridor, was promoted to replace him. Paglin had a genius for planning operations and devising improvised explosive devices, but he was over confident in his abilities and sometimes promised more than he could deliver. On June 29, 1946, Black Saturday, the British security forces carried out raids throughout Palestine and carted away loads of documents captured during the raids. The Hagana and especially their superiors in the Jewish Agency were terrified that the British would discover documents related to the existence of the Hebrew Resistance Movement and that this would result in the imprisonment and even the execution of the Yishuv's leadership. At this time Paglin came up with a plan to blow up British military headquarters, which were located in the south wing of the King David Hotel in Jerusalem. The Hagana signed off on the operation, but Palmakh Commander Yitzhak Sadeh stipulated

The ruins of Jerusalem's King David Hotel, blown up by the Etzel, causing the death of 91 people, July 22, 1946. Photograph by Hugo Mendelson.

that the operation had to take place outside of office hours to cut down on possible casualties.[41]

Due to the necessity of sneaking the explosives in during business hours disguised as milk tins, Paglin planned the operation for the noon hour. The Hagana wanted to give the British only a fifteen-minute warning in order to evacuate the building. Paglin insisted on at least a half hour. But the fuses that Paglin was using were not time-reliable: in hot weather they tended to explode prematurely. Begin had twice postponed the operation at the request of the Hagana, but he refused to postpone it a third time as Paglin was worried about the explosives being discovered. A female Irgun member made the warning calls to the King David Hotel, the French Consulate (to open its windows in order to reduce bomb damage) and the Palestine Post in that order between 12:20 and 12:25. The bomb exploded at precisely 12:37—thirteen minutes earlier than planned. The British disregarded the call as many bomb warnings had turned out to be hoax calls meant as a form of harassment. The explosion killed 91 people: 41 Arabs, 28 British, 17 Jews, and five others. Had the British attempted to evacuate probably even more people would have been killed due to the premature explosion of the bombs. The warning only reached anyone in charge two minutes before the explosion because of the press of other business.[42]

Tragically, the whole premise behind the bombing may have been faulty. The Palestine Police Force had only five detectives who could speak and read Hebrew because most Jews knew English. Most translation was done by Jewish translators who were secret Hagana members and thus destroyed any incriminating documents as a matter of course. The King David Hotel was a legitimate military target and the Etzel did take measures to warn the British. Paglin possibly should have taken into account that the warnings would be ignored, but he was under pressure from the Hagana, which was giving conflicting commands. Begin believed in delegating responsibility to his subordinates and then backing them up after the fact.[43]

The bombing had two major consequences. First, it put an immediate end to the Hebrew Resistance Movement. This resulted in the Etzel and Lehi increasing the tempo of their operations. Second, the British army commander in Palestine, General Evelyn Barker, cut off relations between British troops and the Hebrew economy and did it in such a way ("will be punishing the Jews in a way the race dislikes as much as any, by striking at their pockets and showing our contempt for them") that it lowered American political support for the British position in Palestine. The Etzel posted Barker's order in English and Hebrew all over the Yishuv, thus taking some heat off of them for the flawed execution of the mission.[44]

Two. Menahem Begin, Underground Commander 43

In July 1947 three Etzel members captured in operations were in prison sentenced to death and awaiting execution. Begin had Paglin organize the capture of two British sergeants from the street in the resort town of Netanya. Begin then announced that if the three Etzel prisoners were executed he would execute the two British sergeants who had been tried and found guilty of being in Palestine illegally. The British carried out their executions and Begin did likewise. The bodies were then taken by Etzel members and hung up in an orange grove and the area around them mined.[45]

Begin was making the point that his men were as entitled to the protections of prisoner of war status as were the British soldiers and policemen—whom Begin never deliberately targeted as such. The British ended their policy of hanging captured underground fighters. The Etzel hangings led to soldier riots in Palestine and to anti–Jewish pogroms in Britain for the first time in modern history.[46]

In April 1948 the dissident undergrounds switched from anti–British operations to participating in the Hagana's war against the Palestinian Arabs. Since December 1947 they had been carrying out independent terrorist operations against the Arabs, mostly reprisal bombings of the time they carried out in 1938–39. The village of Deir Yassin (also spelled Dir Yassin) was a small village located west of Jerusalem on the road to Tel Aviv located where Givat Shaul is today. The attack was a way of showing the potential of the two groups in Jerusalem and winning recognition from the Hagana for their independent status. When informed by Jerusalem Etzel commander Mordechai Ra'anan and Lehi commander Yehoshua Zettler of their plans for the attack, Hagana Jerusalem commander David Shaltiel sent letters to both warning that they should hold the village and, if this were not possible, to not destroy the houses under any circumstances.

The attacking force consisted of 132 men: one platoon of Lehi fighters and two platoons of Etzel fighters. Lehi provided the explosives, the Etzel provided the Sten sub-machine guns and the Hagana provided a few rifles and hand grenades in the vain hope that the force might then cooperate on the Hagana attack on the strategic village of Kastel. Most of the fighters had seen no combat in infantry operations—they were veterans of sabotage operations, guerrilla raids and terrorist bombings. The villagers put up a tenacious defense and the attackers suffered four killed and 31 wounded—a one-third casualty rate. The attackers began dynamiting house after house. Villagers were lined up against their houses and shot. Many young girls were raped and executed. The attackers looted jewelry off the bodies hacking off fingers in order to get rings.

The local Hagana commander ordered the dissidents to surrender their weapons after he and his men arrived on the scene. They refused. Yeshurun Schiff, the Hagana commander, refused an order from Shaltiel to open fire on the dissidents as he did not want to provoke a civil war. David Ben-Gurion condemned the massacre and sent a telegram to King Abdullah of Jordan condemning it. Begin had absolutely nothing to do with the planning or the execution of the attack but in later years he defended his organization against charges of a massacre. Originally the figure given by the Hagana and Red Cross for the number of Arab dead was 254. But historians after examining Arab sources have downgraded the number of victims to between 100 and 120. The Arab Higher Committee publicized the massacre and this had the effect of creating the first great wave of Palestinian refugees in April and May 1948. Begin did take credit for this effect. Scheib later took credit, whereas Friedman-Yellin later condemned it. Days later the British were slow in coming to the assistance of a Jewish medical convoy attacked by Arabs in a revenge attack. The British tardiness might have been a reaction to the massacre at Deir Yassin.[47]

The *Altalena* incident occurred as a result of the existence of two separate Etzel organizations: the Etzel commanded in Palestine by Begin and an Etzel operating in America and Europe affiliated with the Hebrew Committee for National Liberation headed by Hillel Kook and Samuel Merlin who had gone abroad at the start of World War II before the split in the Etzel. They considered themselves neutral in the split and mainly busied themselves with public relations on behalf of Begin's Etzel and with procurement of weapons and funds for the organization. To that end they managed to acquire a used American LST (landing ship tank) in France and weapons donated by the French government for the Israeli government and given to Kook and Merlin.

While a complete account of the Altalena affair would be too long for this chapter, I will mention the basic highpoints. On May 30, 1948, Begin signed an agreement to dissolve the Etzel and integrate its soldiers and equipment into the Israeli Defense Forces—the new national army based on the Hagana and Palmakh. The Etzel members would be integrated into their own battalions. Haim Landua of the Etzel met with Deputy Defense Minister Israel Galili on May 15, Israeli independence day, and offered to turn all the weapons on the ship plus allow the Hagana to send a thousand recruits from Europe on the ship. He just wanted $250,000 to equip the soldiers. Two days later Galili informed Landau that Ben-Gurion had turned down the offer. The French government then decided to donate the weapons to Israel, which included: 5,000 rifles, 300 Bren light machine-guns, 150 Spandau heavy machine-guns, five half-tracks, 4 million rounds of ammunition, several thousand bombs and various other equipment. The delay for the sailing of the ship was caused by the loading and the time necessary to get the recruits to the port.

The ship sailed from France on June 11 without Begin being notified first. A truce was in effect and Begin tried to have the ship wait until he could make arrangements with the IDF. Begin wanted to keep 10–15 percent of the weapons for the Etzel forces in Jerusalem, which was not part of the state of Israel and hence not subject to the integration agreement. Ben-Gurion refused to allow any weapons to be diverted to the Etzel. Begin had the ship diverted to Kfar Vitkin, a small settlement north of Netanya.

At Kfar Vitkin Moshe Dayan's 89th Commando Battalion surrounded the beach, although Dayan himself was not present. Begin met the ship and a launch from the ship began to offload the weapons. Begin was given an ultimatum to surrender all the arms within ten minutes or face the consequences. Begin was forced on to the launch by a couple of Etzel members including his former bodyguard, Avraham Stavsky, The launch returned to the ship, but while returning was fired upon by two Israeli Navy corvettes. All but 50 of the Etzel recruits disembarked from the ship and made their way inland to join Etzel units within the IDF. The IDF ordered the Etzel members to surrender. Firing broke out. The Etzel lost six dead

The shelling and burning of the Etzel's Altalena ship by a Palmach detachment off the coast of Tel Aviv, June 22, 1948. Photograph by Hans Pinn.

and eighteen wounded and the IDF took possession of the offloaded arms—about a fifth of the ship's total. The ship then headed south for Tel Aviv.

The captain of the *Altalena* beached the ship about a hundred yards offshore on a sandbar opposite the Kaete Hotel, which was being used by UN observers who had a front row seat to this massive attempted violation of the truce. That morning Ben-Gurion had convened his cabinet and received permission to use force if necessary to effect a surrender. During the night hundreds of former Irgunists had deserted from their units and flocked to Tel Aviv to help unload the ship as word of the fighting at Kfar Vitkin got out. After several hours of stand off during which Begin with a megaphone called for volunteers to help unload the ship, the Palmakh under the command of Yitzhak Rabin opened fire. Palmakh Commander Yigal Allon had turned over control of the situation to his deputy Rabin. At the beach was also one of Israel's four World War I-era artillery pieces. The cannon began shelling the ship and it caught on fire. The captain ordered abandon ship and Begin was dragged against his will and thrown overboard. After wading ashore Begin made his way to a nearby underground radio location and broadcast a very emotional speech to the nation. Israel Scheib urged Begin to attempt a coup d'etat, which Ben-Gurion had always suspected Begin of attempting to do. Begin ignored Scheib and went home. Killed in the fighting was Avraham Stavsky, who had won a reprise from the gallows in 1934.[48]

The crisis occurred because of division within the Etzel, lack of communications between France and Israel, and mutual suspicion and hostility between Begin and Ben-Gurion. Ben-Gurion had already attempted to crush the Etzel in 1945 during the saison, which was renewed briefly in 1947. The *Altalena* affair colored the relationship between Begin and Ben-Gurion until late May 1967, when Begin offered Ben-Gurion the premiership.

Begin through his leadership of the Etzel over four and a half years was able to create a new myth of driving the British from Palestine and liberating Eretz Israel. From 1945 to 1948 338 Britons were killed by Jewish groups. Most were killed individually or in small groups up close. This led to great bitterness. When Britain made its decision to turn the issue of Palestine over to the United Nations in February 1947 this was largely due to two factors. First, the British Empire was broke after World War II as evidenced by London turning over responsibility in the Near East—Greece and Turkey—to Washington that same year. Second, it was not so much the military efforts of the Etzel and Lehi that forced the British to quit as the realization that in the short to medium term (and quite possibly the long term as well) there was no solution that would satisfy both the

Arabs and the Jews. Both the Revisionists and the Arabs rejected partition.[49]

Begin was successful not because he had any great understanding of guerrilla warfare but because he had a very good sense of public opinion and what type of operations would work to win public support. Begin had the good sense to turn military operations over to people who understood military matters and had a talent for it like Ya'akov Meridor, Eitan Livni, and Gidi Paglin.

Begin was also successful because the British had during World War II forgotten most of their colonial counter-insurgency experience. They would reacquire that experience in Kenya, Cyprus and Malaya, but that was too late for Palestine. The political situation of dealing with victims of the Holocaust wanting to get into Palestine while the Arabs wanted them kept out at all cost left Britain in a no-win situation. Many of the soldiers stationed in Palestine after the war had no great desire to be there as they had already spent years in Europe fighting and in occupation duties. By generally operating by a code of warfare, Begin was eventually able to win support for the Etzel from many Jews in the diaspora as well as newly-arrived Jews in Palestine. Begin had a political sense that was completely lacking among his counterparts in Lehi, Israel Scheib (Eldad) and Natan Friedman-Yellin (Yellin-Mor), who, like Yasir Arafat in the 1970s to 1990s, went from one radical ally to another in pursuit of fulfillment of a utopian exclusivist goal. As a result Begin and his former Etzel comrades were much better positioned to reap politically after the 1948 war than were their Lehi counterparts.[50]

Three

A Party Is Born and Grows: From Herut to the Likud

In May 1948, following Israel's declaration of independence, Menahem Begin emerged from the underground, a parade of the Etzel's fighters was held, and Begin declared the formation of the Herut (Freedom) Party. Herut is a classic continuation paramilitary party in which the party is led by those who formerly led the paramilitary organization. In Israel three paramilitary parties emerged—one for each of the main underground militias: Herut; the Fighters' Party for Lehi; and Mapam for the Hagana/Palmakh. The Fighters' Party had disappeared by 1951 after winning only a single seat in the First Knesset. Mapam split in 1954 into two separate parties: Mapam, embodying the haShomer haTzair kibbutz movement, and Ahdut Ha'Avoda (the Unity of Labor), which was the paramilitary portion representing the Palmakh command and haKibbutz haMeuhad kibbutz movement. It continued to exist from 1954 until 1968 when it merged with Mapai and Rafi to form the Israeli Labor Party and was just one faction of that party supporting Yigal Allon and Yitzhak Rabin. Without possibly being aware of it, Israel and Begin were following the model pioneered in the Irish Free State in the 1920s with the two rival factions of the Irish Republican Party that constituted the two sides in the Irish Civil War each transforming themselves into rival political parties.[1]

In the 1950s through the 1970s Herut was known as "the fighting family," a name coined by Begin, because its leaders liked to think of it as a fraternity of former combatants. Initially Begin simply converted the Etzel High Command into the Herut Executive and grafted on a few other people on to its Knesset list to represent other parts of Jabotinsky's movement such as his son Eri and Hillel Kook and Shmuel Merlin of the Hebrew

Three. A Party Is Born and Grows

Menahem Begin and Chaim Landau (sitting), in front of a "homeland and freedom" poster on the stage during a Herut party meeting in Tel-Aviv, August 14, 1948. Photograph by Hans Pinn.

Committee for National Liberation, and Revisionist poet Uri Zvi Greenberg. Begin by himself embodied two of the three main elements of the old Jabotinsky movement: Betar and the Etzel.

There were four different lists from the nationalist Right competing in the elections to the First Knesset in February 1949: Herut, the Fighters' List, Tzohar/Revisionist Party and the State Party. Only the first two made it past the one percent barrier to make it into the Knesset. Begin then had the World Tzohar Union recognize Herut as its Israeli affiliate, leaving Dr. Arieh Altman's Revisionist Party with nowhere to go. It soon collapsed and

(From left) Uri Zvi Greenberg, Esther Raziel Naor and Menahem Begin attending the first Knesset session in Jerusalem, December 12, 1949. Photograph by Hans Pinn.

Begin picked up some of the remnants such as Yohanan Bader. Herut finished fourth in the 1949 election with eleven percent of the vote—much lower than the third that Begin expected to receive. But this was still good by the standards of the Revisionists in the Yishuv.²

Next Begin fell out with some of the intellectuals from his first list who asked questions and expected answers rather than empty pieties. These included Eri Jabotinsky, Hillel Kook and Shmuel Merlin. They soon left the party. Jabotinsky returned to academia and Kook and Merlin turned to writing but largely disappeared. Merlin was party secretary, but left after Begin disavowed the illegal underground that was set up to oppose the German reparations accord through violence.³

Begin's first two years in the Knesset were spent making speeches calling on the government to go to war against Jordan to liberate the East Bank. Ben-Gurion did not think that a Israel that was broke and busy absorbing hundreds of thousands of new immigrants needed to risk its future by taking on London and Washington over Jordan. Begin also had to endure the taunts from Ben-Gurion and the refusal to ever refer to him by name. This would continue until Ben-Gurion retired from politics in

Three. A Party Is Born and Grows   51

1963. Begin seemed to crave the approval of Ben-Gurion, which he could never get. Many of Herut's voters agreed with that as well and in 1951 they abandoned Herut for the General Zionists and Herut was reduced from fourteen seats to only eight. Begin went into a deep depression and began to talk seriously about retiring from politics to practice law and actually retired temporarily for a month in August to September 1951. Begin went abroad on an extended trip. Begin also used his free time to write his first two volumes of memoirs: *The Revolt* was published in 1950 and *White Nights*, his memoir of his time in the Soviet Gulag, he wrote from September 1951 to January 1952 while staying in a guest house in Jerusalem.[4]

It was the reparations negotiations between Germany and Israel in 1952 that both saved Begin from a career as a lawyer and cemented his image as a demagogue with most of the Israeli public. In 1951 when the occupying powers in Germany rejected an application by Israel for financial reparations for the Holocaust, Ben-Gurion filed an application with the provisional government of Chancellor Adenauer in Bonn. Bonn saw this as an opportunity to salvage Germany's international reputation and image and so began negotiations with Jerusalem over financial reparations in March 1952. Arieh Ben-Eliezer suffered a heart attack in December 1951 and Begin returned the following month to organize a series of demonstrations against the negotiations. Begin saw the whole subject of reparations in moral terms, as a form of blood money that would cleanse the hands of the Germans. Begin made some rather intemperate speeches in the Knesset on the issue. He did not stop the negotiations but he did overcome his depression and make a return to politics possible.[5]

Begin ran Herut the same way he ran the Etzel in the underground. He would convene a meeting of the party executive and make a presentation. He would then open the subject up to discussion and after some discussion he would summarize a conclusion without holding a vote on the issue. Begin populated the Herut Executive with Etzel veterans who held staff positions during the Revolt rather than with the independent city commanders or operations chiefs like Gidi Paglin and Eitan Livni. This meant that the Executive consisted of individuals who owed their positions to their relationship with and loyalty to Begin. This tended to ensure a great deal of compliance with Begin's wishes. Begin was in effect recreating Jabotinsky's status within the Jabotinsky movement.[6]

Begin's only real opposition from within Herut came from Shmuel Tamir, a former Etzel commander in Jerusalem who after the war became a brilliant lawyer who fought a number of high-profile cases. Tamir openly challenged Begin's leadership of the party in 1966, following Herut's sixth straight election defeat. This time Herut was part of the new Herut-Liberals bloc known as Gahal, which received fewer seats in the 1965 election than its two component parts received separately. Tamir said that Begin should remain as party leader but that the Old Guard—all the Etzel High Command veterans surrounding him—had to go. Begin made a three-hour speech full of rage and self-pity in which he bared his soul. And then Ya'akov Meridor convened what amounted to a court martial and drummed Tamir out of the party with a year's suspension of his membership. Tamir left with a number of followers including future Prime Minister Ehud Olmert and Eri Jabotinsky and formed the Free Center Party, which ran in the 1969 elections before joining the Likud. The Free Center consisted largely of former Herut intellectuals who despaired of ever being able to reform the party from within. As a result of the Tamir challenge Begin temporarily went into a depression again, from which he emerged only in February 1967 after an eight-month absence from Herut's leadership.[7]

Begin had attempted to make an election pact with the General Zionists before the 1955 elections but was rebuffed because of his reputation as a wild man and demagogue. In 1956 Begin supported Mapai in the Sinai War. Begin began to gradually tone down his rhetoric and he stopped talking about liberating Jordan. When Begin negotiated the Gahal pact in 1965, which was opposed by the first Labor Alignment of Mapai and Ahdut Ha'Avoda, he only laid claim to western Palestine—the West Bank of Jordan and Israel and Gaza. He also indicated that he would not advocate an offensive war against Jordan to liberate territory, but if war were forced upon Israel it would retain the territory. With the formation of Gahal Begin was able to delegate the party's economic and social policy to the Liberals and concentrate on defense and foreign affairs. Previously Begin had farmed this task out to others in the party while he concentrated on defense and foreign affairs.[8]

Herut's first real break came in May 1967 when the Egyptian entry into the Sinai Desert and closure of the Straits of Tiran led to a major international crisis involving Israel, Egypt, Syria, and Jordan. Begin decided that Prime Minister Levi Eshkol, was too indecisive and needed to be replaced. Begin organized an opposition coalition consisting of Gahal, the National Religious Party, and Rafi who demanded that Eshkol give up the defense ministry to Moshe Dayan. Begin originally wanted to bring back his old rival, David Ben-Gurion, as prime minister but after Begin met with Ben-Gurion at the latter's home he changed his mind. Ben-Gurion appeared too old and even more cautious than Eshkol. So Begin championed the idea of a national unity government led by Eshkol that would include Dayan as defense minister. Eshkol was willing to give up the defense ministry but he wanted it to go to Yigal Allon, the hero of the War of Independence and the leader of Ahdut Ha'Avoda. But Allon was away in Moscow when the crisis began and by the time he returned home the momentum in favor of Dayan was too strong to resist.[9]

It has become fashionable among Israeli political scientists to refer to Israel's present political system as a "second republic," as if there were a new constitution or regime. There are various dates that one can argue for the start of the Second Republic, the earliest is June 1, 1967, with the inclusion of Herut in a government for the first time. Ben-Gurion's maxim when forming coalition governments was "without Herut and without the Communists" as he saw both as too extreme. Historian Peter Medding makes the case that Israel's First Republic ended when the first national unity government was formed. American political scientist Amos Perlmutter also made the case for June 1967 but on the basis of Israel's new expanded borders. A case can also be made for 1974 when the Likud became a viable alternative government to Labor, and when a Labor prime minister who was not from Mapai took power in a generational change. The third logical date is May 1977 when the Likud took power for the first time and the labor Zionists were out of power for the first time. What these three dates all have in common is that they revolve around Herut or the Likud, showing the increased importance of the party.[10]

Begin was a minister without portfolio in the national unity government, which carried out the June 1967 war. Begin's main function in the thirty-seven months that Gahal sat in the government under Prime Ministers Eshkol and Golda Meir was to serve as an arbiter of disputes between the other coalition parties. He also served on a number of ministerial committees. Begin himself saw his function as a watchdog of *shlemut hamoledet*—the wholeness of the homeland, by preventing the government from withdrawing prematurely from the captured territory as it did after the 1956 victory. Begin opposed introducing a motion to annex the occupied territories because he thought that it might not pass and then he would have felt obligated to leave the coalition. At the Ninth Herut Conference Begin announced, "Our goal is to ensure that we never withdraw to the June 4 borders." Begin gave a two-hour speech without once touching on economic and social policy. Begin preferred being a minister without portfolio because it allowed him to pursue diverse matters that interested him rather than being confined to a specific ministerial responsibility.[11]

In February 1969 Eshkol suffered a heart attack and died and was replaced by Golda Meir as a compromise candidate between Allon and Dayan. Begin's relationship with Meir was not as cordial as that with Eshkol. In the elections later that year Gahal again won 26 seats. Begin was divided and ambivalent about remaining in the government after the elections until in December 1969 Secretary of State William Rogers announced a new peace initiative. Begin decided that he needed to remain in the government in his watchdog role. Meir offered Gahal six cabinet seats—three for the Liberals and three for Herut. Ya'akov Meridor vacated his seat so that General Ezer Weizman, who was then deputy chief of staff, could join the government as minister of transportation. Weizman went directly from the IDF to the government with no cooling-off period, something that became mandatory afterwards as a result of his example. Begin chose Haim Landau over Yohanan Bader to receive one of the Herut ministries. He preferred personal loyalty over intellectual ability.[12]

Begin was diagnosed as suffering from diabetes after fainting and after being hospitalized in 1969 he gave up smoking. His health remained fragile because of the damage to his health from his confinement in 1940–41 and his years of smoking. In January 1970 Arieh Ben-Eliezer, Begin's closest confidante in the underground and in Herut died of cancer. He had been Begin's designated successor. At the same time Meridor temporarily retired from politics to pursue business interests leaving Begin with no one close to him that he could confide in.[13]

In July 1970 after the government agreed to a ceasefire with Egypt in the War of Attrition that actually ended the war, Begin unilaterally decided to pull Gahal out of the government as he did not want to be a party to the government decision that UN Resolution 242 applied to all fronts. This put Israeli possession of the West Bank at risk. The Liberals as a faction were opposed as were Meridor and Weizman to the withdrawal. So Begin put it to a vote in the Gahal Central Committee and won by a whisker with the support of a few Liberals. Weizman was furious. He had given up his possible chance to become a future chief of staff to sit in the opposition?[14]

Begin promoted Weizman to chairman of the Herut Executive at Meridor's urging in order to appease him. But Weizman was far from appeased. At the Herut annual convention in late 1972 Weizman openly challenged Begin's electoral strategy over the decades. Begin said that he would form his own faction within the party and contest the leadership with other factions. Weizman quickly realized that he had been out maneuvered. Yitzhak Shamir was brought in to replace one of Weizman's appointees on the Executive. Weizman resigned from Herut in 1973 to pursue business interests was kept in cold storage until the 1977 election when Begin finally did allow Weizman to put his ideas on electoral strategy into practice.[15]

In July 1973 Ariel Sharon, the head of Southern Command, was forcibly retired from the IDF when he inadvertently forgot to request an extension of his service. Sharon had in 1969 got just such an extension when he threatened to go into politics. The bluff no longer worked. So Sharon decided to make the best of the situation and he announced in a press conference that he planned to unify the Zionist Right into a single party that would contest the upcoming election. At that time there were four secular parties on the Right and one non-party political pressure group: Herut, the Liberals, the Free Center, Ben-Gurion's State List, and the Movement for the Complete Land of Israel. Sharon had just purchased his Sycamore Ranch near Beersheva and spent the mornings farming in the fields and the afternoons meeting with various party leaders in a bid to organize a merger. Sharon managed to win Begin over with the persuasiveness of his arguments. He said that the new party needed Tamir in to keep him from drawing voters away from the party if he were excluded. He argued that including Yigal Horowitz's State List would give Labor voters permission to vote for the new party.

Sharon's leverage that he used to overcome the hesitation of the various party leaders to compromise was his threat to quit politics and to take Weizman with him. Begin knew that the two were worth several Knesset seats for a party. The solution that Sharon found to simplify the merger was reducing the number of parties from five to three: by merging the State List, the Free Center, and the Land of Israel Movement into a La'am (to the people) faction that would compete with Herut and the Liberals for seats on the combined list. La'am basically consisted of intellectuals and non-party figures from the Left (Ahdut Ha'Avoda and Rafi) as well as the Right. On September 13, Sharon was able to announce that unity had been achieved and the new party was named the National-Liberal Likud (union), a name suggested by Begin. It quickly became simply the Likud. Elections were scheduled for the end of October, but were delayed until the last day of December due to the outbreak of the Yom Kippur War. Sharon was appointed campaign manager and functioned in that capacity until he was mobilized when the war started.[16]

Begin and Meir were actually very similar in their views regarding foreign policy and defense. Both were suspicious of foreigners and perceived non–Jews as hostile. Meir was theoretically prepared to give up territory in exchange for peace but did not believe that the Arabs wanted peace. Meir still had memories of a pogrom that she had experienced as a child in Russia. Both Begin and Meir grew up initially in the shtetl of Eastern Europe, whereas Jabotinsky grew up in a major city with a large Jewish population. Jabotinsky was cosmopolitan whereas Begin was parochial. Jabotinsky read widely; Begin read mostly history and biography, which was actually the reading material of most statesmen and professional politicians. Begin's conceptual world was really emotional rather than rational—

he was haunted by the Holocaust that had taken his family and he saw all of Israel's enemies as potential Hitlers. His economic policy was a vague combination of capitalism and populism. When Begin needed to justify a change in policy he would comb through the writings of Jabotinsky in order to find something that he could use as justification, much as people comb through religious texts for the same purpose or the way Communists use the writings of Karl Marx, Vladimir Lenin, and Mao Tse-Tung.[17]

The new party managed to win 39 seats—a gain of thirteen from Gahal in the last election and of nine from the four parties combined in 1969. Unity was finally paying off! Originally Herut's electorate had been the veterans of the underground and their families and the Revisionists. This included some mizrakhim (Oriental Jews—Jews from Muslim countries), but not as a major constituency. In 1973 with a unified opposition party many mizrakhim perceived the Likud as a viable alternative to Labor and voted for it. Many mizrakhim, especially those from North Africa, felt alienated from Labor from their absorption experience when they were sent from the urban environment that they were familiar with to rural development towns and forced to become Europeanized. Begin had always utilized mizrakhim in the Etzel on a basis of equality with Ashkenazi Jews, as had Stern and Shamir in Lehi. In the underground the mizrakhim were useful because they could easily pass for Arabs and thus foil British security measures. Herut by the 1970s had come to embody all those groups that felt alienated from and excluded by the Labor establishment: Revisionists, mizrakhim, and underground veterans. The Liberals brought in small business owners and industrialists who had been the backbone of the General Zionists. This meant that the party had enough electoral support to win under the right conditions. In public opinion surveys in November 1973 Yigal Allon was the favored politician to be prime minister followed by Begin.[18]

In January 1974 the gap between the two main electoral blocs was twelve seats compared to 28 in the previous election. Begin announced that he would retire from politics if he failed to win the next election. Over the next few years Begin's public image softened even as his ideology remained the same. In 1975 Begin first made public his willingness to compromise over the Sinai, which he did not regard as part of *Eretz Israel* (the land of Israel). Begin following Jabotinsky's ideology tended to conflate the mandatory boundaries of Palestine with the historical borders of Israel, which changed over time.

Sharon's resignation from the Knesset in January 1975 after only a year embarrassed Begin. This probably strengthened him in his distrust of generals as political figures on top of the experience with Weizman.

Three. A Party Is Born and Grows

Likud leader Menahem Begin addressing the Knesset, March 10, 1974. Photograph by Moshe Milner.

But at the same time Begin began to strengthen his personal relationship with Moshe Dayan, whom he admired. Dayan was retired from the government but still nominally a Labor member of the Knesset.[19]

In 1975 Herut was hit with a major financial scandal: the Tel Hai affair. The Tel Hai fund was a bond to fund the party. But the party lacked the funds to redeem the bonds and it was a major source of embarrassment to the party. Begin hit the road traveling abroad to the diaspora to raise funds to repay those who had invested in the party. Both Herut and Labor were in debt, but Herut's problem was more serious because it had both private and public debts and because people assumed that Labor was good for its debts because it would remain in power. The scandal made Begin appear to be out of touch.[20]

Begin got along with Yitzhak Rabin, not as well as he had with Eshkol but better than he had with Meir. Begin promised to support Rabin during the Entebbe crisis in June-July 1976 as he had once supported Ben-Gurion during the Sinai crisis in 1956. This added to Begin's reputation as a statesman and helped to counter the bad publicity from the Tel Hai affair.[21]

In 1976 the Labor government began a slow process of disintegration and collapse as it was hit with several major corruption scandals as well as the ongoing Rabin-Peres feud. Yitzhak Rabin and Shimon Peres were protégés and successors of Yigal Allon and Moshe Dayan respectively, and their feud was a continuation of the personal animosity between Allon and Dayan that had begun in the late 1930s when the pair entered the security establishment as young Hagana officers. The two were competing candidates for the Labor Party leadership in both 1974 when Meir resigned and again in 1977. Rabin won by a narrow margin on both occasions—the last time he would beat Peres until 1992. In his memoirs published in 1979 Rabin would refer to Peres as an "inveterate schemer" and claimed that Peres was "constantly and tirelessly attempting political subversion. He felt that all means were justified in his pursuit of the premiership.... He not only tried to undermine me but the entire government."[22]

In the fall of 1976 former chief of staff and world famous archaeologist Yigael Yadin announced the formation of a new reform party, the Democratic Movement for Change. Yadin made electoral reform his number one priority although he had a number of other suggested reforms. Ariel Sharon also returned to politics with his own Shlomzion party. Both of these parties were basically general's lists: parties created in order to further the political career of a former general. Yadin's DMC featured four former generals on its list. In December 1976 Rabin called early elections after the late scheduling of a ceremony for the arrival of the first F-15 jets from the United States inadvertently caused some of those attending to violate the Jewish Sabbath. The National Religious Party voted against the government when the opposition put forward a no-confidence motion. Rabin won on the motion but decided to expel the NRP ministers on principle causing his government to collapse and forcing him to schedule early elections for May 1977.

Prime Minister Rabin decided to resign from the premiership when a reporter accidentally discovered that his wife was in position of an illegal dollar account in Washington, which dated back to when he had been the Israeli ambassador. His archrival Shimon Peres took over as acting prime minister in early April for the final month of the election campaign. Although many Israelis would look back on Rabin's resignation with nostalgia for a less corrupt era, at the time it seemed to just epitomize his party's corruption. And in addition to the corruption, the economy was doing poorly and the annual inflation rate was running at 38 percent. This caused many voters to blame the poor economic state on the corruption. Corruption is tolerable in good economic times but not in bad times.[23]

In the May 1977 election Labor was reduced to only 32 seats—a record low number to that time. The Likud won 43 seats—a record high. The DMC won 15 seats—nearly all on the basis of Labor voters who temporarily defected in protest against the state of the party. The National Religious Party received a record twelve seats, which deprived the DMC of its blocking role preventing the formation of a coalition without electoral reform. The president of Israel called upon Begin to attempt to form a coalition government. Begin organized one with the Likud, the NRP, the ultra–Orthodox parties, Shlomzion, and Dayan and left ministries open so that the DMC could join later. Begin's coalition controlled 62 seats. There were three basic reasons for the ma'hapakh (upheaval) as the election is known in Israeli historiography: the Rabin-Peres feud, the corruption in government, and the delayed shock of the Arab surprise attack in the 1973 Yom Kippur War. The Likud benefitted from several demographic advantages that were not present in previous elections: more mizrakhim than before, more religious voters than before, and a more prosperous working class. More working-class voters supported the Likud than supported Labor, which was really a middle-class party. In 1977 the mizrakhim were divided upon ethnic lines: more Iraqis voted for Labor than for the Likud and more Moroccans voted for the Likud than for Labor.[24]

Ezer Weizman managed the Likud's election campaign and marketed Begin as a kindly grandfather figure in order to counteract the older image of him as a demagogue from the Altalena incident and the reparations dispute. Begin was hospitalized with exhaustion during the election campaign and then suffered a severe heart attack in the hospital in early March 1977. This kept him out of action, which was really an aid to Weizman in his effort to reimage Begin as the grandfather. The order of Herut's first seven seats on the joint Likud list were: Menahem Begin, Ezer Weizman, Yitzhak Shamir, Moshe Arends, David Levy, Moshe Aridor, and Geula Cohen. With the exception of Weizman who resigned from the government in March 1980 and temporarily retired from politics before leaving the Likud for Labor and of Geula Cohen, who resigned from the Likud in 1979 to form the Tehiya Party, and the absence of Sharon who was on his own list, this was the center of power in the party into the 1990s.[25]

In his victory speech Begin quoted from the Bible and referenced Jabotinsky. He made a reference to the 1931 Zionist Congress election campaign that the Revisionists lost after Jabotinsky campaigned so hard. Begin was really addressing the former underground members of the Right rather than the electorate as a whole. Begin was a movement candidate in the same sense that Ronald Reagan was in the United States. His victory for the Revisionists had a similar meaning to that of Reagan's victory for Conservative Republicans in 1980, but even more so because there had been many Republican presidents before.[26] It is probably more comparable to Lincoln's victory as the first anti-slavery candidate to be elected president.[27]

Four

Begin in Power, 1977–1983

Begin was able to present a government to the president within weeks of the election. His government was chock full of generals: Moshe Dayan as foreign minister, Ezer Weizman as defense minister, Ariel Sharon as agriculture minister and, once his party had decided to join the government after a delay of two months, Yigael Yadin as deputy prime minister. Besides loving generals in the same way that he loved military parades and ceremonies, Begin had a reason for having so many generals in the cabinet. He wanted to scare the Arabs into making peace. Begin had two main goals in the area of foreign policy: to begin the process of massive settlement of Judea and Samaria (as he called the West Bank using the geographic names for the areas) and to make peace with Egypt. The two goals were related and to some seemed mutually exclusive. What Begin wanted to do was to trade the Sinai Peninsula for the West Bank. In order to do this he needed to make a separate peace with Egypt and find a fig leaf to cover Egypt's acquiescence in Israel's de facto annexation of the West Bank.

Begin invited Moshe Dayan of the Labor Party to join his government as foreign minister on May 21, 1977. Dayan's only condition was that Begin agree not to annex the West Bank. Begin saw the May 1977 election victory more in terms of a victory for himself than for his party, Revisionism, or the Etzel so he felt free to invite whomever he wanted to staff the government. Dayan and Begin had three key foreign policy beliefs in common. First, both were opposed to agreements negotiated through an outside mediator rather than in direct negotiations between Israel and its neighbors. Second, both were opposed to the creation of a Palestinian state on the West Bank or in Gaza. Third, both saw the Jordan River as Israel's eastern security border.[1]

Four. Begin in Power, 1977–1983

Dayan was convinced that Egypt was ripe for peace with Israel and that Begin needed someone with his experience and expertise to negotiate the treaty. It was this rather than simply a desire to return to power and attend diplomatic functions—which actually bored Dayan—that motivated Dayan's acceptance of the offer. Outgoing Prime Minister Rabin saw the appointment as a very shrewd move. "Nobody else in Begin's cabinet comes close to Dayan's eminence," said Rabin. Dayan became an independent in Begin's coalition government after it was formed by the Likud, the NRP, and Agudat Israel. Begin had a narrow majority without Dayan and once the Democratic Movement for Change joined a few months later it was a wide margin. Many Labor voters and members felt betrayed by Dayan because he did not return his seat. But Dayan would justify this "betrayal" by the results that he obtained for Israel in his two and a half years in power. Dayan made his acceptance conditional on Begin agreeing not to annex the West Bank, as called for in the Likud platform, while negotiations continued for a peace agreement.[2]

In Begin's first speech as prime minister he stated, "The Jewish people has a historic right to the Land of Israel. It is our ancestral homeland and that right is inalienable." When a reporter asked Begin what style he would adopt as prime minister he replied, "In the style of a good Jew." For Begin this meant settlement of historic Eretz Israel, bringing foreign Jewish communities to Israel, such as Soviet Jews and Ethiopian Jews, and giving refuge to some foreigners needing asylum. In June 1977 Begin gave asylum to 66 Vietnamese boat people picked up on the high seas in the Western Pacific Ocean by an Israeli captain. Begin gave an order to Mossad head Yitzhak Hofi: "Bring me the Jews of Ethiopia." In a televised speech on May 1, 1979, Begin declared that he was working to bring home both the Jews of Ethiopia and the Syrian Jews. Begin had urged Prime Minister Meir to include the freedom of exit of Syrian Jews as part of the ceasefire negotiations with Syria in 1973–74. But Meir did not want to introduce a new complication in negotiations that were already difficult enough. Between 1977 and 1984 some 8,000 Ethiopian Jews reached Israel from Sudan. In May 1991 Shamir airlifted the remaining 14,000 Ethiopian Jews to Israel in a one-day period.[3]

By the late 1970s most Soviet Jews emigrating from the Soviet Union were going to the United States rather than Israel—they wanted freedom rather than Zionism. Begin refused to ask Washington to rescind the refugee status of Soviet Jews. Because Israel was willing to accept any Jew who wanted to come, the Soviet Jews technically were not refugees. Shamir later tried to get Washington to rescind this status although he had no support from American Jews to do so.[4]

Dayan functioned as foreign minister in the same way that he had previously functioned as defense minister and chief of staff: he concentrated on implementing or monitoring a few key policies that were of great interest to him and left the administration of the ministry to others. This is not surprising, after a person develops a leadership style that works for himself or herself there seems to be little incentive to change particularly at age 62—early retirement age in the United States. Dayan concentrated above all on the peace process with Egypt. In the first instance this meant getting the word out to Egypt that Israel was interested in a full peace treaty. No longer would Israel passively wait by the phone for a call that might never come, as it did (or claimed to do) after the June 1967 war. This time Dayan and Begin would actively seek out peace with Egypt.[5]

The first step was finding countries that had ties with both Egypt and Israel and had leaders that might pass on a personal message to Sadat about Israel wanting peace. Dayan met with several foreign leaders in the summer and fall of 1977, but the only real mission that produced results was a secret meeting with Hassan al–Tuheimi, an eccentric political advisor to Sadat who was a mystic, in Rabat, Morocco, on September 4. Morocco had had fairly close covert ties with Israel since the early 1960s when the Mossad began training Moroccan intelligence agents. In 1976 Rabat had offered to serve as a mediator between Israel on one hand and Egypt and Syria on the other. The al–Tuheimi meeting came about as part of this.[6]

Begin and Dayan implemented a strategy separately but in coordination of letting foreign governments know that Israel was serious about making peace with Egypt. At the same time in the White House in Washington was a new Southern Baptist president who had a clear commitment to Middle East peace. President Jimmy Carter, however, was influenced by a Brookings Institution report on Middle East peace and by his national security advisor, Zbigniew Brzezinski, who had served on the committee that wrote the report and by Secretary of State Cyrus Vance. All called for a comprehensive solution rather than a step-by-step approach as Vance's predecessor, Henry Kissinger, had practiced. In August Begin traveled to Romania to meet with President Nicolae Ceausescu, who had friendly ties with President Anwar Sadat of Egypt. Ceausescu then passed on the word to Sadat that in his opinion Begin was serious about wanting peace: "Begin is a hard man to negotiate with, but once he agrees to something he will implement it to the last dot and comma." This resulted in a secret meeting in Morocco between Dayan and Mohammad al–Tuheimi in September.

"I have the feeling of the cantor on the High Holy Days when he stands alone before the Holy Ark and he appeals to the Almighty in the name of the whole congregation…. Therefore, I beseech you, O Lord, make my mission successful," said Begin on becoming prime minister. This illustrates

Four. Begin in Power, 1977–1983

the big gap between Begin and not only his thoroughly secular predecessors in the Labor Party but also Ze'ev Jabotinsky, his predecessor as leader of Revisionist Zionism. Begin was the most ideological and most traditional prime minister that Israel had ever elected.[7]

Begin's main domestic innovation was Project Renewal. This was an urban renewal project to improve the lives of poor urban Jews living in housing projects. It was funded by contributions from the diaspora that were then matched by government funds. That the scheme benefitted mainly mizrakhim who were Likud supporters was an additional benefit. By 1982 the project had built some 30,000 housing units in 80 separate neighborhoods and also provided major infrastructure improvements in terms of plumbing, roads, lighting, etc.[8] By funding this Begin would keep the mizrakhim from questioning the government's support for building new settlements in the West Bank and Gaza.

Begin met with Carter in July and presented an Israeli peace plan and then Dayan met with Secretary of State Cyrus Vance and Brzezinski in Washington in September. Mondale played the bad cop in the meeting grilling Dayan about Israeli settlements in the Palestinian territories and then Carter said that he wanted to reconvene the Geneva Conference that had last met in December 1973. The following month Dayan worked out with Vance the language for the reconvening of the Conference.[9]

When Sadat got word that Carter was planning on reconvening the Geneva Conference he became very worried. This would reintroduce the Soviet Union into the diplomacy of the region where it could use its radical allies like Syria to prevent any progress. There had been a Cold War between Cairo and Damascus since September 1975 when the Sinai II agreement was signed. Sadat decided to preempt Washington and Moscow by getting himself invited to Jerusalem for bilateral negotiations. In a speech to the Egyptian National Assembly on November 9, 1977, Sadat declared that he was ready to travel to the end of the earth to prevent a single Egyptian soldier from dying in combat … even to the Knesset in Jerusalem. Begin was made aware of the speech by a reporter who happened to catch it on the radio. Four days later Begin told a French delegation in Tel Aviv that he was officially inviting Sadat to Jerusalem. Then he issued a formal invitation through the American embassy in Tel Aviv, which transmitted it to the American embassy in Cairo and from there to Sadat.[10]

Sadat was received at Ben Gurion Airport on the evening of November 19, 1977, and traveled by limousine in a special convoy to the Knesset in Jerusalem. At the airport he was greeted by the members of the cabinet and by former Prime Minister Golda Meir. He traded banter with Meir and with Agriculture Minister Ariel Sharon. He was also greeted by Defense

Minister Ezer Weizman, who was on crutches after a serious traffic accident. Weizman used his crutch like a rifle to give Sadat a military salute. It was the beginning of a special political friendship between the two that would last for the remaining four years of Sadat's life. The streets were lined with Egyptian flags, which had been hurriedly produced, and all of Israel's major newspapers issued special editions with a headline in Arabic welcoming Sadat. At the Knesset Begin and Sadat both spoke in English in their respective speeches setting down their terms for peace. Sadat wanted a return of all the Arab land captured in 1967. Begin's reply speech to Sadat was full of biblical references.[11]

Begin and Sadat agreed to set up two committees, one military and one political, made up of both Israelis and Egyptians to work on the various issues related to peace. But beyond this nothing much of a practical nature was accomplished because of the ceremonial aspects of the visit. Two weeks later Dayan again met with al–Tuheimi at the royal palace in Marrakesh, Morocco.[12]

On Christmas Day 1977, Begin, Weizman and Dayan flew to Ismailia, Egypt for preliminary talks with Sadat. Dayan was worried about the total lack of ceremony on the Egyptian side in contrast to the Israeli reception two weeks earlier: no anthem, no Israeli flags, no official ceremony. They also noticed the huge portraits of Sadat that were omnipresent. They were evidence of the Arab cult of personality that existed in all Arab military regimes and was reminiscent of the personality cults of the totalitarian leaders of the 1930s, which held such bitter horrifying memories for the Jews. Little was accomplished at the meeting.[13]

When the two committees started up the following month, Begin managed to inadvertently insult Egyptian Foreign Minister Ibrahim Kamel by addressing him as "young man," which he was compared to Begin but is insulting in Arabic. The delegation was promptly recalled to Cairo.[14] A political rift between Jerusalem and Cairo lasted for half a year with no negotiations and no progress. Weizman managed to keep the peace process from collapsing completely by developing a personal relationship with Defense Minister al–Gamassy and with Sadat himself.

For the rest of the peace process between Egypt and Israel it would be Dayan and Weizman handling the negotiations. Dayan handled the actual formal negotiations and Weizman would go to Egypt to meet with al–Gamasy or with Sadat when the momentum in the process was flagging. Meanwhile Begin and Sharon were busy carrying out the other half of Begin's foreign policy agenda, which to Begin was really domestic policy, the settlement of the West Bank and Gaza with Jews. Shortly after he was elected Begin traveled to the Gush Emunim (Bloc of Believers—a religious

Zionist settlement movement associated with the National Religious Party) squatter camp in Samaria known as Elon Moreh (the teacher's oak) where he declared, "In a few weeks or months there will be many Elon Morehs!" When a reporter asked him if he intended to annex the West Bank, Begin replied, "You don't annex your own territory, you annex foreign territory." Begin had a spot in his heart for Gush Emunim. The number of settlements roughly doubled during Begin's time in office, but Begin acquiesced in a High Court ruling that the expropriation of land to establish Elon Moreh was illegal and the settlement had to be moved.

Sharon personally took charge of West Bank settlement seeing this as a way to advance politically within the Likud as an outsider. He announced plans to settle two million Jews in the West Bank. He had not cleared the statement with Begin and Begin merely explained that it was an unauthorized statement rather than punish Sharon. Sharon became the new Paglin—he would operate independently and Begin would cover for him after the fact. At Dayan's suggestion a statement was issued that there would be no new settlements established, merely military camps manned by Gush reservists. The ruse fooled no one.[15]

Sharon spent the first Begin government mostly working on settlement issues. Within a month of being appointed head of the settlement committee, Sharon had a plan for settling Eretz Israel. In mid–September 1977 Sharon presented his plan, largely based on proposals that he had seen while Rabin's advisor and written by Professor Avraham Wachmann, an architect. The plan had three concentrations of settlements: one in the central mountain ridgeline of Samaria, the second in the Jordan Valley, and the third around Jerusalem. The settlements had three main strategic goals. First, was to protect Israel from the Eastern Front of Jordan, Iraq, and Syria. Second, was to prevent a division of Jerusalem that would allow East Jerusalem to become either the capital of a Palestinian state or a major city within Jordan. Third, was to divide the West Bank and deal with the demographic problem by planting modern Orthodox religious Zionists from Israel and abroad with high birthrates in among the Arabs.[16] Nearly thirty years later Sharon would recognize that this attempt had at least partially failed when he moved to divest Israel of Gaza for demographic reasons.

The first real positive break in the Egyptian-Israeli peace process came at the July 17–18, 1978 summit at Leeds Castle in England. Many issues remained but Dayan came away from the discussions with his Egyptian colleague with the impression that Egypt was indeed serious about making peace with Israel. This feeling and the remaining issues to solve were enough for President Carter to schedule a summit conference with Sadat and Begin and their aides at Camp David in September 1978. Both Begin and Sadat accepted Carter's invitation. This was the first time since January 1978 when he had inadvertently insulted the Egyptian foreign minister that Begin would take a direct part in the diplomacy.

In the summer of 1978, Defense Minister Weizman called for the formation of an emergency national unity peace government. This was a sign that he was becoming very worried about the direction of the peace process. When Begin was asked about this by the press he simply said that his government already was a peace government, thereby defusing the issue. In fact one Begin supporter told *Time* magazine that "Begin is haunted by his heart problem, which means that time is slipping away, and by how history will compare him with his greatest opponent—Ben-Gurion. He is trying to fight his way into the Jewish history books and the leader who brought the peace that Ben-Gurion never could."[17]

The summit opened on Tuesday September 5 and lasted for thirteen days. This was longer than Carter and the American team had anticipated. There was a basic asymmetry between the Egyptian and Israeli teams: on the former Sadat was the moderate and all his advisors were rigid whereas on the Israeli team Begin was rigid and his advisors were flexible. This meant that the American team had to work through Sadat on one hand and through Dayan, Weizman, and Justice Minister Aharon Barak on the other. Sadat and Begin had absolutely no personal chemistry and so were kept apart after an initial meeting out of fear that they would cause the summit to collapse. At the summit the Israeli moderates had different roles: Weizman kept the personal chemistry going and smoothed over any ruffled feathers with Sadat; Dayan would come up with compromise proposals to find ways out of dead ends; Barak then translated Dayan's ideas into legal treaty language while drafting along with Vance. Even though both Brzezinski and Begin spoke Polish (the former's father was a Polish diplomat in the interwar period) they used only English at the summit. Brzezinski was probably the most rigid personality on the American side with his dislike of Begin and his support for a comprehensive peace. The individuals who probably worked the hardest at the summit were Carter, Barak, Dayan, Weizman, Vance and Osama al–Baz, a political advisor in the foreign ministry.

A major sacrifice on Begin's part was his agreement to allow a free vote of conscience on the proposal to remove Israeli settlements in the Sinai when the Knesset voted on it. Weizman got Sharon to phone Begin from Israel and tell him that the Sinai settlements were expendable. With the United States agreeing to pay the costs of Israel building new air bases in the Negev Desert to replace those lost in the Sinai, the issue of Israel's

Four. Begin in Power, 1977–1983

withdrawal from the Sinai was taken care of. The day before the agreement was reached Sadat had threatened to leave and when the Israeli team said it would leave as well. Begin allowed himself to be convinced by Carter to stay on. The Camp David accords called for a bilateral Egyptian-Israeli peace treaty and autonomy negotiations between the two countries in order to implement autonomy in the West Bank.[18]

The Carter administration's top officials on down were biased towards Sadat basically because he was the first Arab leader willing to negotiate openly with Israel, whereas Israel had always been willing to negotiate with the Arabs. Vance saw Begin as a modern-day Pharisee and Sadat as a visionary. Carter told his wife Rosslyn than Begin was a psycho. National Security Advisor Zbigniew Brzezinski reminded Begin of the upper-class Poles who ran Poland before the war. Even Dayan, the Israeli official who got along best with the Americans, saw the administration as biased and told Carter that his people "no longer could be honest brokers."[19]

It took another seven months after the Camp David accords were negotiated to wrap up a peace treaty between Egypt and Israel. Egypt was affected by the resignations of several senior foreign policy officials including the foreign minister. In Israel the problem was that the Likudniks, raised on the philosophy of Jabotinsky and Eretz Israel haShlema (the whole land of Israel), were not comfortable with surrendering territory—even territory that was not considered part of Eretz Israel. During this time Begin and Sadat exchanged very long letters arguing their points of view and replaying their versions of previous conversations that they held In Jerusalem, Ismailiya, or at Camp David. Dayan and Weizman met increasing resistance at cabinet meetings from the Herut Party members of the government. Begin was criticized within the Right for surrendering settlements and agreeing to the language of Palestinian rights in the English version of the treaty. Begin's Etzel comrades were devastated by his giving up the Sinai. Shmuel Katz, who headed up the Etzel office in Paris during the Altalena crisis, broke with Begin over his willingness to return the Sinai and joined Geula Cohen's Tehiya Party. Dayan wanted only security settlements and Weizman wanted settlements only in blocs and without expropriation of Palestinian land. Sadat skipped the Nobel Prize ceremony in Oslo because he had failed to make any gains for the Palestinians. Finally Dayan negotiated solutions to the remaining issues including the priority of Egypt's commitments under the peace treaty and oil supplies for Israel to replace the Sinai oil that it was giving up. A peace treaty was negotiated during shuttle diplomacy by Jimmy Carter and his top aides to Jerusalem and Cairo in early March 1979.[20]

By making peace with Egypt, Begin managed to change his image as

The triple handshake: (from left) President Anwar Sadat, President Carter and Prime Minister Menahem Begin, after the signature of the Israel/Egypt peace treaty in Washington, March 26, 1979. Photograph by Shabtai Tal.

a terrorist into one of a peace maker. But his image would change back again very shortly. At the Nobel Prize ceremony in Oslo in December 1978, Begin attributed his hatred of war to Jabotinsky and accepted the prize in the name of the Jewish people.[21] In reality, if Begin really hated war it was probably because of his family's suffering during two world wars: being forced to move as a child into an abandoned house outside of Brisk, his father's economic status considerably reduced by the war, and then his family wiped out in the Holocaust. But Begin felt a need to attribute everything to Jabotinsky, even as he modified his ideology.

The Begin-Dayan relationship, the key relationship in the first Begin government, changed once the peace treaty was signed on the White House lawn in late March 1979. Begin assigned the task of representing Israel in the autonomy negotiations with Egypt (for Palestinian autonomy in the territories) to Interior Minister Yosef Burg, the head of the National Religious Party. Burg unlike Dayan did not speak or read Arabic or had no knowledge of Arab culture—he was Central European to the core. This led the negotiations to soon reach a deadlock and shut down causing Egypt to implement a policy of cold peace with Israel. It also caused Dayan to

Four. Begin in Power, 1977–1983

Menahem Begin presenting the Knesset with the contents of the peace agreement with Egypt while Yitzhak Shamir listens, March 28, 1979. Photograph by Yaacov Saar.

realize that his time in the government was over and he resigned as foreign minister in October 1979, two years before his death from cancer.[22] This left his former brother-in-law Ezer Weizman isolated. Weizman got tired of being isolated and resigned from the government in May 1980.[23] He went into business and resigned from the Likud. In 1984 he formed his own general's list and won two seats. He then negotiated his way into the Labor Party and spent the last seven years of his political career in Labor before being president of Israel.

In the summer of 1980 Tehiya leader Geula Cohen introduced a bill in the Knesset making a united Jerusalem the capital of Israel. This bill had no practical effect as Israel had already annexed East Jerusalem in July 1967. But Begin's government supported the bill and the Labor Party was afraid to oppose it openly. As a result of the bill's passage, eleven of the thirteen countries that had embassies in Jerusalem moved them to Tel Aviv. This emphasized Tel Aviv's traditional status as the diplomatic capital of Israel.[24]

Labor Party politicians were convinced that the 1977 election was a fluke and with the collapse of the Democratic Movement for Change in 1979 when its two component parts split they would soon return to power.

Prime Minister Menahem Begin at a meeting in Heichal Hatarbut celebrating Zeev Zabotinski's centennial anniversary, June 6, 1980. Photograph by Moshe Milner.

Yadin retired from politics following the 1981 election embittered by his political experience. In 1980–81 as inflation began to increase and internal disagreements within the government increased this view appeared reasonable and was increasingly reflected in the country's liberal media.

At Camp David Weizman came up with the idea of contacting Sharon to get his permission to evacuate the settlements in the Rafiah salient in the northeastern corner of the Sinai. Sharon agreed to support Weizman on the evacuation. In 1981 he razed the city of Yamit in the settlement out of concern that it could cause future security problems for Israel if President Sadat populated it with Egyptians who then infiltrated into Israel looking for work.²⁵

In May 1980 Ezer Weizman quit as defense minister over policy differences with Begin over the implementation of the peace settlement with Egypt. Rather than appoint Sharon to the position as he had appointed Shamir to replace Dayan as foreign minister following the latter's resignation in 1979, Begin assumed the position himself in imitation of David Ben-Gurion and Levy Eshkol. This irritated Sharon who made his feelings plain. But Begin simply joked with reporters that if he did do this he might find the government buildings surrounded by tanks one day. Begin probably did not seriously believe that Sharon would carry out a coup d'etat, but Sharon's rude contact during cabinet meetings, in which he insulted those with other viewpoints, left him feeling uncomfortable about letting Sharon have that sensitive position.[26]

The position of the Likud in the polls deteriorated throughout 1980 and 1981. Begin had reached the zenith of his era in the spring of 1979 when he was praised abroad for his moderation in making concessions necessary for the peace treaty with Egypt. Between 1977 and 1980 inflation increased from 42.8 percent annually to 132.9 percent—more than triple the rate in three years! Privatization was only partially carried out and government spending was not cut. Defense spending could not be cut in light of the continued threat from Syria and the PLO and the cost of moving from the Sinai back to the Negev, and food subsidies were important to Begin's support with mizrakhim.

In 1979 Weizman, Sharon and Levy formed a group to force Begin out of power when he began to act depressed. But this threat revived Begin in time for the Herut Convention and he thwarted them. Weizman then resigned in March 1980. In 1980–81 Begin suffered a stroke and suffered from depression, at least the fifth major episode in his life. Foreign Minister Shamir authorized Weizman, before he resigned, and Levy to form a shadow cabinet to replace the present one if the *party* decided that it were necessary. Simha Erlich, the leader of the Liberal Party, became concerned. Erlich negotiated with Labor to form a Liberal-Labor coalition headed by Weizman if Begin needed to be replaced.[27]

Sharon was worried about reports from the Mossad about progress on the Osirak nuclear reactor in Baghdad. Israel had had a nuclear monopoly in the region since the late 1960s and was wary about losing that monopoly to any Muslim country, particularly a radical nationalist government like that of the Ba'athist regime of Saddam Hussein in Iraq (or the Ba'athist Assad regime in Syria or the Islamic Republic of Iran). Sharon repeatedly urged Begin to react and use the IAF to bomb the reactor. Begin had formed a special committee consisting of himself as defense minister, Shamir as foreign minister, and Chief of Staff Eitan to monitor the situation with Iraq's nuclear potential. On June 7, 1981, Israeli F-16 fighter bombers destroyed the nuclear reactor before it went active and only three weeks before scheduled elections. Three weeks later the Likud won 48 seats, one more than Labor's 47 seats and enough to win the Likud a four year extension in government and Sharon the ministry of defense. Labor had recovered the fifteen seats that it lost to the reformist Democratic Movement for Change four years before, but the Likud attracted enough support from smaller parties to be able to win. Sharon's urging Begin to act was partly responsible for that as well as his settlement activities. The Likud gained three seats since 1977, as well as Tehiya, a splinter party from the Likud. While the National Religious Party had its total representation cut in half from 12 to six, with three going to Tehiya and three to the Likud.[28]

In 1981 Begin ran a campaign of ethnic incitement and demonization against the Alignment (Labor Party and Mapam). Labor Party politicians were pelted with rotten tomatoes and eggs when they went into Likud strongholds. It was the roughest campaign in Israeli political history to date. "The secular worldview and the Alignment's ideas of territorial compromise are alien to this generation, a large part of which grew up in the reality of Greater Israel," explained Aryeh Naor, the secretary in Begin's first government.

Begin was motivated to give the go ahead for the Osirak reactor attack by the potential threat of a nuclear Holocaust in Israel. He likely would have done it even if he was convinced that the attack would cost him the election. In time Rabin and nearly everyone in Labor except for Peres would come to appreciate the wisdom of the attack. The only real negative fallout from the attack was a delay in the United States supplying the IAF with new combat aircraft in 1981–82. Opposition leader Shimon Peres had written to Begin before the attack urging Begin not to go ahead with it and Begin was forced to postpone the attack out of concern that Peres might go public and thereby alert the Iraqis and lead to losses among the IAF pilots taking part. Begin feared that Peres lacked the nerve to carry out the attack if he were elected prime minister. Upon hearing the news of the success, Begin called Ambassador Sam Lewis and after filling him in asked him to pass on the message to President Reagan. Begin reveled in the criticism of the attack in the international press. These were, after all, the same papers that had branded him a terrorist.[29]

Begin's second government was very different than his first government. His first government was a transitional government, an all-talents government that included many figures from the Center as well as From the Right such as Moshe Dayan, Ezer Weizman, Yigael Yadin, and Amnon Rubinstein. The second government by contrast was the first true Likud government in which Herut neo–Revisionist ideology dominated. If the key relationship in Begin's first government was that between Begin and Dayan, in the second government it was that between Begin and Sharon. Sharon like Dayan was someone whose upbringing was not from the Right. He was a Mapainik. Sharon was only given the defense ministry after Moshe Arens and Yitzhak Shamir both turned Begin down when he

Four. Begin in Power, 1977–1983

offered it to them because it would mean presiding over the evacuation of the Sinai.[30]

One of Begin's first acts in his second term was to annex the Golan Heights in December 1981 in response to statements by the Syrian foreign minister and President Assad stating that "[w]e Arabs must not put forth any peace proposal. We must be willing to wait a hundred years and more until Israel's military prowess wanes, and then we shall act." The Golan Law passed in the Knesset by a vote of 63 to 21.[31]

Begin's second term, which lasted for a little over two years, was marked by war. Sharon had begun preparing for a war against the PLO and Syria in Lebanon as soon as he became defense minister in 1981. He took existing defense plans and examined them. Sharon developed two basic plans, Big Pines and Little Pines. Little Pines was for a limited incursion into Lebanon similar to Operation Litani in March 1978, stopping at the Litani River or thereabout. Big Pines meant going all the way to Beirut. Sharon favored Big Pines as he wanted to reshape the political environment of the Middle East using force. He wanted to put the right-wing Maronite Phalange Party into power in Beirut, exile the Palestinians from Lebanon and get the Palestinians to overthrow the Hashemite dynasty in Jordan and turn Jordan into their Palestinian state. He went to Washington in the fall of 1981 and conferred with Secretary of State Al Haig. Haig gave Sharon a yellow light—proceed with caution—which, like many American drivers, he treated like a green light. Begin also understood after Operation Litani that the Palestinians would require a more permanent solution.

Begin saw the Maronite Christians, in power in Beirut and living among the Shia Muslims in southern Lebanon, essentially as Christians rather than as Arabs. The Israeli alliance with the Maronities begun by Peres and Rabin during the Lebanese Civil War in the mid–1970s appealed to Begin morally and psychologically as it involved Jews rescuing Christians rather than Jews being rescued by Christians, as sometimes happened during the Holocaust. Begin saw Yasser Arafat as another Hitler figure—the bad Arab as opposed to the Maronite good Arabs. During a trip to Washington in April 1982, Begin assured Reagan that any future Israeli invasion would be limited to within 40 kilometers of the border.[32]

At the beginning of June Israeli Ambassador Shlomo Argov was shot in the head and severely wounded by an assassin from the Abu Nidal Organization, a Palestinian terrorist group supported at various times by Iraq, Syria, and Libya and that specialized in murdering moderate Palestinians. This was in London while attending a formal function. Sharon won cabinet approval to attack PLO headquarters in Beirut in violation of the ceasefire reached the previous year. The head of Shabak tried to explain to the cabinet that Abu Nidal was not part of the PLO, but Begin cut him short, "They are all PLO." Begin was conflating Palestinian terrorism with the PLO.

The PLO responded by shelling Israeli settlements in northern Israel. The 1981 ceasefire reached by American mediator Philip Habib was in tatters. Sharon then pressed for permission for Big Pines from the cabinet. When Sharon presented the plan he completely ignored the IDF's own casualty estimates for the campaign. The cabinet gave Sharon approval instead for Little Pines and Sharon said that the IDF would only go about 25 miles north of the border and would not go anywhere near Beirut. Begin, like Sharon had wanted the war for a long time. "There is no moral diktat that a nation must, or is entitled to, fight only when its back is to the sea or it is on the brink of the abyss," declared Begin. Begin thought that the war would only last a couple of days.[33]

After winning cabinet approval, Sharon instructed IDF Chief of Staff Rafael Eitan to implement Big Pines. A major problem with the invasion was that Aman, the intelligence branch of the IDF, lacked sufficient up to date information about Lebanon because it had never been a priority. The IDF knew the area between the border and the Litani River from Operation Litani in 1978 and knew Beirut from Operation Spring of Youth, when hit teams went in to take out three top Fatah terrorists in April 1973, and from the earlier attack on Beirut International Airport in December 1968, but did not really know the area between the Litani River and the capital. As a result in the planning far too many divisions were assigned to the invasion than what the roads could support leading to traffic jams that made the soldiers targets for brave Palestinians with RPG-7 anti-tank rocket launchers. And "fuel convoys could not get through, the wounded could not be evacuated, and commanders who went forward to observe ... were unable to return to headquarters," according to military historian Professor Martin van Creveld.[34] Operation Peace for Galilee, as the Lebanon War was officially known, involved: four independent divisions, an amphibious brigade, a two-division corps and a reserve corps. Altogether it was about twice as many troops as had fought on the Southern Front in 1973.[35]

Sharon also assured both Washington and the Israeli cabinet that Syria would be left out of the war. On June 8 Begin told the Knesset that Jerusalem was not interested in a war with Syria and called upon Damascus to refrain from any offensive action. But that same day the IDF attacked a Syrian unit around the town of Jezzine and dragged Syria into the war. The war with Syria lasted for four days until a ceasefire went into effect on June 11. The IAF destroyed the Syrian air force in the skies over Lebanon on June 9 and June 10 by jamming the fire control radars for the

Four. Begin in Power, 1977–1983 75

Syrian surface-to-air missiles and then shot down 90 Syrian combat aircraft without a single Israeli loss. It was an unparalleled feat in the history of aerial warfare in the 66 years since aerial warfare became a major activity in 1916. Until this day this was the last time that the IDF has gone to war against an Arab army in the field. Sharon wanted to teach Damascus a lesson that it would not forget and he did.[36]

Since his days as commander of the Etzel in the 1940s, Begin had always left the operational planning to others: to Ya'akov Meridor, Eitan Livni, Giddy Paglin, and now to Ariel Sharon. Meridor and Livni had not let Begin down, but Paglin had failed to give adequate warning during the bombing of the King David Hotel. But Begin covered for him, and he even covered for the fighters at Deir Yassin, even though that was largely a Lehi operation. Sharon was manipulating Begin during the war by lying to him about his real goals and only telling Begin what he knew Begin would approve of.[37]

Early on Begin told the Knesset that Israeli troops would not be involved in urban warfare and would stay out of major Arab cities, which in turn encouraged Arafat to declare that he would turn Beirut into Israel's Stalingrad. By June 12, six days after the start of the war, the IDF was on the outskirts of Beirut. From this point on it was a matter of Israel putting pressure on the PLO to evacuated Beirut by cutting off the water to the Palestinian quarter of the city while continuing to shell it. Beginning June 14 some four hundred Israeli tanks and a thousand artillery pieces began shelling Palestinian positions within Beirut and this continued for two months. Israeli Navy gunboats also shelled Palestinians positions. The IAF systematically bombed all known Palestinian buildings in West Beirut. Slowly the city was put under siege. On June 25 a number of villages east of Beirut were occupied by the IDF. And on August 4, the IDF took control of Beirut International Airport.[38]

On June 21, 1982, Begin was at the White House to discuss the war with President Reagan. Begin spun the war as a great success for American-Israeli defense cooperation in the struggle against Communism and terrorism. When he returned home, Begin told the cabinet that the summit had been "very important, very warm, friendly." Begin got this impression because Reagan asked him to call him by his first name. Begin took Reagan's natural American informality for friendship.[39]

At this point Reagan sent Philip Habib back into the field again to arrange for a PLO evacuation from Lebanon in exchange for an end to the siege. The problem was that after the PLO had tried to take over first Jordan and then Lebanon, no Arab country wanted to take large numbers of armed Palestinian fighters on its territory. Reagan began "arm twisting" with pro–American regimes and finally a plan was agreed upon to send PLO fighters to Tunisia, Yemen, South Yemen, Syria, Algeria, Sudan, and Jordan. On August 21 international peacekeepers from France, Italy, and the United States arrived and Palestinians began evacuating from Beirut firing thousands of shots in the air to celebrate their "victory" over Israel. The evacuation was completed with 9.000 leaving and the peacekeepers withdrew after about two weeks.[40]

On August 23, Bashir Gemayel was elected president by the Lebanese parliament with Israeli officers advising Shi'ite deputies in southern Lebanon to attend the election and vote. Three weeks later on September 14, Gemayel was assassinated by a bomb placed in the building where he gave a weekly lecture to a Maronite women's group. The bomb was planted by a Christian mercenary in the pay of Syria.[41] The next day Sharon ordered Eitan to let Phalangist militiamen into Palestinian refugee camps in West Beirut in order to clean out any terrorists who may have remained behind after the evacuation. The next day Israeli intelligence officers monitoring what was going on in the camps from nearby rooftops heard radio traffic indicating that something had gone wrong. After several hours of confusion Northern Commander Major General Amir Drori ordered the Phalangists removed from the two camps, Sabra and Shatila. But the camps were never sealed off and new militiamen entered on September 17. Foreign Minister Yitzhak Shamir was informed of the possible massacres by concerned Israeli journalists and did nothing. Sharon finally entered the camps on the morning of September 18 after the Phalangists had been in the camps for three nights and two days. He ordered the last of the militiamen removed and the camps sealed off. By then several hundred to over a thousand Palestinians had been massacred.[42]

On September 24, four hundred thousand Israelis—about a tenth of Israel's entire population at the time—attended a Peace Now demonstration in Tel Aviv and demanded an investigation into the massacres. Peace Now had been founded in March 1978 by reserve officers who thought that Begin's coalition had been slow in taking advantage of Sadat's trip to Jerusalem. After the Camp David summit the organization went into decline until the start of the Lebanon War when it revived with a major rally in July. But the Likud mounted a counter-rally with twice as many attending soon afterwards. But the government could not overlook a demonstration of this size.[43]

A deeply-shaken Begin appointed a three-man investigative committee on September 28. Its head was Supreme Court President Yitzhak Kahan, and its other two members were Supreme Court Justice Aharon Barak, who had served as Begin's legal advisor at Camp David and would

Four. Begin in Power, 1977–1983

be a future Supreme Court president, and retired Major General Yona Efrat as the remaining member. But Begin had only appointed the committee under pressure and continued to regard foreign criticism of Sabra and Shatila as being motivated by anti–Semitism and he remained personally unrepentant about the massacres.[44]

Ambassador Sam Lewis had to interrupt Begin's first vacation in over four years to deliver a heads-up on the Reagan Plan, which was announced on September 1, 1982, and called for Palestinian autonomy within a West Bank ruled by Jordan. It was a plan designed with the opposition Labor Party in mind and based on its Jordanian option and the Camp David accords. In formulating the plan, Washington had consulted with Riyadh, Cairo, and Amman but not with Jerusalem. Lewis's talking points with Begin were identical to those used to announce the plan in the Arab capitals. Begin was enraged to learn that the Saudis had been consulted but not his government. He requested a five- or six-day delay to return to Jerusalem and consult with his government and draft a response before it was officially announced. Reagan did not grant this request, probably because he knew that Begin's response would be negative in any case.[45]

Begin's wife Aliza had been seriously ill with emphysema, which family friends politely referred to as asthma, caused by her life-long smoking habit. For about a year she had been hooked up off and on to a respirator to help her breathe. After the Sabra and Shatila massacre, Reagan cleared time in his schedule to meet with Begin. Aliza became seriously ill and was hospitalized. He went to the hospital and told her that he was cancelling his trip to Washington, but she wrote on a writing pad that he must go. Begin flew to the United States and while he was gone Aliza died in December 1982. Begin returned home immediately without ever having met with Reagan. Begin never forgave himself for abandoning the woman who had stuck with him throughout his life in good times and bad. His foreign ministry aide Yehuda Avner later wrote, "Begin needed three things above all—devotion, tranquility, and companionship, and she gave him all three." The day after returning from the U.S. Begin buried Aliza. At the funeral Israel Eldad, with whom the Begins had lived in Vilna forty-two years before, told Begin as a compliment: "She hated me because of the things I wrote about you. She hated me because she *loved you*." Begin told Eldad softly that she had forgiven him. President Sadat's widow Jehan sent her condolences to Begin through the Israeli ambassador to Egypt.[46]

Begin remained at home in morning even after the traditional thirty-day period was up. He only returned to his office in January 1983. Begin had already been slipping into melancholy while his wife was hospitalized. After her death this turned into depression. In a Knesset speech in response to an opposition motion on June 15, 1983, Begin started out strong but soon lost his focus and appeared very tired. Begin was 70 years old but appeared 80. Ambassador Lewis tried to get Begin to reschedule his meeting with Reagan, but found that Begin had a problem focusing. Finally, in late June 1983 Begin cancelled the Washington trip completely.[47]

The Kahan Commission issued its report on February 10, 1983, which held that the IDF bore indirect responsibility for the massacres. But the report held Sharon *directly responsible* for the massacres. The report called for the removal of Defense Minister Sharon from his ministry, the prompt retirement of Chief of Staff Eitan, the removal of Aman (military intelligence) chief Major General Yehoshua Saguy from his post, and that Brigadier General Amos Yaron not receive a field command for at least three years. The cabinet voted sixteen to one to accept the Kahan Commission report. Sharon was the only dissenting vote. Sharon later spoke to Begin and accused him of handing him over to his enemies as the Hagana had handed over Jews to the British in 1944–45.[48]

During the Lebanon War in 1982 670 Israeli soldiers were killed and another 1,216 died in the subsequent occupation from 1982 to 2000. This compares with some 18,000 Arabs, both Lebanese and Palestinians, and Syrians killed in the war. There were daily demonstrations outside Begin's office by Peace Now and other organizations. Begin saw the casualty figures every day in the press. At one Peace Now demonstration a rightist who was mentally ill threw a grenade into the protesters killing Emil Grunzweig. It was the first political murder of one Jew by another in Israeli history. Wounded in the explosion was another demonstrator, Yuval Steinetz, who later became a Likud MK and minister under Netanyahu.[49]

Whether as a result of his wife's death, guilt over the death of all the Israeli soldiers killed in Lebanon, or guilt over being gone when Aliza died, or a combination of all three, Begin went into a deep depression. He was unable to function mentally and he deteriorated physically losing weight rapidly as he stopped eating. In July 1983 he cancelled a visit to the United States to confer with Reagan over a number of important bilateral matters. On August 28, 1983, Begin assembled the cabinet after he first told his closest aides that he was resigning. He told the cabinet that he felt that it was his duty to resign as he could no longer function as required. When the various ministers begged him to stay he simply repeated, "I cannot go on." He went home. Foreign Minister Shamir and Defense Minister Arens had already been taking up much of Begin's load during his final months.

On September 15, 1983, Begin had Dan Meridor, his political aide, draft a short resignation letter to the president and he signed it and it was sent. Begin continued to live in the prime minister's residence. Meridor

Four. Begin in Power, 1977–1983

and Yahiel Kadishai, Begin's long-term personal secretary and alter ego, managed to find him an apartment in Jerusalem to move into. In December he made the move with their assistance. His unmarried adult daughter Leah moved in with him and began taking care of him. She was a stewardess for El Al. Except for anniversaries of his wife's death when he visited her grave, Begin almost never left the apartment—the only people to visit him on a regular basis where family members, Kadishai and Meridor. In 1984 when the election race between Shamir and Peres looked to be very close Begin declined to make a public endorsement of Shamir, put his name symbolically at the end of the Likud's electoral list or to even go to the polls and vote.[50]

Ya'akov Meridor resigned from the Knesset in 1984, the last of Begin's personal friends from the Etzel to do so. After he retired Begin suffered from diabetes, a stroke, and a heart attack. After Shamir became prime minister in October 1986 he made a habit of stopping by and seeing Begin, usually after he returned from a trip abroad, about once or twice a year. He would brief Begin on the political situation. After Begin went into retirement, he began to have doubts about Sharon and some of the methods he used. Begin was never personally close to Sharon. Begin knew that

Prime Minister Yitzhak Shamir (leading line at right) at Menahem Begin's funeral, March 9, 1992. Photograph by Ziv Koren.

Sharon had overstepped his authority and issued orders without Begin's prior approval during the Lebanon War.

On Passover Eve 1991 Begin gave his first media interview since his retirement. The subject was Jabotinsky's legacy fifty years after his death. Begin said that "the war for the Land of Israel" was what was left from Jabotinsky's teachings still to achieve. He also said that Jabotinsky dreamed of the aliya of Soviet Jewry and of Ethiopian Jewry. In July 1991 he gave his final phone interview on the occasion of the opening of the Etzel Museum in Tel Aviv. The following month on his 78th birthday, Begin had a big party with over 120 acquaintances attending. Begin died on March 9, 1992, and was buried on the Mount of Olives next to Aliza and near the graves of underground martyrs Meir Feinstein and Moshe Barazani.[51]

Before discussing Begin's legacy I would like to look further at his personality. Rabin said of Begin, "I've known him for a very long time and I can tell you that he always puts the national interest above his own." This was to his aide Yehuda Avner urging him to work for Begin as he had worked for him.[52] This could probably not be said of some of those who followed Begin as prime ministers and leaders of the Likud. "History and political biographies are my favorite topics and these I generally read in English," said Begin to Avner. He then cited a number of examples. Begin's other main forms of recreation before becoming prime minister were watching movies at the cinema, particularly American Westerns, and socializing with former members of the Etzel and Lehi. He had to give both of these up upon becoming prime minister. "One could sense his love of words for their own sakes ... a man of passionate polemic and gripping oratory. He loved to debate. He loved to write. He loved to read. He loved to preach. He loved journalism. He loved letters," wrote professional diplomat Yehuda Avner. Begin delighted in inventing neologisms in English, and presumably in Hebrew as well.[53]

As prime minister Begin got only about four to five hours of sleep per night. This might have affected his performance at the start of the Lebanon War, but he was probably more affected by his deference to Sharon as a great military hero. Begin was used to being treated with great deference by his former Etzel subordinates and he treated former generals in the same way. Begin loved to flatter—it did not cost him anything and it might result in goodwill. Begin went all out to receive Sadat in November 1977 with fitting pomp. Most of the 36-hour visit was taken up with ceremonies. But when he issued the official invitations, he issued them for a time on Saturday evening after the end of the Sabbath that would not risk desecrating it. This was both out of prudence for the preservation of his coalition and because of his genuine reverence for Jewish tradition.[54]

Begin was very affected by the Holocaust, as was his successor, Shamir. This is not surprising considering that both lost many immediate family members in it. At a United Jewish Appeal function in May 1981, Begin told the group that Germany was a very emotional subject for him. "I cannot forgive or forget what the Germans did to our people," said Begin. One group member asked him if he ever spoke to Germans in their own language. "No. I know German, but I won't speak their language. We communicate in English." Begin held Chancellor Helmut Schmidt in contempt because Schmidt had served in the Wehrmacht as a young man.[55]

When asked what the lessons of the Holocaust were, Begin was happy to expound.

> I believe the lessons of the Holocaust are these. First, if an enemy of our people says that he seeks to destroy us, believe him. Don't doubt him for a moment. Don't make light of it. Do all in your power to deny him the means of carrying out his satanic threat. Second, when a Jew anywhere is threatened or under attack, do all in your power to come to his aid. Never pause to think what the world will think or say.... Third, a Jew must learn to defend himself. He must forever be prepared for whatever threat looms. Fourth, Jewish dignity and honor must be protected in all circumstances. Fifth, stand united in the face of the enemy. Sixth, there is a pattern to Jewish history ... we rise, we fall, we return, we are exiled, we are enslaved, we rebel, we liberate ourselves, we are oppressed once more, we rebuild, and again we suffer destruction.[56]

This is a very dark vision indeed. These lessons go a long way in explaining the Osirak raid and Netanyahu's attitude towards Iran.

When Begin served briefly as his own defense minister in 1980–81, he relied heavily on his military aide, General Efraim Poran. Poran took him one day to visit a reserve tank brigade in the West Bank. During the visit Begin asked lots of questions of the brigade commander so as to better understand the demands on the men. During the visit, Begin displayed a good understanding of the political dynamics of terrorism, as one would expect of a former resistance leader.[57]

What is Begin's legacy for Israel and for the political Right in Israel? Biographer Avi Shilon writes that Begin was the most consequential prime minister after Ben-Gurion in Israel's history. This is probably correct as Rabin's legacy is tarnished by the failure of the Oslo process. Ben-Gurion's demonization and ridicule of him may have amounted to recognition that Begin was Ben-Gurion's most serious political opponent since Jabotinsky. His Israeli legacy is in three parts. First, by building Herut up through Gahal and into the Likud he created the serious opposition party without which no democracy can function in the long run. By the time of the First Alignment in 1965, Ahdut Ha'Avoda had ceased to function as an opposition to Mapai. The creation of Gahal that same year filled that vacuum.

Second, by making peace with Egypt in 1978–79, Begin took advantage of the opportunity that Golda Meir had overlooked in 1972. That Dayan, Rabin, and Allon had all laid the foundation for this peace through their peace agreements in 1974–75 with Sadat does not diminish Begin's achievement that continues to pay dividends for Israel up to the present. Third, Begin shares with Sharon the responsibility for the disastrous war in Lebanon that reaped very little for Israel but death, wounded, destruction, and a bad reputation. It was not Israel's first war of choice—that was the Sinai War in 1956—but it illustrated a tendency on the Israeli Right to attempt to solve political problems with the Arabs through force. This in turn infected the country as a whole as witnessed by Peres's 1996 incursion into Lebanon and the Olmert-Barak invasion of Gaza in 2008.

Begin's legacy for the Right consists of making the Jabotinsky ideology more marketable in Israel by adding a bit of traditionalism to it. Begin by being pious in contrast to the sabra politicians in Labor, was able to attract the support of large numbers of poor and middle class mizrakhim from the development towns. "He spoke Jewish," was how biographer Daniel Gordis phrased it.[58]

Earlier Begin managed to start the Revolt with Britain just at the time when the British were absorbed with the war effort in Europe and so not in a position to quash it as quickly as they had smashed Stern's revolt in the winter of 1941–42. Begin had the sense to let his military commanders like Meridor, Paglin, and Livni run the operational side of the Revolt while he concentrated on the propaganda side. After having had the good sense not to retaliate against the Hagana-Palmakh in 1944–45, Begin was able to reap the reward in the Hebrew Resistance Movement. After that collapsed in the King David Hotel bombing, both the Etzel and Lehi accelerated their military effort. They could then make a plausible claim that they had driven the British out of Palestine when it was really the financial cost of running the mandate that caused Britain to leave. Begin then took and recreated the Revisionist movement by merging the Etzel and the Revisionist Party into Herut. Begin merged Jabotinsky's ideology with the myth of the Etzel victory over the British to give the Right a political party and myth that could counter that of the Labor Party and the 1948 war. Begin then pragmatically modified Jabotinsky's ideology by quietly shelving the claim to Transjordan as the key to creating the Gahal alliance. He then allowed Sharon to add two new small parties in 1973 and came up with the name for the new party. Shamir then completed the process in the mid–1980s by transforming the Likud from a joint list into a genuine political party. So today's Likud is the product of the efforts of Jabotinsky, Begin and Shamir.

Four. Begin in Power, 1977–1983

Begin's election in 1977 ended the official amnesia towards the undergrounds of the Right and completed the rehabilitation of Jabotinsky that began with his reburial in 1964. Jabotinsky is the most commemorated person in Israel today with at least 57 parks, streets, and squares named after him. Herzl is next with 52, Ben-Gurion and Haim Weizmann tie at 48 each and Begin is next with 43.[59]

Five

Yitzhak Shamir's Preparation

Yitzhak Yezernitsky was born the youngest of three children to Shlomo Yezernitsky in the eastern Polish village of Rujenoy, which is today part of Belarus, on October 22, 1915. Like the city of Brest Litovsk it had passed back and forth through the centuries between Russia and Poland. In the interwar period it was part of Poland. Shlomo Yezernitsky owned a small leather factory and by the standards of Polish Jewry was well off. He was a lover of Yiddishkeit or Jewish tradition and he spent dearly to bring Yitzhak up in Jewish schools. Yitzhak's parents had briefly been involved with the anti–Zionist socialist Bund, a Jewish socialist party in Eastern Europe that was a rival to both Communism and Zionism in the late nineteenth and early twentieth centuries. But his parents quickly became converts to Zionism and spent most of their adult lives as Zionists. In the late 1920s his family moved to the larger town of Volkovysk, which had a population of 10,000 to 15,000 compared to the 5,000 in Rujenoy. There Yitzhak completed two years of Hebrew high school. Later he boarded in Bialystok, a town famous for a pogrom in 1905, where he attended high school. He roomed with another boy from Volkvysk, David Niv, who would later be the historian of Lehi and the editor of the Israeli equivalent of Hansards when Yitzhak Shamir was speaker of the Knesset.[1]

At age 14 in Volkvysk in 1929 Yezernitsky joined the Betar youth movement of Vladimir Jabotinsky, the youth movement that would be the forge out of which he and so many of his future professional acquaintances and colleagues were formed. Jabotinsky had enough of an effect on Shamir that he dedicates five pages to an overview of Jabotinsky's life and accomplishments in his own memoirs. Shamir compresses Jabotinsky's ideology into a single sentence: a Jewish majority in a Jewish state in the complete land of Israel (Eretz Israel haShlema).[2]

In 1932 Yitzhak Yezernitsky moved to Warsaw to study law at Warsaw University. He later admitted to a fascination with Russian revolutionary movements starting with Narodnaya Volya (People's Will), which would later serve as a model for Lehi. There he met a number of his future colleagues including Begin.[3]

In October 1935 after being fortunate enough to receive one of the Revisionist movement's few coveted entrance visas to Palestine, Yitzhak Yezernitsky immigrated to Palestine in order to study law at Hebrew University, thus fulfilling a major dream of his. Initially Yezernitsky worked as a building worker, was unemployed for a short while and then worked as an apprentice book keeper in a Tel Aviv firm. He took a couple of courses in Jewish history at Hebrew University in order to satisfy the terms of his visa and then dropped out.[4]

Shamir, to which he changed his name after one of his underground aliases in the mid–1940s, wrote in his 1994 memoir that he joined Etzel in 1939.[5] This is hardly credible because when he joined the Stern Group in January 1941 he was already in a leadership position and became one of a trio of leaders in the successor Lehi in 1942. A few years later he told Haim Misgav that he joined the Etzel in 1937 when it was still Irgun B (or Hagana B).[6] His biographer journalist Charles Enderlin claims that he joined the organization a few months after arriving in Palestine—so probably sometime in the spring of 1936. I believe that the 1937 date sounds accurate. Shamir wrote that he worked during the day as a bookkeeper and trained nights and Saturdays with the Etzel.

Shamir belonged to the Eighth Company of the Etzel commanded by Arie Yizhaki, who was eager for action. Yitzhaki later accidentally blew himself up while making letter bombs in the spring of 1939; when a British detective asked the dying Yitzhaki for his name, Yitzhaki replied, "I am death." He then died. Enderlin claimed that Shamir participated in the organization's reprisal operations in 1938–39 when he threw a grenade on to an Arab train. In the Etzel and the Stern Group Yezernitsky quickly became a lecturer on various arms and tactics training courses and a segan or the equivalent of a second lieutenant.[7]

When Avraham Stern, who was also from eastern Poland, split off from the Etzel in September 1940, Yezernitsky initially took several months to decide which group to go with. He eventually joined Stern's group largely because his subordinates favored Stern, and probably because as a hardline nationalist and action junkie, Yezernitsky thought it made more sense to join the Stern Group. In his memoirs, Shamir claims that he followed

Stern into the new organization immediately, but this may be misinformation on Shamir's part or simply an error by his ghostwriter.[8]

In February 1939, David Raziel agreed to merge the Etzel and Betar. Stern disagreed with this as he saw the Etzel's role as an independent revolutionary organization. In May 1939 Stern returned to Palestine from Poland to become deputy commander of the Etzel under Hanokh Kalay. The following month Stern directed the Etzel to begin attacking British targets in Palestine. In June 1940 Stern became the de facto commander of the Etzel with Raziel and Kalay both in prison. On August 31, 1940—the one-year anniversary of the arrest of the Etzel's High Command—Stern proclaimed the birth of his own independent organization, Etzel b'Israel, to distinguish it from Etzel b'Eretz Israel. Within a few months it had adopted the name of Lohemei Herut Israel (Fighters for the Freedom of Israel) or Lehi.[9]

After the split, Stern spent several months coming up with an ideology for the organization. He published this as the 18 Principles of Rebirth. Stern had spent much of his time in 1938–39 in Poland organizing connections with the Polish army, founding a Zionist club in Warsaw known as The Jordan, presumably for the purpose of recruiting Zionists into the Etzel, and he founded the Yiddish newspaper *Di Tat* (The Deed) with Shmuel Merlin, who later headed the Etzel's diaspora branch with Hillel Kook during the Revolt. Stern's role in the Etzel during the Arab Revolt was in many ways similar to that latter filled by Begin, or by Scheib in Lehi. It was at this time that Stern adopted the pen name Elazar Ben-Yair after the name of the commander of Masada when it fell to the Romans in 73 A.D. In the underground he became known simply as Yair. Shamir later admitted to having some reservations about a few of the principles but agreed with them in general. Israel Scheib met with Stern shortly after arriving in Palestine in early 1941 and took over the job of writing the movement's ideology. Scheib never edited his writings but printed whatever "gushed forth" as if he were simply a medium.[10]

Most of the senior commanders in the Etzel stayed with Raziel with the junior commanders and their men following Stern into Lehi. Lehi, which had no independent funding, carried out its first bank robbery on September 16, 1940. It would be dependent upon robberies of banks and merchants such as jewelers known euphemistically as "revolutionary appropriations" during its entire existence. This is what led the British to dub it the Stern Gang.[11]

Stern wandered the streets of Tel Aviv in the winter of 1942 carrying a suitcase, which contained a portable cot. After a botched bank robbery in January 1942 in which two bystanders were shot and killed, the citizens

Five. Yitzhak Shamir's Preparation

of Tel Aviv were eager to avenge their deaths by informing on Stern and his men. Stern during this time was totally limited to working organizational matters such as communications with captured members inside the camps and operations. Yehoshua Zetler, who was arrested in 1941, was Stern's deputy until his arrest. His arrest and failure to escape until 1947 opened up space for Shamir to become his successor.[12]

Shamir, who was already playing a major role as a planner for Stern, refused to approve operations that he thought were too risky in terms of collateral damage. After his arrest in December 1941, an operation he had vetoed went ahead with the result that the mayor of Tel Aviv was killed along with two Jewish policemen. This only increased the pressure on the police to kill or capture Stern.[13]

Shamir was arrested twice while in the underground. The first time was in December 1941, when the Palestine Police were rolling up the organization after Stern's premature revolt. He wrote that he learned of Stern's death from a prison guard. He showed up at the apartment of another member who had already been arrested and when he entered the police arrested him as well. It was a common technique that led Lehi to later decree that all senior members should travel in pairs so that if one were arrested the other could warn others and the apartment of the arrested person would be off limits from then on. Shamir was deputy commander in Tel Aviv at the time.[14]

In the few weeks between Shamir's first arrest and Stern's murder on February 12, Stern smuggled a message to Shamir in Mizra Prison that it was his duty to escape "as soon as possible" because Stern was so desperate for qualified men at that point. Pistols as well as messages were occasionally smuggled into Mizra. In one meeting between Stern and Shamir on a Tel Aviv street corner at night before the latter's arrest, Stern warned Shamir that he would be murdered by the police in a completely calm tone, but then added that his death would cause Lehi to flourish.[15]

Shamir claims that he came up with the idea of a collective leadership, haMerkaz or the Center, to replace the unitary leadership that Stern provided.[16] Scheib and Friedman-Yellin had both arrived in Palestine from Poland in 1940–41 and they became the other two members of the leadership. Shamir used the code name Michael after the legendary Irish revolutionary Michael Collins. Friedman-Yellin, a mathematician by training and an engineer by profession was known as "Gra" or "Gera." He ran the Etzel newspaper in the late 1930s. After Israeli independence Friedman-Yellin changed his name to Yellin-Mor, the Mor being part of his wife's maiden name so that they both contributed to their joint married name. And Scheib, a mystical rabbi (he passed seminary but was never ordained) and philosopher known in Lehi as "the doctor" for his PhD degree, took the code name "Eldad," which became his name after he emerged from the underground. Scheib was the movement's ideologue who indoctrinated the new recruits and wrote articles for the organization's newspaper. Friedman-Yellin did the negotiating with the other underground groups, primarily with Begin from the Etzel and Sneh and Golomb from the Hagana. He also issued all communiques. Later Ya'acov Eliav, who had escaped from prison on December 23, 1943, by convincing a gullible guard to let him check the wiring outside of the Russian Compound for a Christmas Tree, which he was erecting as part of his escape attempt, was co-opted into the Center as commander of the fighting force when the Hebrew Resistance Movement began in late 1945. After Shamir was arrested for the second time in August 1946 and exiled to Eritrea, Friedman-Yellin took over some of Shamir's tasks but Ya'akov Banai was put in charge of operational planning until Yehoshua Zettler was released from Acre Prison in May 1947 in the famous combined prison break. Or as Geula Cohen later put it: "Michael" was the organizer, co-ordinator and character of the organization; "Gera" was the tactician, the diplomat and the mind; and "Eldad" was the visionary, ideologist and spirit.[17]

Shamir escaped from the Mizra detention camp near Haifa where he was imprisoned along with Friedman-Yellin. On the night of August 31–September 1, 1942, he arranged an escape from Mizra along with one other Lehi member, Eliahu Giladi. The two hid in a bedding storage closet under a stack of mattresses and then ripped a hole in the fence to escape. Yehoshua Cohen's future wife was waiting in a getaway car outside the camp. She took them to a rendezvous with her boyfriend in the orange groves near Haifa. There Cohen turned over control of Lehi to Shamir. She arranged to supply them with Polish uniforms so that they would not look out of place on the streets in Haifa. There Shamir slowly and methodically began to rebuild Lehi from a base of only six people. Shamir estimated that only 26 Sternists were free. Cohen began to systematically train these 26 in the orange groves. Yezernitsky at the same time transformed himself into Rabbi Shamir.[18]

Giladi soon demonstrated signs of personal instability and became fixated on murdering the leadership of the Yishuv starting with Ben-Gurion. Shamir smuggled a letter into prison describing the problem to Friedman-Yellin who urged him to act as quickly as possible. One evening Shamir and Giladi went for a walk in the sand dunes near Tel Aviv and only Shamir came home. Shamir later described what he did to a group of Lehi veterans and none of them reproached him for his ruthlessness.

Shortly after gaining his freedom, Shamir met with Moshe Segal, leader of Brit Hashmonaim (the Union of Hasmoneans/Maccabees), a rival underground to the Etzel in Jerusalem during the Arab Revolt. Shamir convinced Segal to not only join Lehi but to bring his men with him and thereby the Jerusalem branch of Lehi was created. The two would either meet in Segal's home or in a synagogue in Rehavia.

Shamir personally recruited one by one several new members of the organization to replace those in prison, many of these from the Etzel. He and Cohen then trained them and when Shamir began actively planning operations in 1943–44 he knew the personal abilities and skills of every member of the organization. Shamir reorganized Lehi on a cell basis—so that if a single cell were penetrated only three or four other members would be exposed to arrest. The organization, unlike the Etzel, had no ranks and there was no saluting. Arms were stored in school basements if the principal was sympathetic to Lehi. Friedman-Yellin made the decision in February 1943 that all Lehi members were to go about armed and were to resist arrest by force if it were attempted. This resulted in several Lehi members needlessly losing their lives until the policy was changed some two years later. After Cohen was done training the first group of recruits in the orange groves, Shamir sent him off to Jerusalem to train a second group.[19]

In the early morning hours of November 1, 1943, Friedman-Yellin tunneled out of the Mizra detention camp along with twenty other Lehi members. They could have escaped with more but they had no places to hide them once they were free. Friedman-Yellin arrived in Palestine in August 1941. He was arrested by the British in Syria while waiting to cross into Turkey in order to meet with a German diplomat about a Lehi-German alliance. Stern tried to form alliances with both European Axis powers against the British in 1940–41. After his escape Friedman-Yellin became Lehi's unofficial foreign minister. By 1944 he was advocating an alliance with the Soviet Union.[20]

The Center was all free for only about four months before Scheib was rearrested in March 1944, and it was the first time that all three of them had been free since 1941. The Center met on a weekly basis in a different location each time so that security would be maintained. When Friedman-Yellin met with Eliahu Golomb of the Hagana it was with a pistol on the coffee table in front of him. It was rumored that Golomb had planned to kidnap Stern in October 1940 and hold him until the Hagana command decided that it was safe to mount resistance against the British. The next time that the Center was all free was in June 1946 following Scheib's escape from prison, but that only lasted for another month until Shamir was arrested in late July.[21]

Lehi, unlike the Etzel, believed in personal terror as both a tactic and a strategy. In late 1943 Shamir had drawn up an action plan for a strategy of attacks on key individuals. Initially Lehi carefully planned a number of assassination operations against both administrative figures such as High Commissioner Harold MacMichael and Lord Moyne in Cairo. The organization also planned the assassination of a number of police detectives whose knowledge of Lehi was a threat to the organization. The first was Detective Ralph Cairns, who was killed by a remotely-detonated mine as he walked along his usual route on August 26, 1939, by Etzel members who later joined Lehi. The next was Detective Tom Wilkins who was shot dead by two Lehi assassins who shot him eleven times in Jerusalem on September 29, 1944. Wilkins spoke fluent Hebrew, unlike the vast majority of police detectives, and lived with the daughter of a prominent socialist Zionist leader. "Wilkin had Jewish eyes and a Jewish mind.... Wilkin put his emotions into the fight against us. His Jewish friends liked him and often gave him information unintentionally," said former Lehi member Geula Cohen. "This could mean Lehi men being arrested or killed in ambush. So that's why we had to get rid of him. I'll never forget the sigh of relief we all breathed when we heard that our boys had killed him."[22]

Another example of a key detective who was assassinated was Sergeant T.G. Martin who picked Rabbi Shamir out as Yezernitsky the terrorist when the police knocked on the rabbi's door. While in prison awaiting deportation to Eritrea Shamir got the word out to Friedman-Yellin that Martin had to be eliminated because of his uncanny ability to recognize wanted Lehi members through their disguises. A pair of Lehi assassins shot him on a tennis court before he could go for his weapon the following month. Shamir later wrote and stated that in order to go out and murder a revolutionary must believe that thereby he can change history.[23]

Shamir appointed Ya'akov Bannai to reorganize Lehi in Haifa. Eventually Bannai was to replace Shamir following his arrest. Yehoshua Cohen, who turned command of Lehi over to Shamir in the orange grove in September 1942 at age nineteen, subsisted in the orange groves for years living on a diet of stale bread dipped in boiled water. "He claims no authority. His character is his authority," wrote Scheib of Cohen. Cohen had met Stern only once in a group meeting before Stern's death. Cohen had complained about the lack of action. Cohen later got so much action that the Palestine Police put a thousand pound reward on his head, almost as much as for Stern earlier. Cohen trained the assassins for Lehi's first major assassination in November 1944 and was the trigger man himself in the group's last assassination nearly four years later. He was arrested in late 1944 and exiled to Sudan in December. He remained there until July 1948, before being released following Israel's independence and in time to murder Count Bernadotte two months later.[24]

In the spring and summer of 1944 there was a series of reprisals and attacks between the Palestine Police and Lehi. Then in the summer of 1944 there were five (or seven) attempts made on the life of MacMichael; the first four (or six) attempts were called off without a shot being fired either because MacMichael did not show up as expected or because security foiled the attempt before it could be made. After MacMichael was wounded in the thigh and hand in the final attempt three weeks before leaving Palestine on the way to his farewell party, Lehi stopped plotting to murder him. It was rumored that MacMichael had wanted to eliminate the Jewish Agency as a body advocating on behalf of Zionism. Shamir made the decision to move on to killing Lord Moyne in Cairo and Scheib supported him in this. Shamir had wanted to kill Moyne after he killed MacMichael for maximum shock value, but that plan had to be abandoned. In late 1944 Shamir was also planning the assassination of Sir John Shaw, the chief secretary of the government of Palestine.[25]

The Center was convinced that the British could not keep their promises to both the Arabs and the Jews and that as the Jews were the weaker party they would be the ones to suffer the broken promises. Moyne was seen as being too pro–Arab and unsympathetic to Zionism. Part of the motive for murdering Moyne was to distinguish Lehi from the Etzel by demonstrating that it opposed not just the British mandate in Palestine but British imperialism in general. Moyne was also rumored to have said, "What would I do with a million Jews?" This was after Hungarian Jew Joel Brand brought him an offer from Adolf Eichmann to trade the lives of these Hungarian Jews for 10,000 infantry trucks and some basic foodstuffs such as coffee, tea, sugar, soap, and cocoa etc. Eichmann stipulated that the goods would only be used on the Eastern Front but the Allies had a strict policy of not trading with the Nazis and such a trade would have caused tremendous problems with Stalin if it became known. Moyne was also believed to have requested that Ankara turn back the illegal immigrant ship *Struma* to keep the Jewish passengers out of Palestine before it was secretly sunk by a Soviet submarine operating in the Black Sea in February 1942 only days after Stern's death. "Really those acts by Lord Moyne were without meaning for us," explained Yellin-Mor of Lehi years later. "They were useful only as propaganda, because they allowed us to explain to the people why we had killed him."[26]

Shamir selected Eliahu Khakim and Eliahu Beit-Zouri as the two assassins. Shamir selected the former because he was an excellent shot with a pistol—the best in Lehi, and the latter because he would make a good impression on the witness stand if the two were captured and went on trial. But Beit-Zouri was also a skilled marksman. Shamir had known Beit-Zouri for years as a member of his Etzel squad. One of the two was a companion of Amihai "Gidi" Paglin and had belonged to Paglin's three-man private terror cell before Paglin joined the Etzel in 1943.[27]

Khakim and Beit-Zouri shot Moyne to death at his home in Cairo along with a corporal who interfered with the assassination. They attempted to make their escape on bicycles—Shamir wanted them to use a car but they lacked the money to purchase one—and they refused to shoot the Egyptian policeman who pursued them. Their trial became a sensation in Cairo in the spring of 1945 and they became Lehi martyrs when they were hanged by the British.[28]

The Cairo trial was the first of a series of trials in 1944–45 in which Lehi used the courtroom as a propaganda forum to publicize its existence, the reasons for its war against Britain and the bravery of its fighters. Until then its propaganda efforts had not been very successful, but after that it began attracting more public sympathy and more recruits.[29]

On November 8, the Jewish press in the Yishuv in Palestine called on all Jews to shun both the Etzel and Lehi by denying them shelter and providing intelligence to the authorities. Many Arabists advised a major reprisal against the Yishuv in response to the assassination either in the form of a large collective fine or a policy decision ending Jewish immigration. On November 21, 1944, Ben-Gurion made a speech to the Histadrut (Labor Federation) Convention and in it he called for cooperation with the British authorities.

As a result of the assassination Churchill shelved the plans for partition of Palestine that he had discussed with Weizmann only two days before the murder. He also lost much of his sympathy for Zionism as a result of the murder of his personal friend. The murder was more popular in Jewish America than in Palestine and the pro–Irgun press refused to condemn it. Over the decades the attitude towards the assassins changed within Israel due to the impact of the Holocaust and the two assassins were dug up and reburied on Mt. Herzl with full military honors in June 1975.[30]

As a result of the saison, Lehi basically went on an undeclared truce for six months. When it emerged it began coordinating more with the Etzel so that the two organizations would not interfere with each other's operations inadvertently. On October 31, 1945, when the Palmakh blew up the police boats, Lehi tried unsuccessfully to blow up the Haifa oil refineries. During the period of the Hebrew Resistance Movement Shamir remained in the shadows because he did not trust either Ben-Gurion or the Hagana.[31]

At the time of Moyne's assassination Ya'acov Eliav had just finished

Five. Yitzhak Shamir's Preparation

cooperating in training Hagana and Palmakh commanders in resistance tactics used by Lehi in courses that he ran on five different kibbutzim over the course of nine months. Eliav was told about the assassination by Eliahu Golomb and Israel Galili. Golomb told Eliav that the murder could lead Churchill to put an end to Zionist aspirations unless Lehi was liquidated. Eliav replied that the fulfillment of Zionist aspirations was not up to Churchill and that Lehi had guns and could draw faster than the Hagana-Palmakh. Golomb then used a group of visiting British MPs as cover to transfer Eliav from Kibbutz Yagur to Ramat Gan where Eliav rejoined Lehi.[32]

Upon returning to Lehi, Eliav began teaching a course for Lehi commanders based upon what he learned in Poland in 1939 and from the Palmakh in 1944. The graduates of this course then became the backbone of Lehi's fighting force starting in 1945. Eliav developed a new training program for Lehi based on four principles: ideological indoctrination, character building, weapons training, and underground tradecraft and tactics. Each new recruit was allowed in only after having been vouched for by an existing member who had known him for at least five years. Each recruit was assigned an individual instructor.[33]

Sometime in 1944, probably in late 1944, Shamir married his courier, Shulamit Levy, who had arrived in the country as an illegal immigrant from Bulgaria in 1941. They eventually fell in love and a rabbi known as "the prisoners' rabbi" presided at the wedding ceremony. In August 1945 Shamir's first son, Yair, named after Stern's underground code name, was born. He would grow up to become a pilot and colonel in the Israeli Air Force and eventually an industrialist before following his father into politics. In 1949 the couple had a daughter named Gilada after the man Shamir took a walk with in the dunes near Tel Aviv in 1943.[34]

In the summer of 1945 Lehi began to carry out joint operations with the Etzel and the latter organization essentially taught Lehi how to carry out major paramilitary attacks, which had up until then been its specialty. In February 1946 a Lehi team carried out a raid on a British airfield in Kfar Sirkin near Petah Tikva, while on that same night an Etzel team attacked another airfield. This was to be the pattern for the final two years of its war against the British.[35]

Sometime in early 1946 the Center agreed to let Eliav go to Egypt to organize Lehi cells there before heading on to Europe to run the underground's foreign operations. Eliav organized Lehi cells among members serving in the British army in Alexandria, Ismailia and Cairo. He also plotted to sink the British destroyer *Chevron* in Alexandria but when one of the members involved in the plot was indiscrete the man was arrested before the plot could be executed. Shamir wrote Eliav a long letter about the operational difficulties that Lehi was suffering in Palestine hoping that Eliav would take the hint and return to Palestine. But after thinking about it carefully, Eliav proceeded on to Paris. There he organized a Lehi cell with both operational and propaganda functions. He carried out terrorist operations against London. When the UN voted for partition the Center ordered all its personnel abroad to cease anti–British activities and to concentrate on the upcoming war with the Arabs.[36]

The last operation to be planned and/or approved by Shamir was probably the attack on the Haifa rail yard and repair facility on June 17, 1946. Unfortunately for Lehi, there was an unknown traitor in their midst who revealed their plans to the British. The British army was waiting for them and although they managed to destroy many locomotives the organization lost eleven men killed and eighteen captured, several of whom were then sentenced to death. But the only two Lehi men hanged by the British were the Moyne assassins.[37]

At the end of July 1946, a four-day curfew was imposed on Tel Aviv by the British after the van of the King David bombers was found there. The headquarters for the search was ironically the lawn of the house that Begin was staying in. He had barely enough time to climb into the secret hiding place in the ceiling before the British came to search his house. When he emerged four days later he was so dehydrated that he doused his head in a basin of cold water rather than drink from the tap. Sergeant T. G. Martin spotted Yezernitsky the terrorist by his bushy eyebrows above the beard of Rabbi Shamir and Shamir was out of the struggle. He was the only person arrested during the search who was not soon released.[38]

Within weeks Shamir was flown by plane from Palestine to a prison camp in Asmara, Eritrea, then an Italian colony under British occupation. Sergeant Martin was assassinated on the Haifa tennis court on September 9, about the time that Shamir left for Eritrea. In the prisoner of war camp were three Etzel barracks and one Lehi barracks. Shamir and the other prisoners occupied themselves with lectures, plays, a football team, and of course escape attempts. Before Shamir arrived there had been nine escape attempts, all organized by the Etzel, and twenty men had escaped. A total of seventy would escape before the camp was closed down in 1948 with Israel's independence.[39]

Ya'akov Meridor, who had already led several escape attempts from British camps in Africa after being arrested during the saison, led an attempt by four Etzel members and Shamir on January 14, 1947. The five crawled through a tunnel snuck across a football field, between and under the camp's fences and then walked to Asmara. A Jewish doctor in town and his gentile wife hid the five for several weeks. Arieh Ben-Eliezer, the number three man in the Etzel after Begin and Meridor, went ahead of the others to Addis Ababa, the capital of neighboring Ethiopia. There he searched for a vehicle that he could use to smuggle his fellow prisoners to Ethiopia. Ben-Eliezer located an oil tanker-truck and a driver who would receive the tanker-truck as payment once the five had been transported to Addis Ababa. A special compartment was built between the driver's cab and the oil tank and small holes were drilled in the top for ventilation. But still, Shamir later described the eighty hours that he spent in the truck as the most unpleasant in his life.

In the Ethiopian capital the group split up for the next leg of the escape. Ben-Eliezer and Shamir caught a ride on a freight train hidden among sacks of coffee to the French port of Djibouti in the horn of Africa. The others were arrested in the capital before they could escape and turned over to the British. Yet Meridor managed to make another escape and make it to Europe before Shamir did! After a two-and a half day trip by train Shamir and Ben-Eliezer made it to Djibouti where a French policeman discovered them, turned them over to the custody of the local rabbi and told them to report to the local police station the next morning.[40]

The two spent nearly a year sharing a colonial villa owned by the French colonial governor with a member of the Viet Minh. The latter reminded Shamir of the anarchist terrorists that Shamir used to read about when he was a student at university in Warsaw, and Shamir was not bloodthirsty enough in the eyes of his Asian co-prisoner to be a real revolutionary! Finally Shamir and Ben-Eliezer were guests aboard a small French aircraft carrier that was diverted to Djibouti to pick them up. They were taken in late April 1948 from Djibouti to Toulon, France. After staying about a month in Paris, Shamir flew home to Israel on May 20, 1948, using a false passport smuggled to him by David Shomron, missing by four days Lehi's final parade as its fighters emerged from the underground and awaited induction into the IDF.[41]

Sometime during World War II, Shamir learned that his father was murdered by people whom the latter had known as a child when he returned to his childhood home during the war. This had the effect of making Shamir very anti–Polish and probably increased his suspicion of Gentiles.[42]

Some fifty years later Shamir referred to his days in the underground as "the best part of my life." Shamir spent the summer of 1948 in the Lehi camps in Jerusalem where Lehi had about 120 members divided into three separate camps. After the attack on Deir Yassin on April 9, the Sternists were involved in a joint-forces defense of the Jewish Quarter in the Old City in May and then in a failed attack on the Old City in July. That summer, according to former Lehi member Baruch Nadel, Shamir began to behave like Lehi's first general. He set up his headquarters in Dror Camp in the Katamon neighborhood of Jerusalem. "He told me to keep trailing the UN people, pick up information on Bernadotte's movements," said Nadel. Bernadotte was a Swedish count who had been appointed the UN mediator between the Arabs and the Jews in the late spring of 1948. "Later he told me that it took the Center five weeks to make their final plans. Shamir was a careful planner. Eldad (Scheib) only liked to send others to kill. He didn't know how to fire a gun himself. We used to say that Eldad was built like Lehi, he had a small body and a very big head; Lehi was a small organization with very big ideas," said Nadel.[43]

In July Bernadotte was in Jerusalem for discussions with Foreign Minister Moshe Sharett and Dov Yosef, the Hagana commander in the city. Bernadotte wanted to demilitarize the city but the two refused to give in to his demands. The Central Intelligence Agency in 1948 estimated the total strength of Lehi at 400 to 800, about double the actual size of the organization in the summer of 1948. This was probably because the others in Tel Aviv and Haifa had already been absorbed into the IDF by this time. American Secretary of State George C. Marshall turned down Bernadotte's request for the temporary assignment of a battalion of Marines to guard Mount Scopus in Jerusalem, where the UN had its Jerusalem headquarters, because of the danger posed by the Etzel and Lehi in Jerusalem. Bernadotte pleaded in vain with his superiors in New York for a 250-man guard force for Jerusalem in order to allow him to carry out his mission.[44]

On August 10, Bernadotte gave a press conference at the Belgian consul's villa in Talbiya, located only 300 meters from the Dror Lehi camp that Shamir commanded. During the conference, two Lehi jeeps were parked outside the residence and their passengers held up threatening signs in English, "You work in vain—we are here FFI" (using Lehi's English acronym) and "Stockholm is Yours, Jerusalem is Ours." Baruch Nadel asked Bernadotte a provocative question in Hebrew, which Bernadotte refused to answer after a reporter translated it for him. Bernadotte then whispered into an open mike, "Why do these Jews always ask such insolent questions?" Moshe Dayan, the new Jerusalem theater commander, pulled up in a jeep and ordered the Lehi members out and they withdrew. Scheib openly threatened Bernadotte in a Lehi radio broadcast that night.[45]

Five weeks later on September 17, 1948, Bernadotte's vehicle was stopped by a Lehi checkpoint on a road by one of the three Lehi camps as Bernadotte was passing into the New City. The UN people in the two-vehicle convoy saw four men dressed in khaki uniforms sitting in a jeep on the side of the road. Three of the men approached the convoy. One of them, Yehoshua Cohen, was armed with a Shmeisser machine-pistol, which he thrust into the open window of the car and began firing. He killed both Bernadotte and the French UN captain who was accompanying him. The men then got back in the jeep and drove off. The murder was later claimed by Hazit haMoledet (The Fatherland Front), the Hebrew translation of the name of a former Bulgarian terrorist organization. Shamir's wife Shulamit is from Bulgaria.[46]

The next day operating on orders from Ben-Gurion, Dayan entered the Lehi camps and shut them down, putting an end to the organization's eight-year existence. Dayan also shut down the Etzel—it was again paying the price for a Lehi assassination. So the Etzel came to an end after eleven years as a Revisionist paramilitary organization. Ben-Gurion had the police issue arrest warrants for the Lehi's leadership and Friedman-Yellin and Mattityahu Shmuelevitz were arrested for the murder while Shamir and Scheib went into hiding. Friedman-Yellin and Shmuelevitz received eight and five years respectively for the murder, but were soon pardoned in a wider amnesty. The IDF had given the Etzel some 200 draft exemptions and Lehi fifty so that the leaderships of both organizations could form political parties and run in the elections to the First Knesset in February 1949.[47] In reality it was probably done to keep the undergrounds from infecting the IDF by influencing former members drafted into the new army.

Years later Lehi assassin Yehoshua Cohen confessed to academic Yosef Heller that he knew "we killed the wrong man. The black man [Ralph Bunche, who succeeded Bernadotte as UN mediator] was the right man. He was the man with the ideas." In 1988 Israel Eldad (Scheib), Yehoshua Zettler, the Lehi commander in Jerusalem and the planner of the murder, Makover (one of the assassins) and Hillman (an IDF officer who facilitated the murder), all gave interviews to the Israeli press revealing their role in the assassination. Shamir never denied his role in the murder, but he always downplayed it including in his memoirs. "I don't see Eldad as an important part of this. I see him as a very good propaganda minister. But there is milk in his veins. Shamir was responsible for other such acts. It takes a certain kind of man to assume such responsibility. Shamir is such a man," said historian Shabtai Teveth. Shamir biographer Enderlin wrote that Yehoshua Zettler planned the assassination, but Shamir probably reviewed the plans. Shamir did admit that the Center approved the murder, but not necessarily at a single meeting.[48]

Shamir then threw himself into organizing the Fighters' Party, which ran on an anti-imperialist pro–Soviet platform markedly different from that of the Herut Party. The real purpose of the party was to win the release of Shmuelevitz and Friedman-Yellin from prison. This occurred before the election. Shamir dropped out of electoral politics by the spring of 1949 for a two-decade recess. The party won only a single seat in the election, which was lucky because Lehi at its peak had maybe a thousand members and supporters, just enough for a single mandate in 1949.[49] For the next election in 1951 the quota for a seat increased dramatically due to the large immigration during Israel's first two years of existence and the party folded in 1951 as it split into opposing factions.[50]

Shamir applied for a job as a clerk in the interior ministry, but Prime Minister David Ben-Gurion banned hiring him. Shamir spent the next six years doing various odd jobs to support his family including acting as the head of a chain of cinemas in Ramat Gan and Givatayim. When that did not work out he formed a construction company with three other Lehi veterans, one of them being Yellin-Mor.[51] Finally in 1955 after he complained about his situation to Yaacov Eliav, Eliav told him he was working for the Mossad and suggested that he apply. Isser Harel, the head of the Mossad, Israel's intelligence organization for external intelligence, invited Shamir to join the organization. Shamir requested only that he not be required to do anything that was against his conscience. Harel told him that if this situation arose he should call Harel personally and they would discuss it. Shamir never made the call. Shamir spent the next decade in the Mossad, where he learned French (he had already learned some in Djibouti in 1947–48) and worked in Paris running the European operations for the Mossad. According to Enderlin, Shamir was sent to Paris in 1956 to work with Yaacov Caroz. While there he was entrusted with a number of tasks including planting moles, making timely interventions with the French government, and, according to some sources, with executions. Harel basically wanted Shamir as a consultant: someone who could study the organization and make suggestions for changes based on his expertise and experience of eleven years in the underground. The Mossad ended up hiring at least four other former Lehi members as agents: Ya'akov Eliav, who had run Lehi's European operation in the late 1940s was sent to Spain; Yehoshua Cohen of the orange groves became Ben-Gurion's bodyguard at Kibbutz Sde-Boker, where Ben-Gurion recuperated in 1953–54 while he took a break from politics; Shaaltiel Ben-Yair, who had been suspected of conspiring to bomb a cabinet minister in the early 1950s, was sent under a false identity to Egypt where he became one of Israel's most effective operatives at the time; and David Shomron was posted to Paris. Eliyahu Ben-Elissar became the case officer in Europe for agents in Arab countries.[52]

While in France Shamir was also involved in the case of the search for the son of an ultra–Orthodox family, Yossele Schumacher, who was kidnapped and believed to be in Europe. In March 1962 he was instructed to infiltrate the ultra–Orthodox Satmar sect. He tracked down a rabbi in London who was connected to the affair but the trail ran cold. Eventually Shamir became head of one of twelve "special services" departments within the Mossad.[53]

The decade that Shamir spent in the Mossad from 1955 to 1965 were the spy agency's glory years.[54] It managed to smuggle out and turn over to the CIA a copy of Khrushchev's 1956 Twentieth Party Congress address denouncing Stalin. In the early 1960s it planted two very high agents in both Syria and Egypt. The spy in Syria, Eli Cohen, was an Egyptian Jew who was involved in the July 1954 "mishap" where military intelligence ran a sabotage operation in Egypt aimed at Western cultural targets in a crude attempt to produce a split between the Nasser regime and Washington. The main result of this was a split a decade later in Mapai that caused Ben-Gurion to finally resign as prime minister and in 1965 to form the Rafi Party. Cohen after immigrating to Israel was recruited under pressure by the Mossad. With a dialogue coach he learned to speak Arabic, in which he was a native speaker, with a Syrian accent. And after spending time in Argentina to build up his cover story he went to Syria and became a senior member of the ruling Ba'ath Party. He sent back extensive information on Syrian fortifications on the Golan Heights. In 1965 a Soviet radio transmitter-locater pinpointed his position when he was transmitting back to Israel and he was captured and hanged.[55]

Wolfgang Lotz, known in the literature as the "champagne spy," was a native German Jew who was born in Mannheim in 1921. He joined the IDF and proved his courage in the 1948 and 1956 wars. He was fluent in German, Arabic, Hebrew and English. He was recruited by the Mossad because he was blond, blue-eyed and a native German speaker who also spoke Arabic. In 1957 the decision was made to send him to Egypt but he did not actually go until January 1961. The Mossad gave him a nearly limitless expense account in order to build up his contacts with the Egyptian elite by hobnobbing with them posing as a veteran of the Afrika Korps. Lotz visited many military bases taking photographs and congratulating his hosts on the ingenuity of their dummy aircraft. Lotz made regular debriefing trips to Europe, especially to Paris. Harel was convinced that Egypt was preparing an arsenal of surface-to-surface missiles to target Israel's cities with dirty-bomb (radioactive high-explosive) warheads. Lotz returned to Paris in the fall of 1962 with a list of every single German scientist living in Cairo. After taking power in 1954, President Gamel Abdul Nasser invited in many German scientists to help Egypt build up its defense industries. Lotz also supplied the Mossad with a list of the locations of the scientist's families in Germany and Austria. In 1964 with

Mossad funding, Lotz set up his own horse farm ten miles south of Cairo and next to an Egyptian missile range.⁵⁶

Lotz also helped smuggle in explosives for use by Mossad agents in their terror campaign against the German scientists. The terror campaign was code-named Operation Damocles and Shamir's department was responsible for conducting it.⁵⁷ Lotz's direct role in the terror campaign was limited to writing and sending threatening letters to the scientists. Harel ordered the terror campaign against the scientists in September 1962. A German named Heinz Krug was reported missing. His car was found a few days later and he was never heard from again. Krug had been the manager of the Munich office of INTRA, one of the main suppliers of rocket parts for Nasser's rockets. In November Wolfgang Pilz, a veteran of the V-Weapons projects in World War II, received a letter at his Cairo office. It exploded in his secretary's face injuring her seriously and leaving her blind. A few days later five Egyptian engineers were killed when a parcel addressed to their boss, General Kamal Azzaz, exploded while being opened. Azzaz worked with the German scientists. In February 1963 Hans Kleinwachter, who headed an Egyptian research center for developing missile guidance

An honor guard of Etzel and Lehi underground members beside the coffins of Zeev and Johanna Jabotinsky on the Tel Aviv shore, July 7, 1964. Yitzhak Shamir is at front left.

systems, was shot at from close range. Kleinwachter escaped by grappling with his assailant. In the end the German scientists failed to develop a guidance system.[58]

In March 1963 Ben-Gurion ordered Isser Harel to end the terror campaign because it was putting at risk German weapons shipments to Israel. At the time Germany was Israel's leading foreign arms supplier with used American tanks, helicopters, and submarines. Instead of ending the campaign, Harel escalated it. Harel thought of himself as an unelected deputy prime minister and saw Ben-Gurion as a tired old man by 1963. A week later Ben-Gurion asked Harel to see the raw intelligence for himself so he could judge how much of a threat there was. "If you don't trust me," Harel announced, "I am resigning." Ben-Gurion tried to call and apologize but Harel wouldn't answer his phone. The next day Ben-Gurion received an official letter of resignation from Harel in the mail.[59]

A secret committee was set up in Mapai to examine the reason behind Harel's resignation. Ben-Gurion was fiercely questioned and became angry. Two months later in June 1963 he resigned as prime minister over this and the intelligence mishap in Egypt in 1954. Meir Amit, who replaced Harel as head of the Mossad, was a former chief of military intelligence. Amit and Shamir had a basic personality conflict. The two could not stand one another. So it was not surprising that Shamir resigned from the Mossad about six months after Harel did.[60]

Shamir then returned to the business world as the manager of a rubber plant in Kfar Saba. Shamir quickly became involved in the cause of Soviet Jewry—the struggle for their right to emigrate from the Soviet Union to Israel and the West. This became a major cause in Israel following the June 1967 Six Day War, which served to raise the national consciousness of Soviet Jewry, which had been suppressed since the visit of Golda Meir to Moscow in 1949. Shamir met with Dov Shperling, a Latvian Jew who immigrated to Israel in 1968 after serving two years in the Gulag for Zionist activities. Shamir arranged for meetings between Shperling and journalists and politicians.[61]

In late 1969 Geula Cohen, the former Lehi radio announcer and a disciple of the philosophy of former Center member Israel Eldad, met with the Rabbi Meir Kahane at the office of the Jewish Defense League in New York. Kahane was a former FBI informer and a rabbi of questionable personal morals who liked the limelight. She told Kahane that she and Shamir could supply the JDL with resources if he would redirect the JDL away from attacks on blacks and in support of the struggle for Soviet Jewry. This Kahane promptly did gaining the struggle much publicity in the United States. Until November 1969 the Israeli government did not publicly or privately advocate on behalf of the right of Soviet Jews to emigrate out of a fear of backlash from the Soviet Union in the form of greater arms supplies to Israel's Arab enemies. Golda Meir then changed this policy and it changed more so following the unsuccessful Leningrad hijacking plot in June 1970.[62]

In the fight for Soviet Jewry, Shamir found himself working alongside a number of Herut Party politicians. Party leader Menahem Begin was in the habit of holding an open house Friday evenings in which former underground members would drop by his home and reminisce about the good-old days of danger. Shamir probably attended a few of these after he left the Mossad and was encouraged by Begin to join the party. A number of former Lehi members encouraged Shamir to enter politics including Stern's brother David. Shamir formally joined the party on March 5, 1970, not long after Ezer Weizman joined it in late 1969. Shamir became head of the party's immigration department in 1970 and he became a spokesman for the efforts on behalf of Soviet Jewry. He also became a member of Herut's Central Committee. But he did not receive any salary for the political work he did and kept his old job.[63]

Shamir was almost 55 years old when he started his career in politics—an exceedingly late age to start a political career. Plus as a member of Lehi rather than Etzel under Begin he was a relative outsider in the "fighting family" paramilitary party that was Herut. But he was able to build on his former connections within the small gene pool that made up Revisionist politics in Poland and Israel. He would have known some party members from Betar in high school and at Warsaw University before he emigrated. He would have known others from his three years in the Etzel before the split. He might have known some from Mizra in 1942, although this is not likely as there were few Etzel members in detention in 1942. And he knew Ya'akov Meridor and Arieh Ben-Eliezer, who were Knesset members and senior party members, from Asmara and Djibouti, and Haim Landau from the struggle on behalf of Soviet Jewry.

The only other prominent former Lehi member to make a political career in Herut and the Likud besides Shamir was Geula Cohen. She was the Lehi's radio announcer as a teenager and after 1948 she became an apprentice and pupil of Rabbi Israel Eldad at his magazine *Sulam* (Ladder), which continued Eldad's messianic ideology from when he was a member of the Center. Cohen joined Herut in 1973 and left in 1979 to found Tehiya (Renaissance) in protest over the Camp David accords. It was probably a combination of Cohen's outsider status in the party and her messianism that led to her early exit. Shamir, although a leader in Lehi, was comfortable working in the shadows. He had a slow rise in the party—he was given a safe seat on Herut's list for the Eighth Knesset in 1973. At this point he quit his job and at age 58 became a fulltime politician. In 1977 he was appointed Speaker of the Knesset, not a powerful position, but one with some influence. In early 1980 he was appointed foreign minister by Begin to replace Dayan, who had resigned in October 1979 in protest over Begin's attitude towards the autonomy negotiations with Egypt. This was his reward for abstaining on the vote on the Egyptian-Israeli peace treaty rather than voting no as he really wanted to do. Upon being appointed a minister in 1980, at the age when most people were retiring, Shamir promised to do two things: purchase a tuxedo for formal occasions and improve his English. He did both.[64]

Shamir, in contrast to Begin, was not a polished writer or a great orator, but he knew how to get things done or, in Shamir's case in the 1980s and early 1990s, how not to get things done. He had this in common with Ben-Gurion's protégés like Shimon Peres, Moshe Dayan, Abba Eban, and Teddy Kollek who were known collectively as the bitzuim or "doers." Shamir, like Begin and Ronald Reagan, was an ideologue not a pragmatist. He had a few very important goals rather than an interest in administering or managing policy. Like the Labor Party he was interested in protecting Israel's security as he had done in the Mossad, but he was also interested in the de facto annexation of the West Bank through continued settlement. Criticism by outsiders rolled off of Shamir like water off of a duck's back. He had been called a terrorist when he was younger and it had not deterred him because he believed what he was fighting for was right. The same logic applied to his political career. Shamir's major achievement as foreign minister was a peace agreement with Lebanon in May 1983. But it was an empty achievement as President Hafiz al–Assad of Syria refused to allow the agreement to stand and it was never implemented. Enderlin faults Shamir for not having seen this coming and for not taking the diligence to see that it was.[65] But this was beyond Shamir's power.

Shamir played a major role in the Israeli attack on the Iraqi Osirak nuclear reactor in Baghdad in July 1981. Shamir served on a three-man decision-making committee along with Begin and Chief of Staff Rafael Eitan. Shamir's son, Colonel Yair Shamir, who was then in charge of the IAF's flight testing program, was very involved with the IAF's planning of the attack. But because the attack was classified it was only years later that both learned of the other's role in the attack. Eitan's son was killed in a training accident while training for the attack. The attack squadron that carried out the attack included Yiftakh Spector, one of Israel's leading fighter aces, and Ilan Ramon, who was Israel's first astronaut and who died in the Challenger disaster.[66]

Shamir's big differences with Begin are due not to his origin in Lehi, but due to their differences in personality. Begin was much more religious than Shamir and as a young man had fallen in love with ritual and ceremony. Begin loved the formal trappings of military life: the parades, the drill, the saluting, the ranks, etc. Shamir loved the purpose. As Lehi chief of operations he did away with ranks and formalities. Begin loved to be addressed as "haMefeked" (Commander), whereas Shamir probably was content with a first name or no address. In this Shamir was much more Israeli than Begin, who was famous for his Polish manners. For Begin the concept of *hadar* from Jabotinsky's philosophy was nearly as important as *shlemut ha'Aretz* (consolidation of the land). For Shamir it had very little importance. For Shamir shlemut ha'Aretz and aliya (immigration) were everything.[67]

But Shamir was also modest. When asked by an Etzel veteran who was the greatest person he had ever met, Shamir answered without hesitation. "Menahem Begin was the greatest person I met. Begin was the man because of whom the British left Eretz Israel. Had he not come in the early 1940s, there would not have been a real war with the British and they wouldn't have been chased out of Israel. Lehi alone wouldn't have succeeded and neither would the Irgun without Begin," said Shamir.[68]

When Begin suddenly resigned in September 1983, Shamir was in the same position that Begin had been in in 1943. In 1983 the party wanted someone like Begin who could be trusted to continue to implement his policies. On September 1, 1983, the Herut Party Central Committee elected Shamir to follow Begin by a vote of 436 to 302. His only opponent was Ariel Sharon, who was isolated in the party after losing the defense ministry in February 1983.

Throughout the next nine years the Herut Party and then the Likud was divided into three main political camps: a large centrist camp led by Shamir and Moshe Arens, which also included the second generation of Likud leaders known as "the princes" who were the children of prominent Etzel or Revisionist figures; a camp on the right consisting of Ariel Sharon's supporters; and a camp on the left consisting of North African immigrants from development towns who supported David Levy.

Six

Prime Minister Shamir: The Great Procrastinator

There were two major events worth mentioning that occurred during Shamir's first term as prime minister from September 1983 until July 1984. The first was Bus No. 300. An Egged Bus on route from Tel Aviv to Ashkelon in April 1984 was hijacked by Arab terrorists who diverted the bus to the Gaza Strip. The IDF laid siege to the hijackers and their hostages and eventually stormed the bus. Then it was reported that all four of the hijackers were killed: two killed during the rescue of the hostages and two died from their wounds later. Then it emerged that two of the hijackers were photographed being led away by security personnel in apparently good health. Four senior Shabak officials served as whistle blowers and informed the Justice Ministry investigation that Shabak head Avraham Shalom was lying. They claimed that Shalom had given the order to execute the two survivors so that they would not be the cause of subsequent hostage-taking episodes meant to pressure Israel into releasing them. Eventually Shalom was forced to resign as head of Shabak for having given an obviously illegal order.[1]

In June 1980 three West Bank mayors were targeted in terrorist bombings. Mayor Bassam al–Shaka'a of Nablus lost both legs when a car bomb went off when he stepped on the gas pedal of his car. Mayor Karim Khalef of Ramallah lost one leg from an identical bomb placed in his car. And a Druze bomb-disposal technician was blinded when he accidentally set off a third bomb outside the home of al–Bireh's Mayor Tawil. That same day a grenade exploded in the Arab market in Hebron wounding 11 Arabs. This all happened during the premiership of Begin, but the perpetrators were uncovered only four years later in May 1984 when Shamir was prime minister. Thirty-seven Israelis were arrested and indicted for involvement in the settler underground, which was run by the crème de la crème of Gush Emunim and the settler aristocracy in the territories. Many of the defendants were sentenced to relatively short terms in prison. And they did not even see these sentences through as President Haim Hertzog using his presidential powers to pardon them after they had only served about a third to a half of their sentences, so that they were released in either 1991 or 1994 depending on the crime and the length of the sentence. Hertzog later wrote that he only pardoned those who wrote to him asking for a pardon in their own handwriting and who seemed to display some remorse for their actions. He ended up commuting the sentences of a dozen of the 29 (25 West Bank settlers, two Golan settlers, and two from the civil administration) that were eventually arraigned. Shamir commented in his memoir that he was saddened to think that 36 years after the creation of the state there were still those individuals who thought they were empowered to act as a law on to themselves independently of the state. Despite his support for settlement of the territories he did nothing to impede the investigation or the prosecution of the offenders. He only commented at the time that it was too early to speak of clemency.[2]

In the Likud leadership contest before the 1984 election, Arik Sharon decided to challenge Shamir for the party leadership. Sharon came in surprisingly strong with 42.5 percent of the vote compared to Shamir's 56 percent. This shocked those who had predicted that Sharon would not win more than ten percent of the vote. Shamir knew that following the election he would have to give Sharon a major ministry. It also gave Sharon an incentive to cooperate in the election campaign.

In early elections caused by the defection of the three-man Tami faction from the government to the opposition and held on July 23, 1984, the Likud lost seven seats from 1981 for a total of 41 compared with 44 for the Alignment, which lost three. Neither bloc could very well form a government by itself and so Sharon came up with the idea of creating a national unity government with a rotating premiership. Under the coalition agreement the Labor Party—Mapam defected and so the Alignment came to an end—and the Likud each agreed to hold the prime minister's office for half of the length of the government with Shimon Peres going first. Peres would then become foreign minister when his term was up and Shamir, who was foreign minister under Peres, would become prime minister. Both parties would have an equal number of places in an "inner cabinet" that would set policy for the government in all major areas. This allowed Peres to finally serve as prime minister in his own right.[3]

Yitzhak Rabin was appointed as defense minister for the entire period of the government and had an interest in seeing the government go to full term. Shamir spent most of his term as foreign minister making sure that Peres did not do anything to advance the chances for a peace settlement. In an address to members of the National Democratic Institute—the foreign policy arm of the American Democratic Party—at the Dead Sea in January 1987 he addressed King Hussein indirectly. He said that no international conference could force Israel to do what it did not want to do and that the government remained committed to the Camp David accords.

Shamir's memoirs read much like Rabin's memoirs when the subject is Shimon Peres. Peres wanted to hold an international peace conference along with King Hussein of Jordan sponsored by the great powers. On April 11, 1987, Peres went off to London for a secret meeting with King Hussein of Jordan. They met at the home of Hussein's doctor, who was generous enough to allow his home to be used for the purpose of secret talks on a number of occasions. After several hours of negotiations they came up with a plan for an international peace conference on the Middle East. The agreement specified that the American government would introduce it as its own and the two governments would go along with it. But the problem was that when George Shultz spoke to Israel about it he omitted to talk about it as an American idea. Peres had briefed Shamir on the agreement but refused to let him see a copy of it. Shamir then immediately sent Moshe Arens to Washington to warn off Shultz and tell him that Jerusalem would consider it an unfriendly act to get involved in an internal dispute between two sections of the Israeli government. As a result of this, King Hussein lost all confidence in the ability of Peres to deliver on his promises. In the future he would turn to Rabin to reach a peace agreement with Israel.[4]

In March 1986 at the Herut Party's first party conference since 1979, the party was divided into three rival camps. Shamir's centrist faction controlled half the delegates, just over a third were controlled by David Levy and Sharon controlled the remainder of about 15 percent. Before the 1988 election the two former Gahal parties, Herut and the Liberals, formed a joint Likud Party with one list. This entailed a modest reduction of the Liberals contribution to the joint list in 1984, followed by a virtual Herut takeover in 1988. La'am continued as a small faction that ran as part of the Likud list but did not merge into the party. But it was of declining importance as Ehud Olmert had led the Free Center portion of La'am back into Herut in 1985. And the original two La'am MKs from the State List, Yigal Hurvitz and Zalman Shoval, both left the Likud in 1981 to run with Moshe Dayan on his Telem list. Shoval failed to win election on that list in 1981 and formed his own Ometz list for the 1984 election. So that by the late 1980s the La'am faction was basically defunct.[5]

Shultz was interested in Middle East peace, he devotes several hundred pages in his memoirs to the subject covering the Reagan Plan in September 1982, negotiations for a peace agreement between Israel and Lebanon in 1983, his attempts to negotiate an agreement with King Hussein representing the Palestinians in 1984–85, the London Agreement, and finally the reaction to Yasir Arafat's recognition of Israel in December 1988 just as he was leaving office. But nothing came of it because of the structural restraints on the sides due to ideology and political interests. The Palestinians were unwilling to accept UN Security Council Resolution 242, Israel was unwilling to negotiate with the Palestine Liberation Organization (PLO), and the Likud was unwilling to give up the West Bank. Undoubtedly personal political ambition by Peres to win fame and future office by reaching a major peace agreement with the Arabs played a role. But Peres also believed that a peace agreement was in Israel's interest. Shamir believed that retaining and settling the West Bank and Gaza was in Israel's interest. It was not simply personal ambition but ideological differences—one was a disciple of Ben-Gurion and the other was a disciple of Jabotinsky—that caused the problems.

The other major issue that preoccupied Shamir as both foreign minister and prime minister from 1984 to 1992 was the issue of Taba. Taba was an area of 1.2 square kilometers along the east coast of the Sinai near Eilat where the Israelis had built a resort hotel in the 1970s. Egypt claimed that it was Egyptian territory and Israel claimed that it was Israeli territory. The problem was that the old border between Palestine and Egypt, the Sinai, was poorly marked in the area. Egypt pressed Israel to give up the territory under the 1979 Egyptian-Israeli peace treaty. President Mubarak declared that he would not meet with an Israeli prime minister until the Taba issue was resolved. Peres had plans for wider peace initiatives in the region involving Jordan and the Palestinians for which he needed the assistance of Egypt to support and possibly to mediate between Israel and the Palestinians. Peres threatened to resign and bring down the government if the Likud was not willing to send the dispute to international arbitration.

In accordance with the peace treaty the dispute was finally turned over to international arbitration. This was after a twelve-hour cabinet meeting on January 12, 1986, in which Likud ministers insulted Peres but finally voted in the early morning hours to allow arbitration. In 1989 the arbitrators found in favor of Egypt and an Egyptian buyout of the Israeli owners of the resort hotel was arranged. Shamir complained in his memoirs that he knew that if the issue went to arbitration the finding would be in favor of Egypt. He does not explain in his memoirs how he expected Cairo to remain content with the status quo if it felt that it had a legitimate legal case that the territory was Egyptian. But then Shamir was opposed to the peace treaty in the first place and may not have cared if Israel lost the benefit of the treaty over a small hotel and a few hundred meters of square territory.[6]

In the late afternoon of December 8, 1987, there was a fatal collision between an Israeli truck and a Palestinian car on the Tel Aviv-Gaza highway near the Erez checkpoint that is the northern border of the Gaza Strip when the Israeli driver's brakes failed. The Palestinian occupants of the car were killed. A few days earlier Palestinian terrorists had stabbed to death an Israeli in the Gaza Strip. The rumor now spread, based on a projection of Arab culture on to the Israelis, that this was a deliberate revenge killing by someone related to the Israeli who had been murdered. The accident served as a spark to set off twenty-years worth of tinder that had been building up among the Palestinians. A tinder composed of humiliation, oppression, and victimization in their eyes at the hands of the hated Israelis. Soon the Intifada had spread throughout the Gaza Strip and had crossed over into the West Bank. The scenes in each case were of rock-throwing children confronting Israeli soldiers armed with rifles. The soldiers had two choices: run away or open fire with live ammunition.[7]

The Intifada, meaning shaking off in Arabic, as the revolt was soon named, looked visually very similar to the internal unrest that had plagued South Africa since late 1984 and was still going on as the Intifada began. Defense Minister Rabin had been scheduled to visit Washington the day after the Intifada began and he went ahead with his trip. This contributed to the slow Israeli reaction to what was happening. The Intifada had the effect of speeding up the gap that opened up between Israel and Europe during the Arab oil embargo of 1973–74 and continued to grow as European economic interests lined up more with the Arabs than with Israel. Now with the Holocaust a full forty years in the past, political interests in Europe were starting to realign as well. The Intifada also began to widen the gap between liberal American Reform and Conservative Jews and Israel that had begun during the Lebanon War.

Initially the Intifada was spontaneous and then Palestinians in the territories like Sari Nusseibeh and Faisal al–Husseini, both from distinguished West Bank families that played major roles in politics during the mandate period and in 1948, asserted control and began organizing the supply of services to communities under siege while at the same time lending a political character to the rioting. Finally the Palestinian leadership in Tunis under Yasir Arafat asserted its control over the Intifada and began coordinating with the United National Command that al–Husseini and Nusseibeh had set up. At about the same time the Palestinian branch of

Foreign Minister Shimon Peres (right) and Prime Minister Yitzhak Shamir during a Knesset plenary session, 1988. Photograph by Nati Harnik.

the Muslim Brotherhood in Gaza established itself as Hamas, an acronym meaning zeal in Arabic and short for the Islamic Resistance Movement. Hamas and the PLO soon found themselves in competition for support.[8]

Elections were held as scheduled in November 1988 with the National Unity Government of 1984 going to full term—a rarity among Israeli governments. The campaign was dominated by the antics of various ultra-Orthodox rabbis who promised medical cures and other miracles for those who voted for their parties. These parties held the balance of power in the election and afterwards in the coalition negotiations. On November 1, 1988, the election resulted in the Likud winning 40 seats to Labor's 39. But the Right had a total of 64 seats compared to 56 for the Left. The National Unity Government was extended but without prime ministerial rotation this time. Rabin remained as defense minister and Peres became finance minister in order to help out the kibbutz movement, a key Labor constituency, rather than push for peace as foreign minister. He ignored the advice of his advisor and friend, Michael Bar-Zohar, both to collapse the government before its terms ended and to continue as foreign minister.[9]

Shamir's big diplomatic moment came in 1989. Several months before the elections in July, King Hussein made a speech in which he publicly cut all ties to the West Bank and all responsibility for its fate. No longer would his government pay the salaries of public employees in the West Bank. This pretty much ended the Labor Party's 21-year policy of the Jordanian option of negotiating solution to the West Bank with Amman. In December 1988 PLO leader Yasir Arafat finally decided to bite the bullet and in a statement at Geneva he both accepted UN Security Council Resolution 242 and publicly eschewed the use of terrorism. These were the long-standing American conditions for starting a political dialogue between Washington and the PLO. Secretary of State Shultz took the decision in order to relieve his successor, whomever he would be, of having to make the decision to start a dialogue. George H.W. Bush's secretary of state, James Baker, agreed to continue the dialogue.

But the Israeli Labor Party wanted to be proactive. It decided that it should produce its own peace plan and win government approval for it. Yitzhak Rabin came up with a plan of allowing the Palestinians in the West Bank and Gaza to hold internal elections. Those elected would then serve as Palestinian representatives in a joint Jordanian-Palestinian delegation to hold peace negotiations with Israel. It was not really a new or original plan. Rabin sold this plan to Shamir and it became known as the Rabin-Shamir plan or for short, simply the Shamir plan. Shamir then went to Washington and won American support for the peace plan in April 1989.[10]

But after a terrorist attack on Israel by the Palestine Liberation Front terrorist organization of Mahmoud Abul-Abbas (not to be confused with the later PLO leader and head of the Palestinian Authority known as Abu Mazen), a member organization of the PLO, which Arafat then refused to disavow or reject for internal Palestinian political reasons. Arafat's rejection of terrorism was suddenly in doubt. The Israeli government was also busy settling the West Bank with Baker greeted by a new settlement every time he came to Israel. In frustration, Baker, in a speech to the America Israel Public Affairs Committee (AIPAC) in May 1989, gave out the White House switchboard's number and said, "When you are serious about peace call us." Baker also said, "Now is the time to lay aside once and for all the unrealistic vision of a Greater Israel." AIPAC quickly produced a letter signed by 94 senators calling for the administration to endorse and work with the Israeli government peace plan.[11]

On May 14, 1989, Shamir returned from a meeting in Washington with President Bush. He presented a four-stage plan to the government. The Rabin-Shamir plan was the last stage of the four. The plan won the support of the government. Sharon got together with Yitzhak Moda'i and David Levy of the Likud to pose an internal challenge to Shamir. They wanted to look more nationalistic than Shamir. So they came up with a set of conditions or "constraints" on the peace plan that were then put to the Likud Central Committee. Sharon had begun holding meetings with Likud activists at his East Jerusalem home in order to organize this. The constraints were: no negotiations with the PLO; no Palestinian state under any circumstances; continued Jewish settlement in the territories; an end to the Intifada as a precondition for negotiations; and no participation in the Palestinian elections by Arabs living in East Jerusalem. The constraints were deliberately designed to be deal breakers with the Palestinians.

On July 5, 1989, Sharon convened the Likud Central Committee to discuss Shamir's plan. Sharon chaired the Central Committee and so arranged to hold a vote on both Shamir's plan and his own. If his plan passed it would put an end to the government's initiative. Minutes before the meeting was to begin, Shamir accepted all of the constraints. The meeting ended with Levy standing beaming between Shamir and Sharon. Sharon would later say that Shamir was the biggest constraints minister of them all.[12]

It later became commonplace for diplomats and reporters to speak of Shamir rejecting his own plan. The trio then went on to attack Rabin and compare him sarcastically to Churchill. On October 1, 1989, the three constraints ministers called a meeting of the Likud Central Committee for February 12, 1990. In what later became known as the Night of the Microphones, Sharon had his supporter manning the electronic soundboard and cutting off power to Shamir's microphone when he was speaking so that Sharon could then hijack the meeting. Both Sharon and Shamir ended up losing public support as a result of the spectacle.

The Egyptian government had produced its own set of questions regarding the Israeli plan that Baker then produced answers for. Rabin went to Cairo in September at President Mubarak's invitation to discuss the plan. Rabin said that he had no problem on Cairo consulting with the PLO in Tunis on who should be included in the delegation.

Baker was busy pushing Israel to move forward. At this point Finance Minister Shimon Peres issued an ultimatum to Shamir: either agree to Baker's conditions or we will break up the government. Peres had been busy meeting with representatives from the religious parties and he was confident that he could put together a Center-Left government without the Likud.

On March 11, 1990, at a meeting of the inner cabinet the Shamir plan the Baker's diplomatic efforts were discussed. Shamir refused to agree to allow Palestinians from East Jerusalem in the Palestinian delegation or to allow the delegation to consult with the PLO. Rabin wanted a compromise and suggested that Shamir remove all the other constraints and that the Knesset be allowed to vote about the precondition regarding the participation of Palestinians from East Jerusalem in the delegation. Shamir said no to any compromises and no to a vote. The two parties were now unified on only one point—that there was no unity in the government.

The next day the Labor Party Central Committee met in a meeting called by Peres in anticipation of Shamir's behavior at the inner cabinet meeting. Peres called for a breakup of the government. Rabin told the Central Committee that Shamir was neither interested in a compromise nor in peace, but he did not call for the collapse of the government.

Shamir then seized the initiative instead of waiting around for Labor to leave when it was ready. He fired Peres for trying to undermine the government. All of the Labor Party ministers then withdrew from the government. The Labor Party initiated a no-confidence motion in the Knesset and Shamir's government became the first in Israeli history to lose a no confidence vote. The vote was 60 to 55 against Shamir. Shamir later blamed the fall of the government on the Labor Party's determination to run its own foreign policy involving Amman, Cairo, and Washington without reference to government decisions.[13]

President Haim Hertzog then nominated Shimon Peres to try and form a coalition government. He would have five weeks to try to put together a coalition. If he failed then Shamir would be given a chance. Peres was convinced that he could do it. Rabin had been skeptical only a few days before. Peres spent most of his time negotiating with the leaders of the various ultra–Orthodox parties. Here he encountered their jealousies and mutual antipathies. Half a million Israelis, nearly 10 percent of the population signed a petition to President Hertzog demanding electoral reform. The public was convinced that Peres was trying to buy the needed Knesset votes of the ultra–Orthodox MKs with the public coffers. In the end two MKs from the small Agudat Israel party decided to withhold their support from Peres on the orders of Rabbi Menachem Shneerson of the Chabad-Lubavitch sect in Brooklyn, New York. Shneerson had never even been to Israel and his followers believed that he was the messiah. Rabin labeled the whole period as the "smelly exercise" (hatrargil hamasrikha).[14]

Shamir was then able to quickly form a government with the support of the religious parties, Tehiya, Rafael Eitan's Tzomet party, and Rehavam "Gandhi" Ze'evi's Moledet (Homeland), which called for the transfer of Arabs in the territories and Israel to Jordan. The new foreign policy guidelines for the government were: no negotiations with the PLO, no Palestinian state, Jerusalem to remain united under Israeli sovereignty, and settlement efforts to go forward in the territories by expanding existing settlements and founding new ones. In other words, no to peace with the Palestinians (or with Jordan). It was the most nationalistic government in Israel's history to that point.[15]

The major event in the two-year existence of the Shamir government, which lasted until March 1992, was the Gulf War of January–February 1991. President Saddam Hussein of Iraq invaded neighboring Kuwait in August 1990 and quickly destroyed the country's defenses within hours. President George Bush and Prime Minister Margaret Thatcher of Great Britain took very strong exception to this most egregious violation of international sovereignty and organized an international coalition dedicated to reversing the Iraqi occupation. The Arabs noted the difference between the international community's reaction to the Iraqi occupation of Kuwait and the Israeli occupation of the West Bank, Gaza, and the Golan. The Arab states and the PLO took their positions on the Iraqi invasion based upon their perceived interests. Yasir Arafat's PLO sided with Iraq as Saddam Hussein was perceived to be the newest pan–Arab champion—a worthy successor to President Nasser of Egypt. President Hafiz al–Assad of Syria sided with Washington as Saddam was his bitter enemy because of intra–Ba'athist politics. King Hussein of Jordan sided with Iraq mainly out of fear. This was the one traditional American ally to switch sides in the conflict and not back Washington.

Within days of the Iraqi invasion of Kuwait and the Anglo-American response, Shamir wrote a letter to Bush supporting Bush's resistance to aggression, making note that Arafat had sides with Saddam, and drawing a red line for Iraq, which was the entry of Iraqi forces into Jordan.[16] In December Shamir went to Washington to consult with President Bush about the war. Bush revealed in broad terms his strategy for dealing with Saddam and asked what Israel would do in the event of war. Shamir answered that Israel would defend itself and that he would consult with President Bush. He was indicating that Israel would not immediately react but would do whatever was in the common interest of both Jerusalem and Washington. He also said that Israel had no plans for a preemptive attack against Iraq.[17]

Saddam Hussein's strategy for fighting the war was to try and split apart the international coalition, a combination of Western powers (the United States, Britain, France) and Arab countries (Egypt, Kuwait, Saudi Arabia, Syria) financed by the Arab oil producers and countries like Japan and Korea, by attacking Israel and hoping to provoke it into retaliating and thereby splitting the Arabs off from the coalition when their publics demanded that they not fight against a country fighting against Israel. Washington put great pressure on Jerusalem not to retaliate against Iraqi Scud attacks. The only weapon that Saddam had that could reach Israel were Scud missiles whose range had been increased by welding on an extra stage. These missiles could only be fired from the western desert of Iraq on mobile launchers in order to reach Israel. Both Britain and the

United States had special forces units scouring the western desert looking for these launchers that they would then destroy by calling in air strikes against or by attacking them directly with anti-tank weapons. The United States also sent Patriot tactical anti-aircraft missiles to Israel with their U.S. Army crews to shoot down any Scuds that made it through. At the time the United States claimed almost perfect results for the Patriot missiles in terms of missile intercepts, but after the war when the results were analyzed further it turned out that the Scud missiles had a tendency to break up over Israel as the welding came apart and the Patriot's guidance system had a problem distinguishing the warhead from the fuel stages. The Iraqis aimed at Tel Aviv as this was the largest metropolitan target without a major Arab population. The Iraqis sent missiles equipped with both conventional high explosive warheads and chemical warheads, but the latter were not very effective and contained only non-persistent agents. To protect against chemical weapons the Israeli government had distributed protective (gas) masks to the population and instructed everyone to seal off a room in the house with plastic sheeting that they could enter during an attack. By early February 31 Scuds had been fired against Israel causing 13 fatalities, 237 wounded and 6,500 homes or apartments had been damaged.[18]

At the start of the war the two leaders again talked by telephone. Shamir expressed an interest in the United States allocating it an air corridor so that it could carry out retaliatory raids against Iraq or engage in its own Scud-hunting missions should that prove necessary. Bush replied that this was out of the question as Jordan was completely unwilling to allow Israeli aircraft to overfly its air space. Bush warned that the United States would defend its Jordanian ally's sovereignty if it were threatened. After all, Amman and Baghdad were allies in the war.[19]

Throughout the war Shamir faced pressure from within the cabinet to retaliate coming from a group consisting of Ariel Sharon, Yitzhak Moda'i, Rafael Eitan of the Tzomet party, and Yuval Ne'eman of Tehiya.[20] Shamir was easily able to resist this pressure as he had the votes in the cabinet and he had little respect for those clamoring for retaliation. But there were a number of other ministers who were swing voters in the cabinet and who would vote for either Shamir or with the rebels depending on the situation. These included: Minister of Transportation Moshe Katsav and Minister of Police Ronni Milo. Justice Minister Dan Meridor, Minister of Trade and Industry Moshe Nissim, Interior Minister Arie Deri, and Minister of Religious Affairs Zevelun Hammer tended to vote on the side of caution, and Foreign Minister David Levy was mostly concerned about how any action would impact upon the relationship with the United States.[21]

Shamir, unlike Begin, was reserved and tended to shy away from addressing the nation during a crisis. He did go on television during the fifth day of the war and answer questions. And he defended his policy of restraint being in the national interest of Israel.[22] Shamir does not indicate in his memoirs if he appreciated the irony of someone who had begun his public career carrying out operations in the underground in violation of the Jewish Agency's policy of restraint in regard to Arab terrorism, only to end his career carrying out a similar policy of restraint in regard to Iraqi terror attacks against Israel's civilian population.

Within two weeks of the end of the Gulf War Secretary of State James Baker toured the region to meet with the governments of eight coalition member states and Israel. In his first trip Baker arrived in Israel on March 11 and emphasized the gratitude of the administration for Shamir's policy of restraint during the war, both towards his government and towards him in particular. Baker declared, "A comprehensive peace must be grounded in UN Security Council Resolutions 242 and 338 and the principle of territory for peace. The principle must be elaborated to provide for Israel's security and recognition, and at the same time for legitimate Palestinian rights. Anything else would fail the twin tests of fairness and security." Thus, he made clear the real purpose of his visit. During the visit he met with Foreign Minister Levy, with Shamir, with Defense Minister Arens, with the leaders of the Labor Party, and with Israel's president.[23]

After Baker's visit Washington asked Shamir to send someone to Washington to consult with the administration about the peace plan. Shamir decided to send Justice Minister Dan Meridor, who had been Begin's aide at Camp David and was a favorite of Begin, rather than to send Foreign Minister David Levy, showing how little respect he had for his foreign minister who did not speak English. Meridor met with Dennis Ross and with Baker. He returned to Israel with three questions: Was Israel prepared to negotiate a permanent settlement based on Resolutions 242 and 338? Was Israel prepared to participate in a regional conference called by the superpowers? Did Jerusalem agree to the list of seven Palestinian names (which did not include any resident of Jerusalem and anyone who had been deported) to serve as members of a Palestinian delegation?[24]

Baker would return seven more times to the region in the course of the next seven months in order to kick start a peace initiative that began with the Madrid Peace Conference at the end of October 1991. Baker imitated Henry Kissinger and engaged in shuttle diplomacy between Cairo, Riyadh, Amman, Kuwait City, Damascus, and Jerusalem before returning to Washington on each round. After each round Shamir would convene a meeting with Levy and Arens to discuss how to respond to the demands of Baker.[25]

Six. Prime Minister Shamir

Baker had initially envisaged a major international conference comparable to the great peace conferences of the nineteenth and twentieth centuries such as Vienna in 1814 or Versailles in 1919. But many Arab governments turned down Baker's invitation for them to attend as they did not want to have to sit down with an Israeli delegation unless there was something of direct interest to them. By the end of the fourth round only a Jordanian-Palestinian delegation, Israel and the superpowers had agreed to attend. By July with a little arm twisting President Assad had agreed to a Syrian delegation attending the Madrid Conference. By the end of the July round of shuttle diplomacy Baker had rounded up Egypt and an observer from the Gulf Cooperation Council.[26]

Madrid was an international peace conference, basically ceremonial and symbolic in nature intended to lend legitimacy to American mediation efforts between Israel and the Arabs. Thus it was in the tradition of the Geneva Conference of December 1973, the aborted Geneva Conference of 1977 that Carter tried to arrange, and the aborted peace conference that Peres and King Hussein attempted to set up in 1987. Like his reaction to the London plan of Peres, Shamir's reaction to the Madrid Conference was negative. Baker had to engage in diplomatic arm twisting in order to get Shamir to agree to attend the conference. In September the Bush administration announced that it was suspending for 120 days the granting of Israel's request for $10 billion in loan guarantees to be used to house the immigration of Soviet Jews to Israel. Bush said that granting the request before the Peace Conference could be harmful to it.[27]

Only in October did Washington announce the venue and timing of the Peace Conference: Madrid on October 30. When the government voted on Israel's attendance at the Conference, the vote was only three against. These three were: Sharon, who was still playing his role as the constraints minister, Yuval Ne'eman of Tehiya, and Rehavam "Gandhi" Ze'evi of Moledet. David Levy wanted to attend the conference to represent Israel as its foreign minister. But Shamir did not trust Levy as being sufficiently hardline to protect Israel's interests. Shamir decided that he would attend the conference and Levy would stay at home. This was unusual as the Conference was a foreign ministers' conference. But Shamir told Levy that too much was at stake for Israel to leave it up to him. Levy was very upset with this decision and announced that he would stay home if Shamir led the delegation. Shamir despised Levy as weak and too prone to play the racism card, but he positively loathed Sharon for daring to accuse him of being soft when it came to the Arabs. Shamir decided to bring along Deputy Foreign Minister Benjamin Netanyahu as the delegation's spokesman with the rest of the delegation consisting of professional diplomats and lawyers.[28]

As at Geneva in 1973, each country's delegation made an opening speech after remarks by the superpower hosts. President Bush in his opening address avoided the term "territory for peace" in order not to upset Shamir. Instead he spoke of "territorial compromise," which the Syrians interpreted as meaning a less than full return of the Golan and were upset by. Soviet Foreign Minister Edward Shevarnadze was more concerned with getting economic aid for the disintegrating Soviet Union than he was with the subject of the conference. For the Palestinians a number of Palestinians from the territories led by Hanan Ashrawi, who was a Christian woman from Ramallah and a professor of English, handled the publicity for the delegation and did a very good job. Haidar Abdel Shafi gave a restrained speech laying out the Palestinian case for statehood and calling for reconciliation with Israel. Both the Israeli and Syrian delegations came off looking very hardline. Shamir made a speech in which he accused Damascus of being a major international sponsor of terrorism and one of the most tyrannical regimes in the world, true enough. The Syrian delegation was prepared for this and the Syrian foreign minister held up a wanted post from the 1940s with a photo of Yitzhak Yezernitsky on it. He also accused Shamir of murdering Count Bernadotte in 1948, but by then Shamir was already gone. He who lives in a glass house should not throw stones. In his rebuttals Shamir delivered a targeted message to each of the delegations. He told Lebanon that Israel had no designs on Lebanese territory and only wanted security. To Jordan he said that a peace treaty between the two countries was both desirable and achievable.[29]

The Madrid Conference proved to be the beginning of the end for the Shamir government. Following the end of the Madrid Conference on November 1, the talks reconvened in Washington as a series of bilateral negotiations between Israel and each of its neighbors and multilateral talks on regional issues such as water, the environment, and arms control. Because the Shamir government was no more forthcoming in negotiations in Washington than it had been at Madrid or in the run-up, the 120-day period for the consideration of the loan guarantees was extended. The unspoken American position was "no settlement freeze, no loan guarantees."

Shamir visited Washington in late November and secured only a fifty-minute meeting with Bush at the last minute. Baker had already told Shamir that when it came to the Middle East it was Bush who set the policy for his administration. Shamir had been advised by officials of the America Israel Public Affairs Committee that the Bush administration would not dare to take it on in a fight over the loan guarantees. AIPAC was wrong. Shamir saw George Bush as biased in favor of the Arab position.

Shamir wanted to discuss the loan guarantees but the topic never came up as Bush spent the whole time discussing the venue of the negotiations and Israel's refusal to attend the next round. Shamir was angry when he left. The implicit American position on the loan guarantees was made explicit soon after the Israeli delegation returned home.[30]

In February 1992 testifying before a Congressional sub-committee hearing, Secretary Baker called for a freeze on new settlement construction in the territories. Baker defined construction to include not only buildings but also the accompanying infrastructure such as pipes, roads, sewage systems, etc. Shamir had no intention of complying with this. By this time his government was a caretaker government as the Tzomet Party withdrew from the coalition in December and Tehiya and Moledet parties had withdrawn their support for the government over the reopening of autonomy talks as a result of Madrid the following month, and as a result the coalition was left with only 59 votes. On January 19 Shamir called for new elections to be held on June 23, 1992. Geulah Cohen seemed for some time to be bent on bringing down the government of her former boss, Michael. Shamir never understood quite why this was the case.[31]

Benyamin "Fuad" Ben-Eliezer began a registration drive for party memberships in the Labor Party in November 1990. By the time of the Labor Party's first primary election in March 1992 he had signed up 100,000—65 percent of whom were first-time members and half of whom were under the age of 45.[32]

When Shamir toured the United States he was politely applauded when he spoke in front of Jewish groups. He misinterpreted this to mean support from American Jews on his hardline positions on territorial issues. He knew that the Bush administration had supported Israel on many issues such as cooperating on immigration from the Soviet Union and Ethiopia, support for defense, and the high annual levels of American aid to Israel. He assumed that given time he could iron out the difficulties with Bush in the future after he had been reelected and Bush had won a second term. But it was not to be.

Public opinion polls showed the Likud receiving 48 seats in late 1991 and beating Labor by about a dozen seats. But this was a temporary "sugar high" as a result of the Madrid Conference. Israel was suffering from economic problems and the government, like democratic governments everywhere, would pay the price for that. Because Israel was spending so much on settlement construction in the occupied territories there was a shortage of housing in Israel proper when Jews began arriving in large numbers from the Soviet Union starting in 1989–90. So Soviet Jews, known as Russians no matter where in the Soviet Union they were from, who were naturally predisposed to vote for the Likud because of their dislike for socialism and their belief that Israel was a very small country already and should not give up more territory, ended up supporting Labor in protest at the government's absorption efforts for them. The greater demand for housing drove up housing prices overall thus hurting the traditional Likud constituency of mizrakhim in the development towns and poorer neighborhoods of the main cities. And Shamir was opposed to electoral reform, refusing to vote for the new double voting system that gave every Israeli citizen two votes (one for the Knesset and one for the prime minister) starting in 1996. First, Shamir's opposition had caused the defection of Tzomet in December. Labor had supported this "reform" and it passed by a single vote with Netanyahu's assistance in January 1992, 57 to 56, which ended up backfiring against both major parties and was repealed after only three elections (1996, 1999, 2001).[33]

Both the Right in general and the Likud in particular were hopelessly divided. When he called new elections, Shamir announced that he would run for another term as prime minister at age 73. Although Moshe Arens thought that their centrist camp would beat both the Sharon and Levy camps easily, he was disappointed by Shamir's decision to run for another term. Arens probably suspected that Shamir planned to skip over him as his successor and instead support one of the princes as his successor, as Sharon had hinted at this in 1988. But Arens in his memoirs wrote that Shamir was perceived as being part of the past rather than the future. The same could probably be said about both Peres and Rabin, but at least the Likud would have won some tactical advantage by nominating a younger leader to go up against Labor.[34]

On February 20 the Likud held its leadership election in the Central Committee. Shamir won easily with 46 percent, followed by Levy with 31 percent and Sharon with 22 percent. A week later the panels were chosen that would determine the order of the candidates on the Likud's election list. Neither Levy personally—he ended up in eighteenth place—nor his people did well. Levy went running to the media and cried ethnic discrimination against Moroccans. Then he announced that he was resigning from the cabinet.

On the day he was to resign, Levy met privately with Shamir for almost half an hour. When they finished Levy was reinstated to his former second place on the list and he was guaranteed 30 percent of the safe seats for his supporters. The fix temporarily appeased Levy but alienated Arens. When Arens protested, Shamir threatened to resign and Arens accused him of behaving like Levy. It was at this point that Arens made up his mind to retire from politics following the election.[35]

Six. Prime Minister Shamir

On February 20, 1992, in the Labor primary—the first time that the party's Central Committee had not elected the leader but the party as a whole had—Peres faced Rabin and two minor candidates. Required for a first-round victory was a total of 40 percent. Rabin received 40.6 percent to Peres's 34.8 percent and a total of 24 percent for the other two candidates.[36] Labor was busy preparing for a new general election and its members could smell the possibility of victory and wanted to go with a candidate with a better track record in elections than Shimon Peres. Many Peres supporters imitated Abraham Lincoln in the 1840s. Lincoln was a Whig politician and great admirer of Whig Senator Henry Clay of Kentucky. But in 1840 he supported former Indian fighter William H. Harrison and in 1848 supported Mexican War hero Zachary Taylor. He did this in both cases because both had a much better chance of beating their Democratic Party opponents than did Clay who had a poor election record.[37]

Rabin insisted on formally renaming the party as "Labor led by Rabin." He ran a very personal, American-style presidential campaign that was aimed at picking up votes from alienated Likud voters. Rabin estimated that the party could pick up up to five seats from the Likud. This was a new strategy for Labor. As defense minister Rabin was more popular among many Likudniks than was Shamir during the National Unity Government of 1985–1990.[38]

The settlers ran a record number of separate lists, six, in the 1992 election with the net result that about two seats worth of votes were wasted on three parties that did not make the electoral barrier of 1.5 percent to enter the Knesset. This is in comparison to three small parties on the Left that ran as a joint list, Meretz, and thereby increased the number of seats that they received to a record 12. There were actually more votes cast for parties of the Right and religious parties than for parties of the Center and Left. But in the final count the Center-Left and the Arab parties had 61 seats to the Right's 59 seats.[39]

Shortly after this Shamir decided to give up the chairmanship of the party. Sharon and Levy both saw themselves as Shamir's logical successor, especially after Arens announced his retirement from politics. But several members of the camp known as the princes saw themselves as Shamir's successor. Polls quickly established that Sharon was too far behind to be a serious contender and he dropped out and lent his support to Benny Begin, Menahem's geologist son who had been elected to the Knesset in 1988. On March 24, 1993, Netanyahu won the party chairmanship with 52 percent of the vote, Levy followed with 26 percent, Begin with 15 percent and Moshe Katsav with seven percent.[40]

Shamir never liked Netanyahu much and was very critical of him in the book of conversations that he did with supporter Haim Misgav.[41] Shamir did not appreciate Netanyahu's style of sounding moderate while continuing to function as a hard liner. Shamir, like Begin, was always very transparent in his politics. Sharon and Netanyahu were more opportunistic. Shamir had very little respect for most members of his party after the fighting family disappeared in the early 1970s. Yossi Ahimeir, a former Shamir aide, said, "Shamir believed only in Shamir." His heroes tended to be totalitarian dictators and revolutionaries like Lenin and Mao rather than democratic politicians.[42]

Shamir retired from politics at the end of the Thirteenth Knesset in 1996 at age eighty. When Benny Begin founded his own Herut Party to run against Netanyahu for the premiership in 1999 Shamir supported him and then transferred his allegiance to the National Union (Ihud Leumi) when Herut became part of that. Only when Begin rejoined the party did Shamir once again rejoin the Likud.

Shamir spent his retirement reading, mostly memoirs of revolutionary leaders and underground fighters. He died at age 96 on June 30, 2012.[43]

What is Shamir's legacy for Israel and the Israeli Right? By rebuilding Lehi in 1942–43 Shamir played an important role in providing the pressure that contributed to Britain leaving Israel. The Moyne assassination, however, was a negative act that hurt the Etzel badly and also caused problems for the Yishuv. It prevented an early partition in 1945 that might have resulted in partition having been accepted by the Arabs without a war of independence for Israel, although this is difficult to know. Since Shamir does not reveal much of what he actually did during his decade in the Mossad that too is hard to judge. As foreign minister his main contribution was the aborted peace agreement with Lebanon. As prime minister he both helped to keep Israel secure and at peace but accelerated the problem of the future of the West Bank.

As for the Likud his real contribution was turning it into a united unified party from merely the joint list that he inherited. But because he lacked Begin's charisma he failed to deliver victory in both 1984 and 1992. He probably should have left the party chairmanship in 1987 or 1988 and made room for Moshe Arens then. This would have given Arens a chance to serve as the bridge to the next generation of leaders.

Shamir was the only member of the Lehi's Center to have political relevance after 1948. This was because unlike Israel Eldad and Natan Yellin-Mor he was not a purist. Shamir was willing to choose a party that approximated his ideological worldview and then work inside it pragmatically. Yellin-Mor reversed himself politically after he left the Fighters' Party and became a maverick—too leftist for the mainstream parties and too tied to the Revisionists for the Israeli Left that came to power in Shelli in the 1970s. Eldad was simply off the political spectrum.[44] But Shamir had been quietly fitting in and advancing since he arrived in Palestine from Poland: first in the Etzel, then in Lehi, then in the Mossad, and finally in Herut and the Likud.

Seven

Sharon: A General for the Likud

Ariel Scheinerman was born on February 27, 1928, in the village of Kfar Malal in the coastal plain of Palestine known as the Sharon, from which he would later take his name. His father Samuil was an agronomist, a rare occupation in those days, who had arrived in Palestine from the city of Brest Litovsk, the same city that Menahem Begin came from, on the Polish-Belarus border. He and his girlfriend Vera, had gotten in trouble with the Bolshevik authorities in the Soviet Union and fled to Palestine in 1922. The year before the village that they fled to, Kfar Malal, had been destroyed in the Arab riots. Vera was not a Zionist and had planned on becoming a doctor, a plan she had to give up upon arriving in Palestine because of the lack of universities in the land.[1]

Kfar Malal was a moshav or cooperative village affiliated with the Mapai Party and although Samuil was a registered member of Mapai, he was a contrarian and an individualist. He and his wife had very touchy relations with their neighbors because they dared to be different. Following the murder of Mapai figure Haim Arlozoroff in 1934, which was blamed on the Revisionist Party but was more likely perpetrated by Arab thieves,[2] Samuil expressed reservations about the general consensus. "Revisionists? We weren't Revisionists," said Vera Scheinerman years later. "Whoever knew what that meant around here. It was simply that anyone who tried to demand a bit of order was immediately dubbed a Revisionist."[3]

A decade later, when Ariel was in high school, Scheinerman made him promise to never betray Jews to Gentiles as the Hagana was doing to Etzel members during the *saison* in late 1944 and early 1945 following the assassination of Lord Moyne by the Lehi in Egypt. Schneinerman hinted that he did not want his son to join the Palmakh, which had carried out the *saison* and Sharon honored his wishes.[4]

Sharon made much of this later on during his career in politics. But in the fall of 1947 during what became known as the Little Season when the issue of Palestine was before the United Nations, the Hagana again cracked down on the Etzel and Sharon was an eager participant. "He was very, very active in everything we did against the Etzel," said Dedi Zalmanson in 1983. "He chased after me with a pickax handle," said a former Etzel member. "He smashed up my coffee shop," said Ben-Ami Zamir. Sharon, of course, denied all these allegations categorically. Sharon was working for Hagana Intelligence at the time.[5]

Sharon as a young child was fat. He outgrew this as a teenager, but then would become fat again in the late 1950s as he ceased going on missions in the field with his troops. As prime minister he used to reminisce about how lonely he was as a child. So his childhood figure probably revealed a lifelong tendency to overeat in order to deal with psychological stress. Sharon performed heavy manual labor as a child. Ariel was indifferent to his studies in school but he enjoyed the paramilitary training he received through the Hagana's youth organization, Gadna. Yosef Margalit, a friend of Sharon's from Kfar Malal, remembered, "From his first day in the Gadna, he changed. All of a sudden, with no warning at all, we discovered a totally different Arik." He excelled in all the tasks taught by the Gadna. His mother gave him a love of music and he did attain something of a liberal education at home in spite of the worst of intentions by the local school. Upon his graduation from high school in 1945 he joined the Hagana and went through signal training.[6] Ariel Sharon (he did not change his name until 1953 but for simplicity sake I will use this name throughout this chapter) was a half-generation younger than Dayan and six years younger than Rabin, but that was enough for him to miss out on the pre-independence experiences of the Arab Revolt and the formation of the Palmakh.

Sharon ended up joining the Jewish Settlement Police, which Dayan had belonged to in the late 1930s. He also briefly served as an instructor in the Gadna, the youth division of the Hagana that provided paramilitary training in high schools. Throughout 1947 he was active patrolling by night the area in the Sharon with his local unit. He developed a skill at reading the local terrain. On December 12, 1947, Sharon was mobilized into the Hagana as a fulltime soldier to provide protection to his community in the coming War of Independence, which was in its very early stage. He became a platoon leader in the Alexandroni Brigade.[7]

Sharon was very badly wounded as a young platoon commander during the First Battle of Latrun in late May 1948. His men were trapped and pinned down on the battlefield and he barely made it to the rear with the help of one of his men after he was wounded in the groin. After recovering in the hospital he returned to his unit and served in later campaigns in late 1948. While in hospital he decided to make the army his career. From 1953 to 1956 he first received major attention from his superiors as a leader of commando reprisal raids into the West Bank, Gaza, and even Syria. He formed his own unit of handpicked men who did not fit well into regular units and trained them as Unit 101 in the summer of 1953. Six months later this merged with the paratroopers to form a paratrooper battalion and then a brigade.[8]

Sharon's military career had a severe setback in early November 1956 when during the Sinai War he disobeyed orders and sent his men ahead into the Mitla Pass. They were pinned down by Egyptians firing from the rim of the canyon and took very heavy casualties. Chief of Staff Moshe Dayan kept him from being dismissed from the IDF but he did not receive a promotion for the next eight years.[9] In the mid–1960s he converted from being an infantry commander to being an armored officer after undergoing a conversion course. He served as a commander of an armored division during the June 1967 Six Day War. His capture of the Egyptian town of Abu Agheila at the start of the war was a textbook example on how to defeat Soviet defensive tactics, which is what Soviet military advisors taught to the Egyptians, Syrians, and Iraqis.[10]

Sharon experienced two personal tragedies while he was in the army. First, his wife Margalit, to whom he had been married for about a decade died in a head-on collision with a truck in May 1962. After the funeral, Margalit's younger sister Lily, whom Sharon had adopted as a kind of younger sister, moved into Sharon's house in order to take care of Sharon's young son Gur. The two began dating and fell deeply in love. A year after Margalit's death, Sharon married Lily. They would be together until she died of cancer decades later. She had dreamed of being an artist but took up a job with the police as a sketch artist. There were rumors that she and Sharon had been having an affair while Margalit was still alive and that she found out and committed suicide. It is more likely that Margalit simply suspected such an affair out of jealousy and then committed suicide. Sharon was probably much happier with Lily than with Margarlit as Margalit had her own career as a psychiatric nurse. Lily's true career was being a mother to Sharon's children and then serving as his closest political advisor once he went into politics. She apparently had a crush on him when he was married to her older sister and kept that crush through decades of married life.[11]

In October 1967 Gur was playing with some neighbor children and they took an old hunting rifle that Sharon owned and filled it with gunpowder that they had found along with some scrap metal. One of the boys pointed it at Gur and pulled the trigger. Sharon heard the sound of the gun and found his son bleeding profusely from the head. He picked him up and put him in his car and rushed him to the base hospital. But there was little that the doctors could do for the boy and he died shortly afterwards. Sharon never accepted that the death was an accident and continued to harass the boy and his parents until they were forced to move away. Sharon then buried his grief in work.[12] It may be that Gur's tragic death contributed to the close relationship between Sharon and his two surviving sons, Gilad and Omri, who would serve him as political advisors and confidantes as adults.

Following the Six Day War, Sharon was eventually appointed Southern Commander in December 1969 at the height of the War of Attrition. In 1971, following the end of that war, he began a ruthless counterinsurgency campaign against the Fedayeen groups operating in the Gaza Strip. He divided the strip into grid sectors, assigned a commander and unit to each sector, and stressed using ambushes and aggressive patrolling. He managed to eliminate the problem. As mentioned previously, he left the IDF in July 1973 after he failed to apply for an extension of his service.

After creating the Likud in September 1973, he was mobilized at the start of the Yom Kippur war to command a reserve armored division in the Sinai. After clashing repeatedly with the new theater commander, Sharon with the backing of Haim Bar-Lev, the former chief of staff who was mobilized to co-command in the Sinai, crossed into Egypt by bridging the Suez Canal in the gap between the Second and Third Egyptian Armies. After establishing a bridgehead his unit expanded outwards and was on the outskirts of Suez at the end of the war. Sharon emerged from the war even more of a war hero than he had been in 1967—the perfect way to launch a political career in Israel.[13]

Sharon was still set on being chief of staff someday and was using his political career as a means of fulfilling that dream. He kept his reserve commission as commander of an armored division and actually spent more time seeing to his duties as commander than to his political duties. This caused a number of deputies from the Labor Party to pass a bill prohibiting any Knesset member from serving as a commander at that rank. As Sharon was the only person affected by the bill it was dubbed the "anti–Sharon bill." Sharon ended up resigning his Knesset seat in December 1974 less than a year after having been elected. Sharon was quite happy with the bill because it gave him a handy excuse to give up his boring political duties while claiming that he was being persecuted by the Left.[14]

Sharon's next political venture was to get himself appointed a special advisor to Prime Minister Rabin on terrorism. Rabin and Sharon, although not personal friends, respected one another and Sharon remembered that it was Rabin who had given him his final promotion. Sharon was hoping that this was another stepping-stone in his journey to being chief of staff. Rabin wanted someone who could give him legitimacy with the Right and contribute to a more centrist personal image for himself. Rabin was experiencing problems with the Gush Emunim settlers and needed someone who could talk to them. Sharon had helped to facilitate negotiations between the government and the settlers at Sebastia in November 1974 before he left the Knesset.

Sharon started as an advisor to Rabin in July 1975. Rabin would solicit his opinion on issues relating to terrorism and defense (although Peres had agreed to the appointment on the understanding that Sharon would not be advising on defense matters) and Sharon would give his opinion. Earlier Sharon had objected to Kissinger's two separation-of-forces agreements and was opposed to giving up more territory in the peninsula without a peace treaty with Egypt. Rabin's appointment temporarily neutralized Sharon. After nine months Sharon realized that Rabin had no intention of causing himself political problems by appointing Sharon chief of staff. So in March 1976 he resigned as Rabin's advisor having served a valuable apprenticeship in power.[15] Four months later came the biggest terrorism incident of Rabin's first government and Sharon missed it.

At this point Sharon wanted back into the Likud that he had created three years earlier but Simcha Erlich wanted nothing to do with him. Sharon formed his own list, the first of the general's lists that would become a standard feature of Israeli politics. He named it *Shlomzion* meaning the "peace (or wellbeing) of Zion," which was the title of one of the last Hasmonean monarchs in ancient Israel. Although it initially did quite well in political opinion polls—as such parties tend to do at first—it quickly lost support as Yigael Yadin formed his rival Democratic Movement for Change three weeks later. Politically Shlomzion was all over the map with leftist as well as rightist positions on issues and it called for electoral reform. He held extensive merger talks with first Yadin's party and with the veteran Independent Liberals, a party that split off from the General Zionists a decade before and appealed to German-speaking Israelis. But both rejected Sharon as an opportunist likely to hurt their image. Sharon lambasted the Likud as being no better than the Labor establishment and he promised that he would never go back to it and would stay true to his announced mission even if he failed at the polls.

Sharon, like Ross Perot in the 1990s, preferred to surround himself with sycophants and admirers rather than with professional political organizers who knew what they were doing. His wife Lilly determined who had Sharon's ear in the party and so tended to pick flatterers. Once, Sharon flew to Los Angeles to meet with an American supporter who had written that he wanted to make a contribution. He collected a check in an envelope and when he opened it in his room he discovered that it was only for $25.

But when he failed to attract support on the Left, he went for expansionist nationalism. A couple of months before the election when Shlomzion was polling only one percent in the polls, Sharon conducted talks with Begin about joining Herut. But Yitzhak Shamir could not be located in time to finalize the merger and Sharon was forced to compete as an independent. Shlomzion won only two seats—just over the 1.5 percent barrier for getting into the Knesset.[16]

After the election a relieved Sharon joined the Likud as leader of his own faction, before merging it quickly with Herut. Begin wanted to make Sharon defense minister, but most of those in the Likud objected as Weizman had been in the party since 1969 and had served as the Likud's successful campaign manager in the 1977 election. So instead Sharon became minister of agriculture. Dayan and two other agriculture ministers had gone on to serve as defense ministers. Sharon was also appointed to head the party's committee on settlement.[17] This was the start of an alliance between Sharon and the settlers that would last for nearly three decades (for three decades if one dates it from the 1974 intervention at Sebastia). Sharon now had the second main group in his political following along with his war groupies.

Sharon spent the first Begin government mostly working on settlement issues. Within a month of being appointed head of the settlement committee, Sharon had a plan for settling Eretz Israel. In mid–September 1977 Sharon presented his plan, largely based on proposals that he had seen while Rabin's advisor and written by Professor Avraham Wachmann, an architect. The plan had three concentrations of settlements: one in the central mountain ridgeline of Samaria, the second in the Jordan Valley, and the third around Jerusalem. The settlements had three main strategic goals. First, was to protect Israel from the Eastern Front of Jordan, Iraq, and Syria. Second, was to prevent a division of Jerusalem that would allow East Jerusalem to become either the capital of a Palestinian state or a major city within Jordan. Third, was to divide the West Bank and deal with the demographic problem by planting modern Orthodox religious Zionists from Israel and abroad with high birthrates in among the Arabs.[18] Nearly thirty years later Sharon would recognize that this attempt had at least partially failed when he moved to divest Israel of Gaza for demographic reasons.

At Camp David, Weizman came up with the idea of contacting Sharon to get his permission to evacuate the settlements in the Rafiah salient in the northeastern corner of the Sinai. Sharon agreed to support Weizman on the evacuation. In 1981 he razed the city of Yamit in the settlement out of concern that it could cause future security problems for Israel if President Sadat populated it with Egyptians who then infiltrated into Israel looking for work.[19]

On August 5, 1981, the new Likud government was sworn in and Sharon realized his consolation prize of becoming defense minister after he was denied the senior position in the IDF. Since 1969 the Palestine Liberation Organization (PLO) had operated a protected position in southern Lebanon from which to mount terrorist and guerrilla attacks on Israel. After 1971 this became the main Palestinian front with Israel. On July 24, 1981, American envoy Philip Habib negotiated a ceasefire between the PLO and Israel. The PLO claimed that the ceasefire only governed actions taking place across the border whereas Israel claimed that it was a general ceasefire. Israel also held the PLO responsible for all Palestinian terrorist attacks whether committed by factions belonging to the PLO or not.[20]

When Sharon ran for the Knesset in 1977 his platform called for turning Jordan into a Palestinian state. Because Palestinians are a majority within Jordan—on the East Bank as well as the West Bank, the Jordanian Option of the Israeli Right was to either directly or indirectly get rid of the Hashemite monarchy and turn Jordan into a Palestinian state. This meant for Sharon that the PLO had to be disabused of the notion that it could turn Israel into a Palestinian state. The way to do this was to destroy its enclave of Fatahland and inside Beirut, which functioned as a state within a state. Israel had been cooperating with the Phalangist Maronite Christian militia within Lebanon since the mid–1970s shortly after the Lebanese civil war began in April 1975. Sharon's plan was to smash the PLO in Fatahland and in Beirut and install its Maronite Christian allies in the presidential palace in Beirut. There was suspicion that Operation Big Pines in Lebanon was to be the prelude to Operation Very Big Pines in Jordan: the overthrow of the Hashemite regime.[21]

For the next thirteen years until Jordan signed a peace treaty with Israel during Rabin's second government, Sharon used the slogan "Jordan is Palestine" to advertise his version of the Jordanian Option. Unlike the Dayan Plan ("functional compromise") or the Allon Plan ("territorial compromise") that were advocated by the Labor Party in the late 1960s and 1970s and 1980s, Sharon's version did not involve negotiations with the Hashemite regime in Jordan. Labor negotiated with King Hussein and his advisors on and off for twenty years and never reached an agreement because King Hussein was not willing to make a compromise as he feared that it would cost him his throne as well as being counter to UN Resolution 242. Sharon's efforts in this regard were especially galling to Peres during the National Unity Government.[22]

As related earlier, Sharon took advantage of the attempted assassination of the Israeli ambassador to Britain by the Abu Nidal Organization to attempt to put his plan to rearrange the political map of the Middle East into practice. Sharon was very active in meeting with Lebanese Christian leaders in Lebanon and in going to the front to confer with commanders during the first week of the war and during the siege of Beirut. He had a very adversarial relationship with Philip Habib, the American mediator of Lebanese descent who attempted to restore the ceasefire that Sharon had broken. After Habib had a close call with Israeli artillery he accused Sharon of trying to kill him or at least intimidate him.[23]

Sharon's political career can be divided into three distinct phases: his early career September 1973 to February 1983; rebuilding February 1983 to February 2001; and prime minister February 2001 to January 2006. During his early phase Sharon was full of energy and ambition and short of time. He was eager to get to the top and exceed his old boss, Moshe Dayan, by becoming prime minister. For Sharon becoming defense minister seemed to be psychological compensation for not having become chief of staff. Then after having been forced to resign in ignominy and disgrace from that office he was determined to regain his honor and reputation. The only way to do that was to become prime minister. As his friend and de facto press agent Uri Dan put it, "You did not want him as chief of staff and you got him as defense minister. You did not want him as defense minister, so now you will get him as prime minister." This quote made at the time of Sharon's resignation as defense minister seemed hubristic in the extreme, but Dan knew Sharon well.

Sharon's strategy during this second phase was to take any office that was offered to him and use it as a stepping stone within the cabinet to the next ministry. He also attacked Shamir and Netanyahu constantly from the right by urging more nationalistic positions or solutions. Israeli political scientist Ehud Sprinzak, an expert on the Radical Right in Israel, classified Sharon as belonging to it. Sharon was the champion of the settlers in the West Bank and Gaza and remained so up until 2003. Sharon could be moderate and responsible, but he had to be bribed to be so—bribed with the high offices that he coveted: the defense ministry and the foreign ministry. After Lebanon no one trusted him with the defense ministry. Shamir, who despised him, would not trust him with the foreign ministry. Moshe Arens would under both Begin and Shamir fill the two offices that

Sharon coveted. Under Begin, Shamir became the foreign minister and Arens replaced Sharon as defense minister. Then when Shamir became prime minister Arens was made foreign minister. During the National Unity Government from 1985 to 1990 both the defense and foreign ministries were taken—defense by Rabin and foreign ministry by Shamir and Peres. Then when Shamir formed his coalition of the Right, Arens returned to the defense ministry and David Levy served as foreign minister.[24]

Sharon went into a period of slow recovery that lasted fifteen years until October 1998. Until then he held second-rank ministries in Likud governments. This "exile" was not as severe as Dayan's status in the Labor Party from June 1974 to June 1977 or after October 1979 but more like his status under Levy Eshkol from 1964 to 1967 (or Barak's status from 2001 to 2007). Or, for Americans, it can be compared to Richard Nixon's status between November 1960 and 1968 rather than to his status after August 1974.

The recovery began when Sharon challenged Shamir for the leadership of the party in 1983 and received 42 percent of the vote to Shamir's 56.5 percent. David Levy dropped out of the race to give Sharon a clear shot and this was the start of a de facto alliance between the two. In June 1984 when Labor received 44 seats to the Likud's 41, neither was able to form a partisan ideological coalition. So Sharon conducted talks with Labor leader Shimon Peres about forming a government of national unity. After several weeks they had agreed on a ten-member inner cabinet with five seats each for both parties, a rotating premiership, and a platform. During the talks Sharon made sure that the religious parties refused to enter into talks with Labor. For his reward Shamir gave Sharon the ministry of trade and industry and a seat in the inner cabinet. During the negotiations Sharon was commuting on a regular basis to New York to participate in a libel trial.[25]

On February 14, 1983, *Time* magazine published an article claiming that Sharon had met with Phalange leaders following the assassination of Gemayel and they had agreed on the need for revenge. The author, an Israeli journalist, claimed that this information was contained in a secret Appendix B of the Kahan Commission report. Sharon promptly filed suit for libel in both New York, *Time's* headquarters, and in Tel Aviv. Attorney Milton Gould offered to defend Sharon pro bono. In January 1985 the New York jury ruled that the charge was both false and defamatory but that *Time* had not acted with actual malice, which is necessary to prove libel in America. With the verdict in New York Sharon easily won in Tel Aviv where, as in most of Western Europe, it is not necessary to prove malice in order to prove libel. Sharon's friend Uri Dan wrote a book, *Blood*

Libel about the case. Sharon used the verdict within Israel to create the feeling that he had been wronged by the Left.[26]

In 1983–84 the rehabilitation within Likud of Sharon seemed as likely as the rehabilitation of Robert McFarlane or Oliver North within the Republican Party after the Iran-Contra affair. Begin, like Reagan among movement conservatives in the United States, was regarded by Likudniks as their ideological figurehead and standard bearer. Sharon was held responsible for his retirement from depression by son Benny Begin and others. Shamir was elected his successor as he was seen as largely a Begin copy.

Sharon could take credit for expelling the PLO from Lebanon. Although Arafat and many of his followers infiltrated back into Lebanon over the course of the next year, Assad conspired with dissidents within Fatah to provoke a revolt against Arafat that led to Arafat's final expulsion from Lebanon in November 1983 in two stages: first from the Beka'a Valley and then from Tripoli in the north.[27] Arafat spent the next decade in exile until the Oslo process led to his return to mandatory Palestine in May 1994. From Tunis Arafat had no possibility of conducting a real armed struggle against Israel and was forced to finally sue for peace. Over the next two decades Sharon would remind audiences of his role in humbling Arafat while ignoring his grandiose plans of 1981–82.

Sharon in his first decade in politics had bounced from side to side across the political landscape like a bumper car in an amusement park ride. His fortunes had gone drastically up and down in a roller coaster fashion. This, surprisingly, is not atypical of former generals when they enter into politics in Israel. Rabin experienced the same phenomenon from 1974 to 1984, as did Ezer Weizman between 1969 and 1979 (and even until 1985) as did Barak from 1995 to 2007. This is because, I believe, these generals rely on their instincts in a new environment in which they have not yet developed the knowledge to act instinctively. They receive too much power too fast and make major mistakes in the full glare of the public spotlight. This is why only in dictatorships are civilians made overnight into generals.

Sharon had a somewhat smoother journey during his second decade in politics. Although he was twice forced to issue letters of apology to Peres for defamatory public statements that he made about Shimon Peres, he remained as Shamir's minister of industry and trade for six years. Sharon had claimed that Peres had conspired with Saddam Hussein to hold an international conference on Israel. On July 23, 1988, he told *Ha'Aretz* that the Intifada would never have broken out if he had been defense minister instead of Rabin.[28]

Prisoner of Zion Anatoly Scharansky (center, in sweater) standing between Prime Minister Shimon Peres (right) and Vice-Premier Yitzhak Shamir (center), shaking hands with Minister Ariel Sharon, Ben Gurion airport, February 11, 1986. Photograph by Nati Harnik.

Lilly and his two sons became Sharon's principal political advisors and together they decided whom to support and whom to oppose in the party. Sometimes Lilly and Sharon would talk all night about party politics. In March 1987 Sharon beat Levy's candidate, Ovadia Eli, for the position of chairman of the Likud Central Committee by the margin of 66 percent to 34 percent. Only a year before, Benny Begin had gone on the political talk show *Moked* and claimed that there was no Sharon camp in the Likud. But after the November 1988 election gave the Likud 40 seats, the Sharon camp was represented in the Knesset only by Sharon and two other MKs.[29]

In May 1988 Sharon's mother, Vera Scheneirman, died at the age of 88. She had seen her son rise to the top of the defense establishment—and then self-destruct. She would not witness his ultimate triumph. Sharon spoke to the press of the favorable influence that she had on his development as a child. Sharon had first his father as a role model, then his mother. After Sharon's second marriage, his source of psychological support was transferred to his wife Lilly. Once she was gone, he would be profoundly lonely.[30]

In August 1988 the Likud was transformed from a joint list similar to its Gahal predecessor to a united party. No longer would each faction within

Seven. Sharon: A General for the Likud

Housing Minister Ariel Sharon (left) and his wife, Lily, host Prime Minister Yitzhak Shamir at their ranch in the Negev, August 27, 1990. Photograph by Tsvika Israeli.

the two component parties appoint its own representatives to agreed-upon positions on a common list, but a 3,000-member Central Committee dominated by the members of the Shamir-Arens faction and the Liberals would decide upon the composition of the Likud's election list. Sharon decided to get the press to attack him in order to boost his prestige within the party. He said that he would annex parts of the West Bank to deal with the Intifada. Labor publicized this in its election campaign.[31]

In December 1988 when Secretary of State George Shultz recognized the PLO after it had fulfilled America's long-standing conditions for such recognition, Sharon denounced the Reagan administration for having done so. He also denounced Labor for not having prevented this. Sharon proposed an enhanced version of the Allon Plan, which dated back to July 1967, as an alternative to negotiating with the PLO over a Palestinian state. Later Sharon compared the 1989 Baker Plan—a modification of the Rabin-Shamir Plan—to Munich 1938. Sharon did not care that such comparisons made him look ridiculous in Washington as his constituency was in Israel and on the West Bank.[32]

At a scheduled meeting of the Likud Central Committee, which Sharon

Prime Minister Yitzhak Shamir (left) and Housing Minister Ariel Sharon during a visit to a housing construction site near Sderot in the Negev, August 27, 1990. Photograph by Tsvika Israeli.

chaired, on February 12, 1990, Sharon suddenly announced his resignation from the government. Shamir ignored this announcement and delivered the speech he had already prepared on his diplomatic efforts. When Shamir finished his speech and read out the text of a resolution of support, Sharon jumped to his feet and read out his own resolution, which ended with the question "Who is in favor of eliminating terror?" This went down in Likud history as "the battle of the microphones" or "the night of the microphones." Four months later Sharon returned as minister of housing in Shamir's new government more refreshed for having had a vacation.[33]

In 1990 Sharon used his rabbinical connections to help oppose the formation of a Labor government by Peres. Sharon had bodyguards keeping one Aguda (ultra–Orthodox) MK from attending the Knesset vote on Peres's proposed government. On April 15, the other Aguda MK, Avraham Werdiger, phoned Peres to say he could not vote for such a dovish government. Shamir appointed him minister of housing when the Likud-led coalition was sworn in. This was just in time for a major exodus of Jews from the former Soviet Union as emigration was allowed freely for the first time in decades. Sharon presided over the commencement of the construction of over 170,000 housing units and hundreds of thousands of apartments to house all the new immigrants as they arrived in the biggest aliya since Israel's first decade. In the meantime Sharon made sure that trailers were available to house the immigrants until their apartments were constructed.[34]

During the Gulf War in January-February 1991 Sharon and Yitzhak Moda'i demanded of Shamir that the IAF retaliate against Iraq for Scud attacks. Defense Minister Moshe Arens pressured Shamir from inside the cabinet to arrange for an IAF corridor across Jordan for such a retaliation. Sharon said that Israel should unilaterally notify Washington and dispatch the IAF and also commando units to hunt down the Scud launchers in western Iraq.[35]

Sharon's performance as housing minister in Shamir's government during the large Soviet Jewry immigration was severely criticized by the government comptroller in his report issued in April 1992. The report implied that Sharon let out contracts on a partisan basis during the 1991 housing crisis. Sharon got the shells of buildings completed in record time but because he neglected to arrange for infrastructure work (plumbing, electrical wiring, etc.) the houses and apartments remained unoccupied for long periods until they could be completed. "There is no justification for a government ministry using government money to flout laws and regulations," said the report.[36]

Sharon's political advisor advised him to go for the party leadership within moments of Shamir losing the 1992 election. "Whoever gets there first will take the party. Go there and show leadership," he advised Sharon. Sharon's excuse for not competing was, "For me politics is an option, not an obsession." Later the same advisor told him, "If you run against Bibi, it will be over my dead body. You've got no chance, Bibi has conquered the Likud."[37]

In March 1993 the Likud held a leadership election to elect a replacement for Shamir. With Moshe Arens having retired at the same time as Shamir, the leadership was being passed to the next generation. The three candidates were: Benjamin "Bibi" Netanyahu, a protégé of Arens who had served in the Sayeret Matkal and was the brother of slain Sayeret Matkal commander Yonatan Netanyahu and a successful hasbaran or spokesman; Benny Begin, geologist son of the former Etzel commander and Herut and Likud leader; and David Levy. Netanyahu won with 52 percent, more than twice that of his nearest rival, Levy. From the start Sharon and Netanyahu formed a rivalry and mutual antipathy reminiscent of that between Rabin and Peres. Sharon considered Netanyahu to be a lightweight with no real accomplishments and a liar to boot. Netanyahu considered Sharon to be a has-been and a loose cannon.[38]

After Rabin signed the Oslo agreement with Arafat on the White House lawn in September 1993, the Likud came out in bitter opposition to the new arrangement. Sharon met with Rabin on several occasions and warned him that Arafat could not be trusted to keep his word. Despite Sharon's outbursts during the national unity governments when Rabin was defense minister and the debacle in Lebanon, Rabin still had respect for Sharon's opinions. But Rabin pressed ahead and Netanyahu and Sharon, despite their mutual antipathy, found themselves sharing the speaker's platform at many anti–Oslo rallies in 1994 and 1995 in which settlers appeared with posters portraying Rabin in a SS uniform or dressed in a keffiya like Arafat.[39]

Sharon formed a good relationship with the newspaper *Yediot Ahranot* when it was the leading newspaper in Israel. Sharon wrote fairly regularly for Yediot and his better articles he sent to the *Jerusalem Post* where English translations of them would run. Sharon argued repeatedly in these articles and in political speeches that the second Rabin government lacked legitimacy as it was dependent on Arab votes for its majority in the Knesset. He argued that Arab MKs should not have the right to vote on territorial issues. This anticipated later arguments by the Radical Right regarding the loyalty of the Arab minority. But actually it was Rabin who had coined the term "Jewish majority."[40]

Sharon argued that only the Right could be entrusted to implement autonomy for the Palestinians. He argued that in reality autonomy had been merely a fig leaf to allow Egypt to make peace with Israel. "Autonomy in the days of Rabin and the Left is not the same thing at all as autonomy under Mr. Begin and the Likud," he wrote. Sharon advocated dividing the West Bank and Gaza into a series of non-contiguous Arab enclaves that accounted for only 30 percent of the area of the territories. Sharon's opponents on the Left dubbed these enclaves "Sharon's bantustans" after the apartheid homelands in South Africa.[41]

Rabin would take time out of his schedule to hear Sharon argue against Sharon. "He always had a soft spot for Sharon. Don't forget that they went back decades together," said Rabin aide Eitan Haber. "It was a way of re-examining his own positions, by submitting them to the rigorous criticism of someone with mirror-image views, but with experience and detailed knowledge that he really respected," said Haber. Sharon always regarded Oslo as "a historic mistake of monstrous proportions." And he always regarded Arafat as an unreformed terrorist.[42]

Sharon along with Netanyahu was guilty of incitement against Rabin through his speeches at settlers' anti–Oslo rallies. Sharon attended an anti–Oslo rally in Zion Square in Jerusalem on October 5, 1995—a month before Rabin was murdered by Yigal Amir. There were placards there depicting Rabin in an SS uniform and wearing a keffiyah—in other words demonizing him. Sharon compared Rabin and Peres to Marshal Pétain, the leader of Vichy France during World War II, in a *Penthouse* magazine interview in 1995. In an interview with a Haredi (ultra–Othodox) magazine in 1995 he referred to Rabin and Peres as collaborators. "Rabin and Peres are a couple of collaborators who in any normal country would be put on trial," claimed Sharon. "Being a *moser* (informer) and a snitch is part of the spiritual ethos of the Israeli Left," wrote Sharon in a settler magazine. This was an obvious reference to the saison, which Sharon pretended he did not take part in during 1947. Sharon later excused his conduct by arguing that the Left had incited against him over Lebanon in 1982–83 and that this was fair payback.[43]

In December 1995 Sharon announced that he would not challenge Netanyahu for the party leadership. During the election campaign he called for a government of national unity following the election—with the people he had been calling traitors and collaborators. During the campaign Sharon made an alliance with the Habad Hasidim sect of ultra–Orthodox Jews. He talked them out of staying neutral in the election by promising them more funding for their yeshivas if the Likud were elected.[44]

During the election campaign of 1996 Netanyahu promised Sharon one of the top three positions if the Likud won. Sharon did not believe that he would follow through. Sharon worked hard campaigning for the ticket and induced both Raful Eitan of Tzomet and David Levy of Gesher to run as part of the Likud. After Netanyahu narrowly nosed out Peres in May, he decided not to give Sharon a ministry at all in the new government. But David Levy announced to reporters the promises that Netanyahu had made to Sharon and not fulfilled. Levy threatened to leave the coalition with his faction ten minutes before the government was to be sworn in if Sharon were not given a ministry. A ministry of national infrastructure was custom built for Sharon by stripping functions from several other ministries. "There was no rational conversation. This is Israeli politics," explained Netanyahu of his conversation with Levy.[45]

In the summer of 1997, Netanyahu pushed out Finance Minister Dan Meridor, another leading prince, who Netanyahu probably viewed as both too dangerous and too liberal. Netanyahu then turned to Sharon and asked him if he would take the ministry and Sharon agreed. But Sharon never got the office. Netanyahu's *modus operandi* was to promise the same office to several people and then give it to the one to whom it would most benefit Netanyahu to give it to. Netanyahu called Sharon to his office. Sharon stood in the doorway and said, "A liar you were and a liar you have remained."[46]

In June 1997 Sharon invited Mahmoud Abbas (Abu Mazen), who was one of Arafat's two top political advisors, to his Sycamores Ranch for a long private conversation. The details of the meeting were not publicized only its occurrence. It was the first step in Sharon's campaign to change his image from man of war to man of peace. This was at a time when Palestinian independence was still anathema to much of the secular Right and heresy to the religious Right. Sharon later announced that he had cleared the meeting with Netanyahu, which was an implied snub towards Foreign Minister Levy. This was Sharon's biggest ideological transformation since Shlomzion in 1977. In August 1997 at Netanyahu's request, Sharon met with American Mideast envoy Dennis Ross. This was Sharon's first meeting with a senior American official in over a decade. Sharon left an impression of "moderation and pragmatism."[47]

In January 1998 Foreign Minister David Levy quit the coalition over the budget, which he claimed slighted the disenfranchised. By then Sharon and Levy were back to being bitter rivals and Sharon had no thought that he owed anything to Levy. This left Sharon as the second most important person in Netanyahu's coalition. Netanyahu kept the foreign ministry for

(From left, facing the camera) Defense Minister Mordechai, Prime Minister Netanyahu and Foreign Minister Sharon meeting Palestinian Authority Chairman Arafat, U.S. Secretary of State Albright and President Bill Clinton at Wye Plantation, October 20, 1998. Photograph by Avi Ohayon.

himself while he bided his time. In October 1998 he was scheduled to attend a summit in the United States to decide upon territorial concessions as part of a scheduled Israeli redeployment under the Oslo accords. On October 13 Netanyahu appointed Sharon as his new foreign minister on the eve of departing for the summit in exchange for Sharon's support for whatever concessions were necessary to make at the summit.[48] This was Sharon's first chance at the limelight in fifteen years.

After being appointed as foreign minister, Sharon flew to Minnesota from Israel to visit King Hussein of Jordan who was being treated for cancer at the Mayo Clinic in Rochester. Sharon had earlier accompanied Netanyahu to Amman in September 1996 when Netanyahu was forced to deal with the botched Mossad assassination attempt against Hamas leader Khaled Mashal. Afterwards, Sharon was full of praise for Netanyahu's handling of the crisis. The Mayo visit signaled Sharon's acceptance of the Hashemite monarchy and likewise Hussein's acceptance of Sharon's new role in the government. Sharon then spent the weekend in New York before traveling on to the Wye River Conference in Maryland, which was already in progress.[49]

At the Wye summit, Sharon sat directly opposite Arafat but never acknowledged his presence directly and always referred to him in the third person. Arafat was not upset by this treatment—Sharon was as much a devil for the Palestinians as Arafat was for the Israelis. During the conference several Clinton administration senior officials including Secretary of State Madeleine Albright, National Security Advisor Sandy Berger, and CIA Director George Tenet worked to draft compromises by which the Palestinians would agree to specific security arrangements in exchange for Israel giving up territory on the West Bank. A very ill and pale King Hussein flew down from the Mayo Clinic to urge everyone involved to make the necessary sacrifices for peace. Less than four months later he was dead. Prime Minister Netanyahu agreed to transfer 41 percent of the West Bank over the next three months from Area C—under total Israeli control—to Areas A and B: under total Palestinian control in Area A and under Palestinian civil control and Israeli military control in Area B. The thirteen percent being transferred directly to Area A included the city of Hebron with its Jewish enclave. The agreement was signed on October 23, 1998, after nine days of talks at Wye and a year and a half of negotiations with the Clinton administration. The Knesset ratified the Wye agreement the following month with Labor and Meretz supporting as the former had with Camp David.[50]

Sharon supported Netanyahu at Wye River, but upon returning home he urged the settlers to seize new land near their settlements. In January

During a cabinet tour of Judea and Samaria, Prime Minister Benjamin Netanyahu talks with Infrastructure Minister Ariel Sharon, December 28, 1997. Photograph by Avi Ohayon.

1999 Sharon made official visits to the United States, France, Germany and Russia. In Russia Moscow proved eager for new relations with the Jewish State and Prime Minister Yevgeny Primakov, an Arabist by training, laid out the red carpet for Sharon. Sharon used his tenure as foreign minister as preparation for becoming prime minister, something that most people thought was not possible. He made sure that he was well briefed on all foreign issues and met repeatedly with American officials.[51]

After the death of King Hussein in Jordan in February 1999, Sharon attended the funeral representing Israel. At the funeral President Ezer Weizman shook hands with terrorist leader Nayef Hawatme, for which he was soundly criticized at home. He defended himself by arguing that Arafat was also a terrorist.[52]

Netanyahu's coalition was in a state of collapse. Right-wing ministers were upset over the territorial concessions at Wye. On December 21, the Knesset voted for new elections in May 1999. Defense Minister Yitzhak Mordechai resigned from the government to join the new Center Party being formed by former Chief of State Amnon Lipkin-Shahak and Ron

Milo, a Likud prince, in January. Mordechai, a mizrakhi, soon took over as the party leader as polls showed him more popular than either Shahak or Milo. Netanyahu replaced Mordechai with Moshe Arens as defense minister.

In April 1999 Sharon made his third visit as foreign minister to Russia. He was trying to prevent Moscow from selling anti-aircraft missiles to Tehran, which could complicate an Israeli strike against Iranian nuclear facilities. While there Sharon came out against independence for Kosovo in order to appease the Russians, because the Serbs had supported the Jews during the Holocaust and because he feared that it could serve as a precedent for a future Palestinian state. Sharon also made a show of correcting his Russian interpreter and portraying himself as an expert on Russian culture in order to win the support of Russian Jews back home.[53]

Netanyahu negotiated with Syria about a return of the Golan Heights in exchange for peace. This was done through a number of different mediators with the most intensive effort coming during August and September 1998. Sharon later claimed that he stopped Netanyahu from sending a detailed withdrawal map to Assad. Netanyahu denied this and said the negotiations were conducted through the defense minister. Defense Minister Arens said that both Bibi and Sharon were in on the deal, which collapsed because Netanyahu never sat down with Assad in person before his government collapsed.[54]

The May 1999 election resulted in a majority for the Center-Left. The Labor Party, campaigning as One Israel, received 26 seats with former Chief of Staff Barak imitating Rabin with a personalized campaign. Barak formed a wide cabinet with the religious parties as well as Meretz and the Center Party. David Levy had reformed his Gesher Party and joined as part of the One Israel coalition. He was then appointed by Barak as foreign minister.

Netanyahu quit temporarily as party leader and retired—temporarily—from politics. Sharon was elected as the Likud leader on September 2, 1999, with 53 percent compared to 24 percent for Ehud Olmert and 22 percent for Meir Shitreet—by then all his serious opponents had left either the party or politics: Levy had defected to Labor; Netanyahu had retired; Benny Begin had formed his own Herut Party. Sharon got by on four hours of sleep a night during the leadership contest. The Likud had been left with only 19 seats and no one seemed to want the task of rebuilding the party except Sharon. Sharon was seen as only a temporary party leader at this time. All the polls showed Netanyahu as the only Likud politician who could defeat Barak. No one in the Likud took Sharon seriously as a future prime minister at this time. Sharon was seen as someone who would rehabilitate the party so that Netanyahu could return and assume power.[55]

But Sharon was faced with several personal tragedies. His wife Lilly was diagnosed with lung cancer. Sharon spent much of his time caring for her. Than in December 1999 a short-circuit in some wiring caused a fire that burned down his home at the ranch. Lost in the fire were many personal records, notes, and photographs. In January Lilly was hospitalized in poor condition. Lilly died on March 25, 2000, in a Tel Aviv hospital leaving Sharon alone after 37 years of marriage. Now he had only his two adult sons, Omry and Gilad, to rely on for advice about politics and government and when they disagreed he would have to decide for himself. So they made a division of tasks: Gilad advised his father on economics, strategy, and ideology and Omry on party politics. Sharon seemed almost rejuvenated after Lily's death as he channeled his grief into politics. His love of her may have been largely narcissistic.[56]

Barak's attempts to negotiate a peace treaty with Syria collapsed in Geneva in March 2000, causing him to turn to the Palestinian track. On the eve of the Camp David summit in July 2000 Barak lost his majority in parliament. In the aftermath of the failed Camp David summit Barak was vulnerable. Polls showed that Netanyahu would beat Barak in an election. In June 2000, Sharon had met with professional political advisor Arthur Finkelstein who advised him to concentrate on a single campaign theme. Sharon chose a united Jerusalem and accused Barak of wanting to divide the city. Sharon told the Knesset on July 24, 2000, that "no prime minister has the right to make concessions over Jerusalem." If this sounds like Arafat at Camp David that month, Sharon too noticed the comparison. "Arafat says, and I must say I really admire him for this ... that in the matter of Jerusalem he needs the approval of the Arab and Muslim worlds. Barak, on the other hand, doesn't understand that before he signs anything, before he agrees to anything even verbally, he must have the consent and approval of the entire Jewish people, in Israel and in the Diaspora."[57]

After getting permission to do so from Barak, Sharon decided to visit the Temple Mount to demonstrate that the Temple Mount remained under Jewish control. Barak gave Sharon permission as he feared being attacked politically by Sharon if he did not. Both Arafat and Abu Ala'a, one of his top advisors and later his prime minister, urged him to cancel permission for the visit. Arafat said that it would "destroy everything." "You know it's very dangerous, it might result in bloodshed," said Abu Ala'a to Gilead Sher, the chief Israeli negotiator with the Palestinians. Interior Minister Shlomo Ben-Ami informed Palestinian security chief Jabril Rajoub who said it would be okay as long as Sharon made no attempt to enter either of the two mosques on the Mount. He later denied saying this.[58] Rajoub may have been disingenuous as he realized that this gave Arafat a perfect rallying cause to spark a new Intifada—the Al-Aksa Intifada. As the whole area of the Noble Sanctuary (Temple Mount) is considered to be one giant mosque, having a large number of booted security guards and politicians would definitely be considered a serious violation.[59]

Sharon entered the Temple Mount at 7:55 a.m. on the morning of September 28 accompanied by five Likud MKs and dozens of elite police officers with over a thousand police on stand by in the Old City in case they were needed. The visit lasted only forty-five minutes and resulted in Sharon helping to spark off a new wave of unrest. Palestinian protesters attempted to claw their way through the police escort to get at Sharon who sweated in his bulletproof vest. Former Chief of Staff Amnon Lipkin-Shahak, who was a minister in Barak's government, claimed that Sharon made the visit to punish Barak for having made concessions on Jerusalem.[60]

Within a day seven Palestinians had been killed in riots. Arafat went on the radio to call for Palestinians to defend the Al-Aksa Mosque. With negotiations deadlocked he fancied that violence was more likely to advance his cause than more talks. And with falling living standards due to a stalled economy, the Palestinian territories were ripe for a new Intifada. By October the Intifada was in full gear. Neither Barak nor Sharon saw the outbreak of the Al-Aksa Intafada as being spontaneous.[61]

Barak resigned as prime minister by calling for new elections for prime minister on December 9, 2000. Because the double-voting system was still in effect, Barak could either have his entire government resign or just resign personally. He decided to resign personally bringing about the only election in Israel history for just the prime minister in February 2001. Likud MKs introduced a special bill to allow a non–MK—that is Netanyahu—to compete for the premiership. It seemed likely to pass. But then Netanyahu announced that unless Barak would call a full election—for the Knesset as well—he would stay in retirement and not run. The Knesset passed the Netanyahu law on December 18, 2000, but Barak refused to call for a general election. The way was clear for Sharon.[62]

Based on a scale devised by Arthur Finkelstein, Sharon's campaign manager Reuven Adler measured Sharon's rating on the Arab question as 4.7 where 5 was the extreme Right and Meretz was 1. Adler's pollster determined that the general Israeli public was between 2.6 and 3.2 on the scale. Adler determined that Sharon needed to be perceived as about 2.7 in order to win. So he came up with the slogan "Only Sharon Will Bring Peace."

By early January 2001 Sharon led by twenty points in the polls. Late in the campaign the Sharon team switched the slogan to "I have confidence in Sharon's peace." This depended on the deliberate double meaning of the word *bitakhon,* which means both confidence and security in Hebrew.

In January 2001 Barak went into final negotiations with the Palestinians at Taiba in Sinai, but the move smacked of desperation. Even though he broke off the negotiations a week before the election it did not help him. Sharon concentrated on mobilizing three groups of voters for the election: settlers, the ultra–Orthodox, and Russian immigrants. With only Sharon and Barak in the race the Likud did not have to worry about these groups voting for other parties like Shas and the National Religious Party. Sharon was also portrayed in his campaign as a grandfather and farmer rather than as a controversial former general and career politician. It was very similar to Weizman's makeover of Begin in 1977. Sharon declined all interview requests during the campaign. On February 6, 2001, Sharon beat Barak by a margin of 62 percent to 38 percent or 24 percentage points—even more than Barak had beaten Netanyahu by in 1999.[63]

Eight

Netanyahu: King of the Princes

Prime Minister Benjamin Netanyahu's family has a long history as Zionist activists. His grandfather, Nathan Mileikowsky, was an Orthodox rabbi from Lithuania who became a Zionist with Herzl and then broke with him over the Uganda offer in 1903. Mileikowsky became a follower of Jabotinsky in 1905. In 1908 he moved to Warsaw and became principal of the city's Hebrew high school and was also a Zionist lecturer throughout Poland, Benjamin's father Benzion was born in 1910. In 1920 Nathan Mileikowsky moved his family to Palestine. Benjamin's maternal grandfather, Abraham Marcus, immigrated to Palestine in 1896. Mileikowsky settled in Jerusalem and changed his name to Netanyahu—God gave him or God's gift. Nathan died of typhoid and heart disease at age 55.

Benzion joined the Revisionist Zionists in 1928 at age 18 and remained with them for his entire life. He founded and became the first editor of the Revisionist newspaper, *Hayarden* (The Jordan), while still a student at Hebrew University. He was close to Abba Ahimeir while a student, but after Jabotinsky denounced Ahimeir he sided with Jabotinsky. In 1940 he followed Jabotinsky to America to serve his as his personal secretary. After Jabotinsky's death he became the head of the New Zionist Organization in America and remained for eight years before returning to Israel.

In America Netanyahu edited and published a monthly newsletter known as *Zionews*. In the February 1944 issue Netanyahu wrote, "The partition of the land itself is an utter impossibility." In a 1943 essay Benzion called the Arabs a "semi-barbaric people, which lacks any democratic tradition and is fired by religious fanaticism and hatred for the stranger. The tendency towards conflict is the essence of the Arab. He is an enemy by essence. His personality won't allow him any compromise or agreement....

His existence is one of perpetual war." Benzion looked to Ottoman rule as a model for treating the Arabs. Thus, he became an advocate of "transfer" or Arab removal from Palestine/Israel. His essential views changed little throughout his adult life.[1]

In 1945 Benzion married Cela Segal, a law student from a distinguished Petah Tikva farming family. Benzion's oldest son, Yonatan (Jonathan) was born in 1945 and named for Colonel John Patterson, Jabotinsky's long associate and former commander. In November 1948 the family returned to the Talpiot neighborhood of Jerusalem. Begin snubbed Benzion Netanyahu as a shirker from the struggle against the British and refused to offer him a position in Herut. Benjamin, nicknamed Bibi as a child, was born in October 1949. He was raised to perceive Begin as the enemy for having snubbed his father at a time when Begin was considered to be the Right in Israel, especially by those from a labor Zionist or General Zionist background. Benzion became the assistant editor of *Encyclopedia Hebraica* until 1962. In 1962 he moved his family to Ithaca, New York to take up a position as a researcher into Spanish Jewry during the Inquisition at Cornell University.[2]

The Netanyahu family remained in the United States for sixteen years. Bibi as a teenager worked to finance annual trips back to Israel for the summer so that he could hang out with his childhood friends there. For nine months out of the year he was a transplanted Israeli and did not date American girls. At age 16 he fell in love with Micki Weissman, who eventually became his first wife. Bibi's only friends in high school in Philadelphia, where his father had relocated to teach at a university there, were members of the haShomer haTzair youth group. But Bibi spoke the fluent accentless American English that he speaks today. His older brother Yoni returned to Israel in 1964 to enlist in the IDF as a paratrooper. Bibi graduated from high school in 1967 but skipped his graduation to catch an early flight so that he could see his brother before war broke out in 1967. Yoni was badly wounded in the elbow during the war but recovered full use of his arm, fortunately for his future military career.[3]

In August 1967 Bibi went into the IDF. He intended to follow his brother into the paratroopers, but was intercepted by a recruiter for Sayeret Matkal (Headquarter's Reconnaissance—the elite scout and anti-terrorist unit of the IDF). In those days the Unit, as it was universally known, consisted mainly of kibbutzniks. This was okay as most of Bibi's Israeli friends as a youth were from a Mapai background. He completed his basic training in November 1967. He first saw action in March 1968 at the Battle of Karameh. Yoni then quit Harvard University, where he was studying following his initial mandatory IDF service to return to Israel to become a platoon commander in Sayeret Matkal. Bibi took part in the raid on Beirut Airport led by Rafael Eitan in December 1968 and helped to blow up one airliner. The following May he almost drowned in the Suez Canal during a commando raid as part of the War of Attrition. His boat was hit by machine-gun fire and he had no time to get rid of the machine-gun ammunition that he was carrying around his neck before he went into the water. He was saved by a naval commando who held his head above water until they reached the shore. Decades later this would make that individual subject to ribbing among his former comrades.[4]

Bibi initially had problems with navigation but by working with his team leader, Amiram Levine, he mastered the technique of night navigation. In mid–1969 after having graduated with honors from an officer's course he returned to the unit as a team leader. Bibi divided his free time hanging out with his brother Yoni, with his girlfriend Micki, and reading history and politics. After Netanyahu was elected prime minister in 1996 his future opponent and former commander Ehud Barak praised him as a conscientious young officer who could always be counted on to complete the mission. "The Unit contributed a great deal to my life, the thoroughness and care taken in preparing missions. I learned to understand the need to make changes and improvise…. My experience was unique. I learned not to run away from hardships, that one must overcome them," said Netanyahu years later of his military experience.[5]

During the Sabena airliner rescue of May 1972 Bibi rushed to Lod Airport upon hearing word of the hijacking on the radio. Barak agreed to allow him to participate as an ordinary soldier in the rescue on Barak's team. Bibi was wounded in the arm when a fellow rescuer pistol-whipped a female hijacker and the gun went off wounding Netanyahu. Bibi left the IDF on June 19, 1972, after nearly five years of service with the rank of captain. He had extended his service by two years in order to become an officer. In the summer of 1972 Bibi's younger brother Iddo joined the Unit, making the Netanyahus only the second family to have three brothers serve in Sayeret Matkal. The first family to do this feat was the Brog/Barak family.[6]

Bibi left to Boston with Micki Weissman to study architecture. In only 2.5 years he did a BA in architecture and then did an MA in architecture and business administration at the Massachusetts Institute of Technology. At the same time Micki did a BA in organic chemistry at Brandeis University. The two shared an apartment together and then got married. After they married they changed their name to Nitai, a pen name that Benzion Netanyahu had used decades before. Yoni liked the name and so also legally changed his name to Nitai and in fact this was the name on his military identification card when he was killed at Entebbe in 1976. The family had to petition the IDF to have him buried as Netanyahu. Bibi took it for granted that Yoni would someday make chief of staff so he decided to make his reputation in business. Several of his uncles were industrialists so that this appeared to be a logical decision.[7]

In 1973 Bibi became a Zionist activist at MIT. He became good friends with Uzi Landau, the future government minister and son of Herut minister Haim Landau, and with Colette Avital, Israel's consul in Boston. Bibi rushed back to Israel at the start of the Yom Kippur War in October 1973. He flew back on the same flight with Ehud Barak. He spent most of the war guarding tanks in the Sinai and then along the Northern Front. Bibi's first television appearance was in a debate with Professor Edward Said, the Palestinian activist, on American television in late 1973. Bibi loved the cameras and the cameras loved him. Avital had arranged the appearance for him. In June 1976 Bibi went to work for the Boston Consulting Group with a $60,000 annual salary. There he met future Republican presidential nominee Mitt Romney, although the two were never close friends.[8]

The death of his older brother Yoni at Entebbe on July 4, 1976, profoundly affected Bibi's life. It had a deep psychological effect on him and probably led to the breakup of his first marriage. Bibi started an affair with Fleur Cates, who eventually became his second wife. When Micki found out she divorced him. Bibi managed to have a good relationship with his daughter Noa from his first marriage. But when he started seriously dating his third wife, Sara, she created a rift in the relationship with Noa. The second major effect was that Bibi later spun his own service with Sayaret Matkal and his brother's death to become an anti-terrorism expert by founding the Jonathan Institute for the Study of International Terrorism.[9] This would help to give him the inside edge to win the leadership of the Likud from the other competing princes.

At the end of 1978 Bibi returned to Israel and interviewed with Rim, a furniture retailer in Israel. By the early 1980s Bibi controlled a network of dozens of shops and marketing outlets all over Israel and he spent most of his time on the road. Fleur Cates and Bibi married in New York. She was born in Germany to a Christian family but raised in England. She underwent a Conservative conversion to Judaism, and later in Israel underwent an Orthodox conversion. She lived in Boston and he lived in Israel and every third week he would fly to Boston to spend a week with her. While in America he would call home to the office every day to help run his business long distance.

During this time, Bibi's father Benzion was a fierce critic of the Camp David accords and Israeli-Egyptian peace treaty from the Right. He was much closer to the splinter Tehiya Party of Geula Cohen than to the mainstream Likud Party. This resulted in Begin dismissing him as a "right-wing extremist." In 2009 he told the Israeli newspaper *Ma'ariv*, "We should conquer any disputed territory in the Land of Israel. You don't return land."[10]

Why is this important? Many politicians, after all, have different politics than their parents or evolve politically. But Bibi had been raised to revere his father and was quite close to him as an adult. "He worries that his father will think that he is weak," said one family friend to the *Atlantic*. "His father has a huge influence on him," said a former advisor. "Always in the back of his mind is Benzion." As a result his father ran interference for him with the Right by arguing that his 2009 Bar Ilan speech in favor of a Palestinian state was just something that he said to please the Americans. "He doesn't support a [Palestinian state]. He supports the sort of conditions that they will never accept."[11]

At the start of 1982 the post of political attaché became vacant at the Israeli Embassy in Washington. Ambassador Moshe Arens's first choice turned down the job and Bibi accepted immediately when offered the job. Bibi's father and Moshe Arens had worked together closely in the U.S. in the late 1940s and Benzion had been a witness at Arens's wedding in 1948. Bibi had met Arens at a political function once and Arens thought of him when the position became vacant. Bibi returned to Israel in June 1982 at the start of the Lebanon War, But he soon left after he was not given anything to do—he had missed too much reserve duty to stay active with Sayeret Matkal. He spent most of the war in Washington defending Israel in the American media.[12]

Fleur moved to Washington to live with Bibi and to become part of his diplomatic career. Every weekend the two would rent three television cameras and a spotlight and then turn their living room into a television studio. Bibi practiced giving interviews and soon was giving interviews on American television using sports metaphors and also in the corridors of Congress. Bibi became personal friends with *Nightline* host Ted Koppel, with *New York Times* columnist William Safire, and with George Will, former Washington editor of *National Review* and a columnist for *Newsweek*. Bibi became a regular guest on *Nightline* and befriended George Nader, a Syrian-American who was close to the ruling Ba'ath Party in Damascus.[13]

Bibi criticized the Israeli Foreign Ministry for not setting up a quick reaction public relations office in Jerusalem. He blamed Foreign Minister Shamir for this oversight. After Sharon's resignation as defense minister in February 1983 Arens was appointed as defense minister. Arens recommended that Bibi be appointed as the Israeli ambassador in Washington. Neither Begin nor Shamir was enthusiastic about this suggestion, so for six months he served as acting ambassador. In this capacity Bibi arranged a three-day conference at the Jonathan Institute in 1984 with prestigious political lecturers from England, Israel, and the U.S. In 1985 the proceedings were published in Hebrew in Israel and in 1986 in English in the United States as *Terror: How the West Can Win.* The book contained chapters on the Soviet, Arab, and Muslim contributions to international terror and how the West could counter the use of terrorism for political gain. The chapters were well written but everything was from a conservative point of view. There was no analysis of how to use political fixes to solve conflicts that served as catalysts for terrorism. In fact in the sequel, published a decade later and written entirely by Netanyahu, Bibi was scathing about attempting to do so. After the publication of the book, Bibi was given personal protection by Shabak, the General Security Service, and later by American bodyguards out of fear that Arab terrorists would try to murder him for the sin of drawing attention to state sponsorship of terrorism.[14]

Shamir disliked Netanyahu and refused to promote him. This dislike might have stemmed from Bibi's complaint about the lack of p.r. in 1982, or from Bibi's love of the media, or from old internal politics within the Revisionist movement in the 1940s. Shamir appointed Meir Rosen, the legal advisor to the Foreign Ministry and a former Begin advisor, to become Israeli ambassador to Washington. Bibi regularly undercut his superior by stealing media opportunities through his numerous personal contacts. The first act of Israel's National Unity Government in 1984 was to appoint Netanyahu as ambassador to the United Nations. Elyakim Rubnstein was upset at being passed over for the job, but he did not let it affect his legal ruling when years later when serving as justice minister he decided not to prosecute Bibi for involvement in a shady affair. As UN ambassador Bibi became a regular guest on *Larry King Live*.[15]

While in New York Bibi developed a taste for expensive Cuban cigars and Italian and Indian food. In his tastes he had much more in common with Jabotinsky than with Begin or Shamir. His cigar habit cost the Israeli taxpayers $40,000 a year. Whenever invited out for drinks or coffee, Bibi always expected the other party to pay. Bibi began to get out of shape from when he was a commando running or walking tens of miles a day, and by age 49 he had heavy jowls and a thick waist. *Ha'Aretz* reporter Akiva Eldar did the first serious media profile of Netanyahu in 1984 when he was appointed ambassador to the UN. It was very critical. Eli Tabor wrote a much more favorable piece a year later in *Yediot Ahranot*.[16]

Bibi tried to scuttle the massive prisoner exchange that Shimon Peres arranged with Ahmed Jibril's Popular Front for the Liberation of Palestine-General Command in May 1985 that traded over a thousand Arab prisoners from Israeli prisons for three Israelis being held in Lebanon. Decades later Netanyahu would make a similar swap to release a single Israeli soldier, Gilad Shalit, being held captive in Gaza by Hamas. Bibi just ignored orders that he did not agree with like referring to the West Bank by that name rather than as Judea and Samaria or to continually referring to Arafat as a blood-drenched terrorist. It was at this time that both Sharon and Levy began to see Netanyahu as a potential future rival. Rafael Eitan offered him the number two position in his Tzomet party but Bibi was not interested. He wanted to be prime minister some day and for that he needed a large party like the Likud. Netanyahu's ideas were conventional Likud ideas but he delivered them in a much more confident manner than did most Israeli politicians who lacked his native fluency in English. Bibi's former New York aide Eyal Arad returned to Israel in 1988 and began preparing Netanyahu's camp within the Likud. The two of them had formulated a plan for taking control of the Likud while Arad was still in New York.[17]

Bibi decided to compete for the fifth place of the Likud Knesset list in 1988. He was seen as a pushy outsider by veteran party activists for competing for such a high ranking when he was so new to politics. But Benny Begin was unorganized and took his crown prince status for granted. Bibi used Yaffa Motil, a veteran activist as his connection to the party's activists. He ran his campaign on a budget of $40,000. For the general 1988 election Bibi imported Republican Party pollster Frank Lunz from America. Three days before the election, on October 30, 1988, Palestinian terrorists attacked an Israeli bus near Jericho and burned a mother and her three children to death. The attack contributed to a slight Likud majority in the election.[18]

Netanyahu belonged to a group that the media dubbed the "Likud Princes"—these were the second generation of Likud members who were the children of prominent figures in the Herut Party, the dissident undergrounds and the Revisionist Party who entered the Knesset in the 1980s and 1990s. They included: Benny Begin, geologist son of Etzel commander Menahem; Netanyahu, son of Jabotinsky aide Benzion; Dan Meridor, the son of an Etzel veteran and Herut MK (but not Ya'akov Meridor) and M. Begin's long-term aide; Ron Milo, who was the brother-in-law of Hassia Begin, Benny Begin's sister; Ehud Olmert, son of Etzel parents and a longtime MK from the Free Center and Herut parties; Uzi Landau, son of Etzel High Command member Haim Landau; Tzahi Hanegbi, son of Lehi member, Herut and Tehiya MK Geula Cohen; and Tzipi Livni, daughter of Etzel Jerusalem commander Eitan Livni. Three of these princes were appointed ministers in the National Unity Government following the 1988 election. Shamir appointed Netanyahu deputy foreign minister under David Levy.[19]

In March 1989 Fleur returned to America to work for cosmetics king

Ron Lauder, who still remains close to Netanyahu and later did a mediation mission for him with Syria. They got a friendly divorce as she simply did not want to be a politician's wife. After Fleur returned to the States, he started dating an El Al stewardess, Sara, who became his third wife after she became pregnant. She is still married to him and this has been his longest marriage. Netanyahu was also dating another woman at the same time.[20]

Bibi campaigned to end the fledgling dialogue between Washington and the PLO in 1989. Bibi succeeded but Secretary of State James Baker retaliated by breaking off all relations with Netanyahu. "I have no interest in him, and I don't ever want to see him or hear him again," said Baker. Bibi told others privately that the George H.W. Bush administration had conspired with Peres to bring down the National Unity Government.[21]

Bibi's honeymoon as deputy foreign minister under Levy fell apart after a few weeks and Levy ostracized him. Levy, who spoke French instead of English, felt inferior to Netanyahu and was afraid of being shown up by him on American television. Bibi became Israel's leading spokesman during the Gulf War in 1991 with Shamir's consent. Levy forbade his For-

Likud MK Benjamin Netanyahu addressing the Knesset during the debate on the Israel PLO agreement, September 21, 1993. Photograph by Avi Ohayon.

eign Ministry from helping Shamir prepare for the Madrid Conference in October 1991, but Bibi ignored this and was brought along by Shamir to serve as the delegation spokesman. This should have been a warning to the other princes, but they continued to underestimate him and did not take him seriously before the 1992 election.[22]

Bibi voted against his party and with Labor in voting for the new direct elections for prime minister law in the spring of 1992. Bibi was convinced that with his mastery of the media that introducing a law that would produce American-style presidential elections in Israel had to help him. Likud dropped to only 31 seats in 1992 but this did not bother Netanyahu as he was near the top of the list. No one was prepared for Moshe Arens's surprise resignation announcement. This opened up the way for Netanyahu to contest the party leadership. On June 29, 1992, Bibi announced his candidacy for the leadership. David Levy failed to take the announcement seriously.[23]

In 1996 Ha'Aretz columnist Yoel Marcus wrote that Bibi was as clever and skillful a politician as was Moshe Dayan, but with a much greater drive and work ethic than Dayan. He also wrote that he was not pompous like Levy nor outspoken like Sharon. Avigdor Lieberman, who would later become Netanyahu's chief rival for leader of the Israeli Right, took over as Bibi's new office manager and political advisor after Sara forced Eyal Arad out. She suspected Arad of facilitating Bibi's relationships with other women.

During the campaign Netanyahu admitted to an adulterous affair with another woman on Israeli television after someone tried to blackmail him. Bibi publicly accused the Levy campaign of trying to blackmail him. The fallout from this admission was a signed agreement between him and Sara in which he agreed to take her on all of his trips, include her in all his social activities, etc.[24] She simply did not trust her husband.

In the party leadership contest on March 24, 1993, Netanyahu received 52 percent of the vote, Levy 26 percent, Benny Begin 16 percent, and Moshe Katsav 6.5 percent. Thus Bibi received more votes than all of his opponents combined. Sharon stayed out of the contest after it became clear to his pollster that Netanyahu would win by a landslide.[25]

For three years Bibi had a weekly lunch with Yitzhak Shamir in which he asked Shamir for advice and showered him with respect. This immediately ended as soon as Netanyahu was elected prime minister in 1996. Bibi had inherited a party that was financially broke and millions in debt. Bibi appointed Lieberman as party general manager in order to manage the party's finances. Netanyahu went on an overseas tour and raised $1.5 million from Jews and Israelis living overseas. Many of Bibi's plane tickets and hotel bills were paid for by wealthy supporters from Australia, Europe and the United States.[26]

In 1993 Netanyahu wrote and had published *A Place Among the Nations*, a combination Zionist history and polemical apology of the type that Abba Eban used to write but from a Revisionist or neo–Revisionist viewpoint. Israeli-American academic Ilan Peleg dubbed it "Revisionism for the 1990s." In the book Netanyahu used more rational and historical arguments to make the same type of arguments that Jabotinsky and Begin used. By writing the book, On September 5, 1993, the *New York Times* published an op-ed piece by Netanyahu entitled "Peace in Our Time?" which was essentially a summary of the book. Netanyahu could go on a book tour on the American media to flog the book and at the same time keep his name and image in the media in Israel by defending Israel abroad. It was reissued in a slightly updated version in 2000 under the title *A Durable Peace,* with some maps reflecting the Oslo accords. In the book Netanyahu makes the case that Israel needs to control the central mountain range that runs through Samaria for its own defense. He also makes the case for Palestinian autonomy as the solution to the conflict.[27]

Imagine the bookshelf of a middle-class Likud activist in Israel or a Likud supporter in the United States who can read English easily. It would contain Menahem Begin's *The Revolt* and possibly *White Nights* as well, a quality biography of Begin by Avi Shilon or Amos Perlmutter, Yitzhak Shamir's memoir *Summing Up,* and possibly Haim Misgav's *Conversations with Yitzhak Shamir* as well, one of the biographies of Ariel Sharon, Hillel Halkin's new biography of Jabotinsky and Netanyahu's book. One could do without the Jabotinsky biography and the Sharon biography, and maybe even the Shamir memoir or conversations, but the Begin books and Netanyahu book would be indispensable for understanding the party.[28]

In 1992 Netanyahu invited Benny Begin, Dan Meridor, Ron Milo, and Moshe Katsav to a working meeting to plan a strategy for the centrist camp in the Likud. Only Milo showed up. The other princes regarded Bibi as an outsider and a pretender to the throne. At the Likud Party conference Bibi defeated a motion not to recognize agreements signed by the Rabin government. Netanyahu, Meridor and Milo all committed themselves to honoring all of Israel's agreements.[29]

Bibi was campaigning for the Likud leadership when the Oslo accords were announced by the Rabin government in September 1993. Bibi panicked. The first anti–Oslo demonstration was held by settlers on October 5, 1994. About 35,000 people attended the rally. As party leader Netanyahu would be in the forefront of anti–Oslo protest efforts right up until Yitzhak Rabin's assassination thirteen months later. Bibi started to move

Eight. Netanyahu: King of the Princes

Likud leader Benjamin Netanyahu eulogizing slain Prime Minister Yitzhak Rabin during a special Knesset memorial session at the end of the 7-day mourning period for Rabin, November 13, 1995. Photograph by Tsvika Israeli.

to the right after the rally demonstrated to him that he could only rely on the settlers to actively oppose Oslo. His name became actively linked to elements from the extreme Right such as Elyakim Ha'etzni and the Kahanists.

In late December 1994, Netanyahu led Rabin by two percent in the opinion polls. In late February 1995 when Netanyahu heckled Rabin while the latter was speaking in the Knesset, Rabin said to him, "You just shut up. When Menahem Begin made the decision to withdraw from the Sinai, you weren't even here. You have never in your life filled any kind of position involving responsibility for security." After this Netanyahu stopped relating to Rabin as a symbol of Israeli security, and treated him merely as another rival politician. In July 1995, Bibi headed a "funeral" procession with a coffin for Rabin at an anti–Oslo rally at Kfar Saba. After the rally Shabak head Carmi Gilon met with Bibi to go over warnings of an assassination plot to kill Rabin. He asked him to tone down the rhetoric. Bibi did not heed the warnings and kept up the rhetoric. Sharon denounced the warning as a "Stalin-like conspiracy on the part of government."[30]

"Only when we are planning something really extreme do we go to him and put him in the picture," explained Netanyahu aide Uri Aloni. The anti–Rabin campaign reached its peak in October 1995. There was another rally with a Rabin coffin at Ra'anana. "We are burying Prime Minister Rabin," shouted the protesters. At a huge rally at Jerusalem's Zion Square a month before the assassination protesters carried Photoshop pictures of Rabin in an SS uniform and Rabin in a keffiyah. "Rabin is a murderer" and "Rabin is a traitor" were repeatedly yelled.

Bibi issued a statement on the morning of the November 4, 1995, Peace Now rally requesting that his supporters let the Peace Camp demonstrate in peace. American Ambassador Martin Indyk informed Netnyahu of Rabin's assassination. Bibi issued an immediate statement to the press condemning the murder in his own name and the name of the Likud Party.[31]

Bibi was concerned that his political career would be over if Peres called for early elections immediately following the murder. Every Friday evening Bibi got together with his political advisors to eat, drink, go over the data and strategize about the future. After the Rabin murder some of his advisors thought that Peres would want to call elections later so that he could win in his own right and that if this happened then the Likud stood a good chance of winning.

In December Peres led Netanyahu by 20 points in the polls. Bibi recruited Sharon to campaign for him and Sharon put his heart into it. Then one day on the trip from Jerusalem to Tel Aviv he recruited Dan Meridor to campaign for him. Arthur Finkelstein, the American Republican pollster who had advised Senator Alfonse D'Amato in New York, began analyzing polling data that Netanyahu sent him in America. "You're in the picture. You can win the election," Finkelstein advised him. Bibi figured that if he could make fewer mistakes than Peres he could win. "Peres will make his share of mistakes," he told his advisors. "We'll just have to be there when he does."[32]

In the March 29, 1996, Likud primaries Sharon came in second behind newly-retired Yitzhak Mordekhai to earn the fifth spot on the Likud list behind Netayahu, David Levy, Rafael Eitan, and Yitzhak Mordekhai. He had beaten Benny Begin in the biggest comeback in Israeli politics since Rabin's return to the premiership.[33]

Bibi decided to recruit personalities to his campaign in order to raise the morale of his team and campaign. He recruited former General Yossi Peled, former Mossad head Gideon Ezra, and former Northern Commander General Yitzhak Mordekhai, who retired from the IDF in 1994. Mordekhai wanted to join Labor but Peres refused to give him a government ministry so he joined the Likud instead. Bibi promised him the defense ministry and appointed him as his campaign manager rather than Sharon.

Ya'akov Levy, the Gallup CEO in Israel, designed for Bibi a strategy that he called 60/60. Sixty percent of the electorate wanted to keep the Golan and 60 percent wanted peace. So if Bibi could satisfy both groups he could win the election. So Bibi's 1996 election campaign was built around the twin themes of peace and security, much like Rabin's 1992 campaign. This combined theme proved to be very effective in attracting floating voters. Bibi also tried to find disenchanted former Labor voters, but this effort largely failed.[34]

Bibi also campaigned for the religious vote by visiting synagogues, the gravesites of the righteous, and meeting with prominent ultra-Orthodox rabbis. Rabbi Ovadia Yosef, the spiritual leader of the Shas Party, instructed his followers to vote for Shas for the Knesset and for Netanyahu for prime minister. A few days before the elections a new bumper sticker appeared: "Bibi is good for the Jews."

Bibi missed his former patron Moshe Arens's seventieth birthday party in order to fly to New York and meet with Arthur Finkelstein in private. Because the meeting was a secret, Bibi could not explain his absence to Arens and lost him as a friend. Finkelstein charged Netanyahu $1,000 an hour plus expenses, but Ron Lauder had agreed to pick up the tab for Finkelstein. When Finkelstein arrived in Israel he assumed complete control of Bibi's campaign. Finkelstein designed a campaign based around three themes:

- Peres will divide Jerusalem;
- Peres will withdraw from the Golan; and
- Bibi means a secure peace.

The campaign ads depicted Peres as Arafat's partner, a man willing to trust the terrorists with Israel's security. Finkekstein's ads depicted Bibi as a born leader. He advised Bibi to simply attack Peres at every opportunity during the debate no matter what the question was.[35]

Halfway through the campaign Finkelstein was forced to leave Israel due to prior commitments, but he stayed in phone and fax contact with the Netanyahu campaign and appointed his personal assistant as go-between with the campaign. Finkelstein limited ads to 30 seconds and constantly repeated them to drive them into the minds of voters. This approach saved the Netanyahu campaign both time and money so that the workers ended up working shorter hours than those in the Peres campaign. Limor Livnat made a few ads with disappointed Labor voters that aired. Sara Netanyahu insisted on making her own ad. So they humored her by shooting her several times, but they always said that the ad was never quite ready until after the election. She was convinced that her husband was having an affair with Limor Livnat because the Israeli satirical show *Eretz Nehederet* ("Wonderful Country," the Israeli version of the British *Spitting Image*) hinted at it for satirical purposes and this fed into her paranoia. Bibi had to get Finkelstein to convince her that it was not true.[36]

Sharon held a summit with Habad rabbis thirteen days before the election. As a result the movement came out for Bibi in a major way during the final two weeks of the election campaign by putting up banners, standing on street corners, and handing out Netanyahu stickers in ultra–Orthodox neighborhoods.

The 1996 election was the first held under the new double-vote system. As a result of the "reform," Shas went from six to ten seats, the National Religious Party went from five to ten, and Israel B'Aliya, the veteran Russian party, won seven seats. Bibi received 50.6 percent of the prime ministerial vote to 49.4 percent for Peres. Early on the vote tended to favor Peres, so many people went to bed thinking that Peres had won only to wake up and see that Bibi had won. What really cost Peres the election was his decision in April to shell southern Lebanon in Operation Grapes of Wrath in response to Hezbollah provocations in order to prove how tough he was. An artillery shell went astray and killed over a hundred people sheltering near the village of Kfar Kana. As a result many Israeli Arabs boycotted the elections and stayed home giving Netanyahu the margin of victory. Or it may have been Arafat's decision to return to terrorism in February 1996 accompanied by a number of Hamas revenge bombings for the Israeli assassination of Hamas bomber Yahya "the engineer" Ayyash, ordered by Peres.[37]

Bibi's first task after being elected was forming a coalition and filling his cabinet. Netanyahu formed a coalition with Shas, the National Religious Party, United Torah Judaism, Israel B'Aliya, and The Third Way, a new party of former Labor Party supporters who wanted to retain the Golan Heights. The Likud won only 32 seats—two seats less than Labor and a record low for a ruling party to that point in history. Bibi's promises of jobs made before the election soon turned out to be worthless. Avigdor Lieberman was determined to keep Meridor out of the government as a potential threat to Netanyahu. He also saw Benny Begin as a potential threat to Bibi and advised him to cut short both of their political careers. Sara hated Limor Livnat and was determined to keep her out of the cabinet. She threw a tantrum when she learned that Bibi had appointed her to the government. Levy received the foreign ministry back again, which he had held under Shamir, but he left in 1998 after a budget disagreement with Netanyahu.[38]

Bibi's first major problem after forming his coalition and cabinet was deciding what to do about the Oslo process. He was torn between his

Eight. Netanyahu: King of the Princes

commitment to the ideology of Jabotinsky and his promise to honor all of Israel's international commitments. He had built his political career on the demonization of Yasir Arafat from 1982 to 1996—now he had to decide if he would be Arafat's partner for peace. If he did, he risked becoming the subject of ads by a future Likud rival like Sharon or someone from another party on the Right like he had produced against Peres. As a result Bibi did everything he could to delay implementing the Oslo accords once he was in office.[39]

Irving Moskovitz, an American Jew from Miami, pressured Netanyahu's government to open up a tunnel that ran parallel to the Western Wall and was discovered by archaeologists to tourists. For nine years the Muslim Waqf had denied permission for opening the tunnel because it involved knocking down a wall in the Christian Quarter, which might serve as a future precedent for Israeli actions in the Muslim Quarter. The government decided to compromise by only opening up one end and leaving the end near the Temple Mount closed. Netanyahu did not consult the heads of the security establishment before making the decision because he and his advisors did not trust them because they mostly came from Labor backgrounds. Arafat organized riots to protest the decision and the net damage was more than a hundred Palestinians killed and hundreds more wounded and 26 Israeli soldiers killed in the fighting. The Palestinian Police, many of whom were former Fedayeen, sided with the rioters and opened fire on the Israeli soldiers trying to squelch the protest. The incident seriously damaged the relationship between Arafat and Netanyahu, never good to begin with, and Arafat was no longer prepared to work with him.[40]

In the spring of 1997 Shimon Peres proposed a National Unity Government with the Likud to Bibi. Negotiations on the NUG were quite advanced in March and April with Netanyahu agreeing to make Peres the minister for peace and Barak defense minister. Peres and Netanyahu even agreed on a joint platform for the government. But then the Israeli Police recommended indicting Netanyahu, Arie Deri, the political leader of Shas, and Lieberman for abuse of confidence (corruption). Once this occurred Labor pulled out of the deal. Attorney General Elyakim Rubinstein decided not to indict Netanyahu due to lack of evidence.[41]

On September 25, 1997, an attempted Mossad assassination of Hamas political leader Khaled Meshal in Amman failed badly after a Mossad member injected a poison into Meshal's neck but got into a scuffle with Meshal's bodyguard. The Mossad agents sought refuge in the Israeli Embassy in Amman. A crisis between the Israeli and Jordanian governments ensued, which neither Israel nor Netanyahu could afford. Netanyahu was forced to provide the antidote to the poison and make a number of concessions to King Hussein that had the net effect of further empowering Hamas. Bibi maneuvered to place the blame on Mossad head Danny Yatom, a Rabin appointee, who was forced to resign. A former deputy head, Efraim Halevy, was brought out of retirement to head the Mossad. The incident badly damaged Netanyahu's reputation with both the Clinton administration and with King Hussein. Bibi admitted to Ross that it had not occurred to him that anything could go wrong when he approved the plan.[42]

At the Likud conference in November 1997 Netanyahu attempted to eliminate the primary system and revert to the Likud Central Committee choosing the Knesset list. He secretly supported Lieberman's attempt to abolish the primaries while attempting to appear to be above the issue. By the end of 1997 Bibi was polling at 30 percent approval rating compared to 40 percent for Ehud Barak who had just been named the new head of the Labor Party. On the second anniversary of Rabin's murder half a million Israelis marked the occasion in a rally in Rabin Square.[43]

Netanyahu negotiated two agreements with the Palestinian Authority during his first term as prime minister. The first was an agreement over Hebron signed in the spring of 1997. Because of the poor relations between Netanyahu and Arafat, American Middle East envoy Dennis Ross was upgraded from being merely a facilitator as he had been when Labor was in power to being a full mediator similar to the role that Henry Kissinger and Jimmy Carter played in the 1970s. Here is what Ross wrote about the difficulties of working with Netanyahu.

> Bibi would often protest that Arafat should be made to understand the constraints upon an elected prime minister. I agreed, and worked hard to convince Arafat, Asad, and other Arab leaders of the new to reach out and condition the Israeli public. But Bibi's cabinet did not reflect the cabinet per se; it was much more the captive of the far right and thus less representative of the country as a whole. It surely could not be ignored, but if Arafat saw Bibi yielding to pressure from within the cabinet, he would see the value of pressuring him as well.[44]

In the fall of 1996 between the tunnel riots and the American election in November 1996, Ross conducted a marathon 23-day negotiating session but got nowhere because neither the Israelis nor the Palestinians were eager for a deal at that time. Arafat thought that Netanyahu faced more pressure to make concessions than he did and so would cave first. On January 17, 1997, an agreement for Israeli redeployment from 80 percent of Hebron was signed. Even after the agreement the Israeli military remained in control of the city, but markets were reopened and security arrangements were reached between the IDF and the Palestinian Authority. Only some 400 Jewish settlers lived in the area that remained under Israeli control amid some 140,000 Palestinian residents. Ross in his account wrote that Netanyahu failed to deliver when he promised to deliver Israeli concessions on six separate issues that Arafat had declared to be of prime importance.[45]

Benny Begin resigned from the government in January 1997 in response to the Hebron agreement. He was protesting a Likud government giving up any of the land of Israel. For this gesture he won Shamir's support for the rest of his political career.[46] Begin was the first of three Likud ministers to resign within a year. Dan Meridor resigned in June 1997, and David Levy in January 1998. This had the effect of leaving the government less moderate.[47] So then Netanyahu tried to appease the Right by giving permission for the Har Homa settlement located in between East Talpiot and Bethlehem in southeastern Jerusalem. Shimon Peres had cancelled plans for the settlement, around since the early 1980s, because of Palestinian opposition. But in February 1997 the Netanyahu government approved the settlement.[48] This strategy of appeasing both sides was also used by Prime Minister Tony Blair in the Northern Ireland negotiations after 1998 where he would first bribe Sinn Fein to honor its commitments and then bribe the unionists to assuage their anger. This had the effect of raising American pressure on Israel to make a major withdrawal in the next further redeployment on the West Bank that Labor had committed Israel to in 1995.[49]

In two separate interviews in the Israeli press in May 1996 Netanyahu stated that in his opinion agreeing to give back the Golan Heights was not the way to make peace with Syria, because regaining the Golan was actually a low priority for the Assad regime. He said it was "a fourth priority." He suggested instead reconvening the Madrid Conference and discussing different issues of bilateral importance between the two countries with the Syrians.[50] And the non-return of the Golan, annexed by Israel in December 1981, was part of the Likud platform in 1996. So it would seem strange that in 1997–98 Netanyahu devoted more effort voluntarily to the Syrian front than he did under compulsion to the Palestinian front. Netanyahu used cosmetics billionaire Ron Lauder, a personal friend, to mediate between Israel and Syria during 1998. Netanyahu was willing to give up most of the Golan but wanted to keep an Israeli intelligence presence on Mt. Hermon. This was unacceptable to President Hafiz al–Assad who had to show that his steadfastness had gotten back all of his territory, just as Anwar Sadat got back all of the Sinai, but without making humiliating gestures like going to Jerusalem. Netanyahu also used Miguel Moratinos of Spain, who was serving as an European Union mediator, and an

Omani mediator. But Netanayahu was never willing to commit up front to returning all of the Golan before he knew what he would receive in exchange. He did question at length whether the "Rabin deposit" made by Prime Minister Rabin in 1993 and confirmed by Peres in 1996 was a legal commitment on the part of the Israeli government. American mediator Dennis Ross told Bibi that an agreement with Syria was impossible without first agreeing to return all of the Golan. But Assad was unwilling to sit down with Netanyahu before the latter's government finally collapsed.[51]

The major negotiation of Netanyahu's first government was the Wye River Plantation Summit in October 1998. The summit took place at a former slave plantation in Maryland located on the Wye River and close to Washington. This site was later used for negotiations between Israel and Syria as well. Under the Oslo accords the Rabin government committed Israel to making three further redeployments between the redeployment that followed the Oslo II agreement in October 1995 and the final settlement of the conflict. The Palestinians argued that the IDF should make each redeployment 30 percent of the territory on the West Bank so that borders would not be an issue in the final settlement negotiations.[52] Israel, naturally, wanted to retain as much territory as possible going into the final settlement negotiations so as to give it the maximum amount of bargaining leverage. In December 1997 Netanyahu told Ross that Israel could only afford to give up 13 percent more of the territory in Zone B to the 27 percent that the Palestinians already controlled in Zone A. Bibi wanted the IDF to remain in control of 60 percent of the West Bank.[53]

So basically it was up to the United States as the mediating power to determine how much traffic each side's metaphorical bridge could bear and determine how much territory should be given up in each of the further redeployments. Israel committed itself to giving up 9.1 percent in the first of the FRDs and carried this out. Washington wanted Jerusalem to commit to somewhere close to 15 percent for the second and Netanyahu wanted to give up no more than 10 percent. There was also a question of which zones the territory would come out of: Zone A, the area of total Palestinian control in the major towns; Zone B, the area of mixed Palestinian civil control and Israeli military control in the smaller towns and villages; and Zone C, the area of total Israeli control in the rural areas of the West Bank. Going into the summit Washington and Jerusalem had already agreed to an Israeli redeployment from 13 percent of the West Bank to be composed of 10 percent transferred from Area B to Area A and 3 percent from Area A to be made into a nature reserve. The summit was just to nail down the exact territory involved and a number of security measures that Israel demanded from the Palestinians in exchange for this.

Eight. Netanyahu: King of the Princes

During most of the eight days of the summit, Clinton was gone doing fundraising appearances for Democrats running for Congress in the midterm elections. Most of the mediation duties fell to Secretary of State Madeleine Albright, National Security Advisor Sandy Berger and Middle East envoy Dennis Ross. The first two were convinced that Netnayahu was deliberately attempting to undermine the Oslo process through obstruction.[54]

Immediately after arriving in Washington on October 15, 1998, Netanyahu was put on a helicopter and whisked away to the Wye Plantation before he had a chance to meet with Republican members of Congress and line up support against pressure from the Clinton administration. At the plantation Secretary of State Madeleine Albright was waiting along with CIA director George Tenet, and CIA Israel station chief Stan Moskowitz were waiting for him. The following day Defense Minister Yitzhak Mordekhai and Foreign Minister Ariel Sharon joined Netanyahu and Commerce Minister Natan Sharansky at the plantation.

The day after in a meeting with Clinton and the Palestinians, Bibi announced that he would go home unless there was a security agreement with the Palestinians. This ignored the fact that days before Mordekhai had pronounced himself satisfied with the security plan presented to him by Palestinian Security Chief Mohammed Dahlan. But Reserve Major General Meir Dagan, who served as a personal anti-terrorism advisor to Netanyahu, pronounced himself dissatisfied with the plan at the start of the summit.[55]

King Hussein of Jordan arrived at the summit on October 20 from the Mayo Clinic in Rochester, Minnesota where he was undergoing treatment for cancer. Clinton warned everyone that they would have to use a special disinfectant before having any contact with the king so as not to accidentally infect him. Hussein was there at Clinton's request.[56]

On October 21, Netanyahu announced that he was going home because there was no security plan. That evening he has a conference call with the Israeli consuls in the United States and announces, "I've got them by the balls." But when the American protocol chief asks Netanyahu what type of ceremony he wanted for his departure he realized that his bluff had been called and backed down. Dahlan had already told him to go ahead and leave.[57]

The next issue was haggling over the number and type of prisoners that Israel would release in a promised prisoner release. Israel agreed to release 500 prisoners and the Palestinians wanted a thousand. Netanyahu agreed to release a hundred Fatah prisoners and 400 others provided that they were not members of Hamas.

At 3 a.m.—the negotiations on the last day began at 10:30 a.m.—the two sides had agreed on a compromise of 750 prisoners. But Netanyahu announced that he intended to build a new Jewish quarter on Har Homa. He also wanted Palestinian General Ghazi Jebali arrested by the PA for murder of Israelis. He said he would drop this demand if the Palestinians would drop their opposition to the Har Homa settlement.[58]

Finally at 5 a.m. Netanyahu agreed to the terms proposed. But he then announced that Clinton had agreed to release American traitor Jonathan Pollard from prison for espionage on behalf of Israel. George Tenet strenuously objected to this as did House Speaker Newt Ginrich, a Republican congressional leader, and it was off. Netanyahu signed anyway.[59]

Now came the hard part: Bibi would have to sell the agreement to his government and his party. The danger involved is illustrated by a barb that Arafat hurled to Bibi at the agreement signing ceremony: "I can't picture you in a keffiyeh!" This was an allusion to the posters of Rabin in a keffiyeh carried by the settlers in the anti–Oslo rallies before Rabin's assassination. On November 17, the Knesset gave its approval to the agreement with 75 members voting in favor. Of this majority, only 30 came from the government. As with the Camp David accords, a Likud-negotiated agreement owed its approval to the opposition parties. Two days later, the government by a vote of six in favor, five against, and three abstentions gave its approval to carry out the first phase of the agreement.[60]

On November 24 Rafah airport, the first Palestinian international airport was opened in Gaza. On December 13, President Clinton landed to pay an official visit to the PA and witness the meeting of the Palestinian National Council where the Palestinian Covenant would be modified to eliminate its clauses inconsistent with the peace process with Israel. A three-way meeting between Clinton, Arafat, and Netanyahu at the Erez checkpoint went badly. Netanyahu and Saeb Erekat read off lists of items that they thought demonstrated that the other side was not in compliance with the Wye agreement. Before Clinton left Washington, Ross flew home to brief him on the perilous situation of the Israeli government before he left on his trip. Netanyahu then stopped implementation of the Wye River agreement until the Palestinians met five Israeli security demands.

Clinton was facing possible impeachment by the House of Representatives over his lying under oath about the Lewinsky affair. He was also planning a bombing offensive against Iraq over Saddam Hussein's noncompliance with international nuclear inspections, which were part of the 1991 ceasefire conditions. Netanyahu was facing a possible collapse of his coalition over the implementation of the Wye agreement, and the Palestinians were upset because many of the prisoners being released were ordinary criminals and not terrorists. By the time Clinton returned to

Washington, Berger and Ross were in agreement that they needed a new Israeli government in order to save the peace process.[61]

Netanyahu's attitude was that the Palestinians must adhere strictly to the Wye timetable but that the time table was flexible for the Israelis. Bibi's government was being sustained by Labor votes on the implementation of Wye, but he feared that at any moment Labor could choose to vote against him and his coalition would collapse. Bibi faced an unholy alliance of the Israeli Left and Right—the Left because it did not trust Netanyahu and the Right because it was opposed to peace.[62, 63]

On January 4, 1999, the Knesset voted to dissolve itself and call new elections for May 17 by a vote of 85 to 27. Labor had finally decided to stop supporting Netanyahu in office now that he was no longer implementing the peace process. At the same time the Right with Labor's help passed a law requiring a majority vote in a popular referendum and a 61-vote majority in order to give up the Golan.

In his first outing as prime minister Netanyahu was torn between living up to his own ideology and winning the support of his "political tribe" and being perceived as a peace maker by the Israeli security establishment. He was torn between the ideology that he had learned from his father and his political mentors like Moshe Arens and Shamir, and his socialization into the elite of the IDF from his own service and that of his older brother. In an earlier period he could have performed like Moshe Dayan or Yigal Allon. But now he was faced with making existential decisions. "No, Begin had it easy. I will make the hard decisions like Ben-Gurion," he told Ross once.[64]

Some academic analysts like the English academic Neill Lochery took the Hebron agreement and the Wye River summit as evidence that today's Likud "is not your father's Likud," to paraphrase one car commercial.[65] But this judgment proved to be premature because the fall of his first government fundamentally resolved Netanyahu's cognitive dissonance in favor of his Revisionist roots.

The election campaign was largely a matter of dueling imported American strategists, Arthur Finkelstein for Bibi and James Carvile and Stan Greenburg for Barak. Carville, Greenburg, and Barak read the polls as closely in 1999 as Bibi and Finkelstein had done in 1996. With the divided vote many of Bibi's religious supporters on the Right voted for their religious parties for the Knesset and did not vote in the prime ministerial contest. Barak beat Bibi by thirteen percent and in the Knesset election Labor won 26 seats to the Likud's 19 and Shas's 17 seats. Barak then faced the task of governing when the Center-Left (Labor and Meretz) controlled little more than a quarter of the seats in the Knesset.[66]

Nine

"You will get him as prime minister": Sharon as Prime Minister

---

First Sharon formed a government of national unity with Labor (26), Shas (17), Israel B'Aliya (6) and the Likud (19). He offered the defense ministry to Labor. Barak seemed inclined to take it, but after his party revolted he was forced to surrender it to former Brigadier General Benjamin "Fuad" Ben Eliezer. Sharon made Peres his foreign minister and Eli Yishai of Shas his interior minister. Sharon soon had a coalition of 68 votes and the National Religious Party, the Center Party, and Gesher were all ready to serve in the coalition if necessary.[1]

Sharon's government assumed office in early March 2001. Its first goal was to end the Intifada on terms favorable to Israel. There was an unprecedented wave of terror attacks during Sharon's first hundred days in office, more intense even than the wave in 1996 that helped to elect Netanyahu. But this worked to Sharon's advantage when the 9/11 terrorist attacks occurred in the United States in September. President George W. Bush, who had been Sharon's guest on a guided tour of Israel in 1999 when he was governor of Texas, was receptive to the message that Arafat was just a local version of Al Qaeda leader Osama Bin-Laden. In March Sharon had traveled to Washington to meet with Bush and had spread the word that he was ready for peace and compromise but would not negotiate under fire.[2]

Peres agreed to form a National Unity Government with Sharon soon after replacing Barak as Labor leader in the late winter of 2001. Peres took the foreign ministry and Benyamin Ben-Eliezer defense—the job that

Prime Minister Ariel Sharon speaking at reception in honor of Israel Prize recepient Yitzhak Shamir, Hilton Hotel, Jerusalem, April 26, 2001. Photograph by Amos Ben Gershom.

Yitzhak Shamir and Prime Minister Ariel Sharon at the reception honoring Shamir for the Israel Prize, Hilton Hotel, Jerusalem, April 26, 2001. Photograph by Amos Ben Gershom.

Barak initially contemplated taking. Sharon refused to give Levy, the man who had saved Sharon's career in 1996 and who helped to collapse the Barak government in 2000, a job.[3]

On September 23, 2001, Sharon became the first Likud leader in history to say he was ready for a Palestinian state in a speech at Latrun. But Sharon's state was composed of only about 42 percent of the West Bank and resembled more a South African homeland like KwaZulu than the map of the state that the Palestinians had in mind. But, nevertheless, many Likud Central Committee members regarded it as a betrayal of principle just as many Palestinians regarded the Oslo agreement as a betrayal. On October 13, 2001, National Union leader Rehavam Ze'evi and Israel Beitenu leader Avigdor Lieberman resigned from the government. Before their resignations could take effect officially Ze'evi was assassinated by terrorists from the Popular Front for the Liberation of Palestine as his home in the Old City of Jerusalem. Netanyahu called for an all-out war against the Palestinian Authority and the exile or killing of Arafat.[4]

In June 2001 after the Dolphinarium Disco bombing in Tel Aviv that killed twenty-one people, Sharon ordered the IDF to prepare to enter the casbahs of the West Bank. When Chief of Staff Shaul Mofaz objected to

Nine. "You will get him as prime minister": Sharon 171

this, Sharon yelled, "This is war, in case you haven't understood until now." Sharon spent hours with the mid-ranking officers, battalion and brigade commanders, going over maps and strategy in order to determine how to fight the Intifada. His message to field officers was: surprise the enemy, throw him off balance, attack, attack, always attack. But in general Sharon was much more restrained than he had been in the 1950s, in the 1970s or in 1982. "But in intimate consultations I saw how he thought about the ramifications of every move. I saw that this was a complex man, not the simplistic advocate of brute force that one had been led to believe," said his military aide Moshe Kaplinsky.[5]

In January 2002 Israeli naval commandos captured the Palestinian arms ship *Karin A* on its way from Iran to Gaza. It was boarded in the Red Sea. Arafat denied any knowledge of the ship but documents from the ship were produced and shown to several Western leaders that refuted this story. On January 14 Sharon said that Arafat would not be allowed to leave Ramallah until he arrested Ze'evi's killers and those responsible for the *Karin A*. That same day Sharon signed a death order for Ra'ad Karmi, a Palestinian terrorist from Tulkarem who belonged to Arafat's Fatah movement. Sharon was reviving a policy first used when Peres was prime minister in 1996 of "targeted killings" or assassinations of terrorist leaders who were operationally involved in terrorism rather than merely endorsing its use. The idea was to retard the enemy's capability of carrying out terrorism by depriving it of the experience of veteran operatives.[6]

In order for targeted killings to work Israeli intelligence, usually Shabak, had to have information about the location and movements of the target and be able to transmit this information and get a decision to kill back in time to execute the attack, usually by attack helicopter or fighter jet in time. This meant taking account of possible collateral damage—innocent civilians killed or injured in the attack. As several former heads of Shabak later admitted in the film *The Gatekeepers* the target killings were a tactic intended as a stop gap measure in order to buy the government time to come up with a permanent solution in the form of a political solution. But Sharon never really envisaged a political solution with the Palestinians. He thought wholly in terms of whatever Bush would allow him to do.

On July 23, 2002, the IAF bombed the house in Gaza of Salah Schade. He was the leader in Gaza of Hamas's military wing, the Izz al–Din al–Kassem Brigades, named after a resistance leader killed fighting the British in late 1935 when Sharon was seven years old. (Ironically, Kassem was a hero of Arafat.) The house had been bombed with a one-ton bomb that killed twelve people in addition to Schade. On March 22, 2004, Sheikh Ahmed Yassin, the spiritual leader and ideologue behind Hamas, was killed by Israeli rockets fired from a plane as he left his mosque from mourning prayers. This was a departure from the previous policy of only hitting operational leaders and was an Israeli declaration of war on Hamas. Less than a month later his successor, Abdel Assis al–Rantissi was also killed by the IAF in a targeted air strike on April 17. These two would be the first of many senior Hamas members to be killed and would result in Hamas not publicly identifying its leaders. In June 2004 the U.S. House of Representatives passed a resolution by a vote of 397 to 5 supporting Israel's right to use targeted killings to defend itself.[7]

In March 2002 a suicide bomber blew himself up in a hall in Netanya where a passover seder was taking place. He killed 29 people and injured 140, twenty of them seriously. The killer was from Hamas and his name was on a list of known terrorists given several times to Arafat for apprehension. Sharon reacted by ordering an invasion of the West Bank cities evacuated under the Oslo II agreement in late 1995. Israeli tanks poured into the cities and Israeli soldiers made their way from house to house checking for terrorists. In Jenin there was a very destructive battle as several houses had to be destroyed to protect the troops going in. The Palestinians claimed that 500 people had been killed. It later turned out that the figure was about 50 Palestinians, about double the number of Israeli soldiers killed. In October 2002 Ben-Eliezer pulled Labor out of the coalition in order to put distance between it and the Likud before the general election. Ostensibly the pullout was caused by the Likud allocating too much of the budget to settlements at the expense of the poor, but it was really a political decision that was poll driven. Polls indicated that it might disappear if it remained in the coalition. Labor chose Avram Mitzna, a former major general in charge of Central Command during the first Intifada and later mayor of Haifa as its candidate for prime minister. Sharon easily won the Likud primary for the leadership and named Netanyahu to replace Peres as foreign minister and former Chief of Staff Shaul Mofaz as defense minister to replace Ben-Eliezer. Mofaz, a hardliner, became Sharon's protégé.[8] Operation Defensive Shield, as the invasion was officially called, lasted for forty days and 29 Israeli soldiers were killed and about a hundred were wounded.[9]

Sharon sent troops into the six main Palestinian towns in an attempt to root out terrorism. Bush was preparing to wage a coalition war in Afghanistan and so could not risk condoning Sharon's moves openly. Sharon was warned to have his troops out of the towns before coming to Washington on a scheduled visit. In November Sharon rescheduled the visit rather than prematurely pull his troops out. Crown Prince Adullah of Saudi Arabia flew out to Bush's ranch in Crawford, Texas in April 2003 and demanded that the siege on Arafat be lifted. Operation Defensive Shield ended that month with 260 Palestinians killed, thousands wounded and nearly two thousand arrested.[10]

Sharon ran on his record of combatting terrorism and used the terms peace and security almost interchangeably in his election campaign. Sharon beat Netanyahu in the Likud primary by a 16 percent margin. But his supporters did poorly in the primary and the Likud list was mostly composed of Netanyahu supporters. Netanyahu had agreed to serve as Sharon's foreign minister on the condition that Sharon call early elections. Sharon agreed after his pollster showed him with an eight percent lead over Netanyahu for the party leadership. Before the primary Netanyahu said that he would support whomever the winner was. Labor candidate Amram Mitzna was too much of a dove in the new Israel that had emerged as a result of the failure of Camp David and the Al-Aksa Intifada. Because the Sharon "brand" was much stronger than the party brand, the Likud ended up running a personalized campaign much like Rabin ran in 1992 and Barak ran in 1999. During the campaign Mitzna called for a unilateral Israeli withdrawal from both the Gaza Strip and the West Bank if agreement with the Palestinians was not possible. On January 28, 2003, Sharon was reelected prime minister. The Likud doubled its number of seats from 19 to 38, Labor lost seven seats to have only 19, Yosef "Tommy" Lapid's Shinui party gained nine seats for a total of 15, and Shas lost six seats to end up with 11, and the dovish Meretz had its seats halved to six.[11]

Sharon formed a coalition with 68 seats composed of the Likud (38), Shinui (15), National Union (7), and National Religious Party (6) on February 28, two days after his seventy-fifth birthday. Ehud Olmert, a personal friend of Tommy Lapid, handled the negotiations with both Lapid and with NRP leader Effie Eitam. Olmert convinced Eitam that Lapid was not anti-religious but only anti–Haredi. Sharon after he had his coalition of the Right was much more interested in implementing a strategy than he had been before. For the remainder of his time in office Sharon concentrated on two main projects: the building of the Separation Barrier—a combination of fence and walls that separated Jews from Arabs and ran inside the West Bank so that the main settlements were included behind it, and the disengagement from Gaza. The barrier was authorized by the government in June 2002. Sharon considered the route of the barrier to be the basis of Israel's future eastern border. Later the Israeli Supreme Court made the government modify the route of the fence to minimize the nuisance to Palestinians along the route. The International Court at the Hague ruled the whole barrier—which it called a wall—illegal because it was built on Palestinian territory.[12]

"Restraint is strength" became Sharon's new motto. Sharon now projected an image as prudent, calm, long-suffering and complex—the opposite of the pre–1982 Bulldozer. Waiting until after 9/11 for his major retaliation against Arafat had worked. By 2005 Sharon had created an image as a national father figure—reliance and admiration became how Israelis saw him. "Restraint is strength" paved the way for the later disengagement.[13]

During the spring of 2003 Sharon also had to contend with the Road Map. This was an attempt by the Bush administration to revive the Israeli-Palestinian peace process through the Quartet (the U.S., Russia, the European Union, the UN) by creating a "road map" for what needed to be done to ensure security and ensure compliance under the Oslo agreement. The problem was that neither side trusted the other and neither was really interested in a negotiated peace. But Bush was under pressure from British Prime Minister Tony Blair to revive the peace process as a condition for British participation in the invasion of Iraq in March 2003. On May 23, 2003, the Israeli government officially agreed to the Road Map "in principle" but with so many qualifications as to mean a rejection in practice. Sharon only agreed to it because he knew that the Palestinian Authority would not comply with it. The Road Map passed the cabinet by a vote of 12 to 7 with four abstentions. Of the fourteen Likud ministers half voted for it and half voted against it or abstained.

The Bush administration forced Arafat to appoint Mahmoud Abbas as his prime minister. In June Sharon said of him, "Abu Mazen, too, is still an Arab." In other words he was not to be trusted. Arafat was a ruler who did not really want to share power—this was not the Arab model. So he used his control over his security chiefs to frustrate Abbas until he finally resigned in September. Arafat then appointed Ahmed Qurei, also known as Abu Ala'a, as the new prime minister. At a Likud Central Committee meeting three days after the cabinet vote on the Road Map, Sharon was heckled by demonstrators and Netanyahu was greeted by a friendly crowd chanting, "Bibi, Bibi."[14]

The Bush administration indicated repeatedly that Arafat was off limits to Israel—he could not be killed or forced into exile. So Sharon kept him under siege in his compound in Ramallah, known as the Mukata. Sharon was itching to have Arafat killed, but he gave his word to Bush that he would not do so. But Arafat was politically dead or irrelevant as far as both Sharon and Bush were concerned as the latter indicated in his speech on the Middle East on June 24, 2002, which called on the Palestinians to choose a new leader untainted by a connection with terrorism. Sharon and his aides had a role in drafting the language of the speech.[15]

Nine. "You will get him as prime minister": Sharon

In his final months in 2004, Arafat was back in his element as if he were back in Beirut under siege by Sharon in 1982. This was Sharon's fourth and final round of confrontation with the Palestinians. The first was on the West Bank and in Gaza from September 1953 to October 1956, the second was in Gaza in 1971–72, and the third was in Lebanon in 1982–83. The only other native-fighter politician to have such a long confrontation with his native enemy was Andrew Jackson who fought Indians off and on from 1788 to 1837 when he resigned as president. Other than in appearance, the two men had many other personality traits in common. But Sharon, unlike Jackson, could not intimidate rivals by challenging them to a duel or simply shooting them, he had to stick to lawsuits and bullying.[16]

Sharon, according to his confidante and attorney, Dov Weisglass, had thought that upon taking office he could negotiate a 25-year truce with the Palestinians. Then he concluded that he had to eradicate terrorism first and wait for a successor to Arafat. But in the meantime the opposition was busy attempting various peace initiatives with moderate Palestinians. Ami Ayalon, a former head of both the Israeli Navy and Shabak, got together with former Intifada organizer Sari Nusseibeh to mount a petition drive. More serious was a negotiation between elements in Labor and Meretz on one hand and members of the Palestinian Authority on the other, to continue the negotiations where they left off at Taba in January 2001 in an attempt to reach a peace agreement. The Swiss government underwrote this initiative financially and the final agreement was signed in Geneva in August 2003. An infrastructure was appointed to publicize the venture among Israelis and Palestinians and took the name of the Geneva Initiative.[17]

This was in concept very similar to an initiative carried out by the parliamentary opposition in apartheid South Africa in the mid–1980s known as the KwaZulu/Natal Indaba or simply the Indaba for short. This was a negotiation between the former provincial government of Natal (before it was abolished by the government's constitutional reforms) and the government of the KwaZulu homeland and numerous third party groups. The Indaba was rejected by the National Party government as being a form of majority rule—which it was not, it was power sharing—but it caused a number of independent candidates to challenge the National Party in the next election. One of these was elected and a second lost by only 39 votes to a senior government minister. This in turn influenced President F.W. de Klerk to institute major reforms once he took power in 1989. A similar dynamic operated in Israel with the Geneva Initiative.[18]

Sharon in 2003 saw himself under some pressure from Washington to do something. National Security Advisor Uzi Dayan, a former deputy chief of staff and the nephew of Moshe, briefed Sharon about the demographic challenge to Israel presented by the combination of the higher Arab birthrate and the occupation. Sharon decided to partially alleviate this problem by withdrawing from Gaza.[19] Settlers later charged that Sharon was merely trying to solve his legal problems by withdrawing from Gaza so that the liberal legal establishment would quash the investigations against him because he supported their political agenda. All those who knew Sharon refute this allegation. The one settler leader who really knew Sharon personally, Ze'ev Hever, concluded that Sharon carried out the disengagement because he saw it in Israel's national interest to do so.[20]

There were three separate corruption investigations pursued against Sharon and his family. The first was the Annex Research affair involved illegal campaign contributions to the Sharon campaign by international corporations during 1999 and 2000. Eventually his son Omry was indicted and convicted for receiving illegal campaign contributions and served some six months in a minimum-security prison.[21] The case against Ariel Sharon was closed by the prosecutor for lack of evidence. The second was the Cyril Kern affair. Kern was an old friend of Sharon's who had helped to save his life by rushing him to the hospital after he was wounded in the Battle of Latrun. Kern then became a financier and made his fortune in casinos in the homelands of South Africa, which became a playground for South African whites under apartheid. Kern made a loan to Gilad Sharon to finance Sharon's leadership bid in the 1999 Likud contest. Sharon claimed that it was a loan with interest and was paid back including the interest charged. The third scandal was known as the Greek Island affair and involved David Appel paying Gilad Sharon a major fee ($400,000) and an annual $20,000 salary to promote his investments on the Greek island of Patroklos and in the city of Lod in Israel. The police thought that this was an influence-peddling scheme whereby the investor, David Appel, was paying for Sharon's influence through his son. In April 2005 the charges in the Greek Island affair were dropped because of insufficient evidence to prosecute—a weak case. It would seem that the Gaza disengagement did not prevent Omry from serving time in prison and that the other matters were dropped due to a lack of evidence. On June 15, 2004, Attorney General Menahem Mazuz closed the case against Sharon over the Greek Island Affair. He first informed Sharon and then held a press conference to inform the nation that he was dropping the case due to insufficient evidence. Mazuz ruled that there was no criminal intent on the part of either Sharon or his son Gilad, who never tried to conceal the salary that he was being paid.[22]

On October 16, 2003, Gilad Sharon wrote a position paper for his father in which he expounded on the principle of unilateral action as a

Nine. "You will get him as prime minister": Sharon

means of dealing with Israel's security problems. He did not mention anything in particular but only the principle. With this in mind Sharon went to Italy for three days on a secret trip on November 17. There he met with Assistant Secretary of State for Near Eastern Affairs Elliot Abrams at his hotel. This was the first occasion on which Sharon spoke of the possibility of a withdrawal from Gaza. A week later his personal attorney, Dov Weisglass, met with Elliot Abrams and National Security Advisor Condoleeza Rice in Washington. Weissglas briefed Sharon back in Israel on November 26. The Americans were concerned that the disengagement might clash with the Road Map and they did not want anything to interfere with that—even though Arafat had declared the Road Map to be dead on September 2. They later decided that this unilateral move would not interfere with the Road Map.[23]

Three government ministers including Finance Minister Benjamin Netanyahu and Foreign Minister Silvan Shalom publicly opposed the disengagement plan and led the movement to defeat it. On November 21, 2003, Israel's Channel 2 announced in its newscast that Sharon intended to carry out his disengagement from Gaza by the end of the summer of 2004. On December 18, 2003, at the Dan Hotel in Herzliya, Sharon made a speech on disengagement in which he defended it as a means of reducing both terrorism and friction with the Palestinians. He started out by speaking in favor of the Road Map plan, but stated that if the Palestinians did not soon endorse the Road Map and began to implement it he would be forced to act unilaterally.[24]

The settlers took Sharon at his word from the moment he made the speech. On January 12, 2004, 120,000 settlers and their supporters demonstrated in Rabin Square in Tel Aviv (the square where Rabin was assassinated in 1995) against the disengagement plan under the slogan "Arik Don't Fold." The demonstration was organized by the Yesha Settlement Council, the governing body for the settlements.

In February 2004 Sharon had breakfast with *Ha'Aretz* reporter Yoel Marcus. Because *Ha'Aretz* was the newspaper of the political and business establishment in Israel—the equivalent of the *New York Times, the London Times,* or *Le Monde*—Sharon figured it would be the ideal vehicle to announce his plan to withdraw from 17 settlements in Gaza and four on the West Bank. The media soon got behind Sharon's initiative, but he had problems with his own party. Sharon met with Bush at the White House on April 14, 2004, and got his support for the Gaza disengagement. Bush and his advisors tried to get Sharon to broaden the disengagement on the West Bank. Bush also handed Sharon an official letter in which he made three crucial recognitions of Likud positions:

- No return of Palestinian refugees to Israel;
- A de facto recognition of the legitimacy of the settlement blocs;
- And no return to the 1949 armistice lines.

On May 4, the Quartet met in New York and endorsed the idea of the disengagement as being consistent with the Road Map.[25]

His son Gilad later wrote that the disengagement was the main order of business for the Israel government from its announcement in December 2003 until its execution in late August 2005—and even afterwards until the election of March 2006.[26] The next major step was getting an endorsement from the Likud Party. Sharon decided to conduct a referendum on the disengagement open to all party members. Sharon knew that he could never win support for the plan from the party's Central Committee. But he figured that with his personal reputation and speaking ability he could sway ordinary Likud members. A referendum was scheduled for May 4, 2004. Ten days before the referendum Netanyahu and then Shalom came out in favor of the disengagement. But then the tide of opinion began to shift. Three days before the referendum polls showed the opposition ahead by 3 to 9 percent. The Yesha Council divided up the Likud voters registry and every West Bank settler was given a list of five Likud members to lobby in opposition to the disengagement. On May 4 party members were asked a single simple question, "Are you for or against Ariel Sharon's political plan?" Sharon was trounced by a 59.5 percent to 39.7 percent margin on the day of the referendum—almost exactly a 3:2 ratio, with half of eligible voters turning out. On the day of the referendum, a combined Palestinian Islamic Jihad and Al-Aksa Brgades team murdered a settler family as they drove out of the Gush Katif settlement bloc in Gaza. They claimed that this was revenge for the Sheikh Yassin assassination and had nothing to do with the referendum. Sharon decided he had to bypass the party and win support in the government and the Knesset for the disengagement.[27]

On May 15 a pro-disengagement rally was held in Rabin Square and attracted 150,000 people. The next day President Moshe Katsav admitted that there was a national majority in favor of withdrawal. Sharon decided to hold a vote on the disengagement plan at the regular weekly cabinet meeting at the beginning of June. First, he decided to improve the odds by firing two ministers, Benny Elon and Avigdor Lieberman, of the National Union who were opposed to the disengagement. The two decided to stay away but were found and served with legal papers announcing their firing. The government voted 14–7 to authorize disengagement, but not evacuation of the settlements. They would do that on another occasion.[28]

On October 25, 2004, the Knesset voted 67 to 44 in favor of the disengagement plan with all of the Left voting in favor of the plan. Sharon was repeatedly interrupted with heckling as he announced the plan. Two Arab Mks voted in favor of disengagement, the other six from the Balad (nationalist) and Hadash (Communist) parties abstained. The political atmosphere in Israel was eerily similar to that of nine years before. There were terror attacks by Hamas and Islamic Jihad with Israeli targeted killings in response. The settlers held mass demonstrations in opposition to the disengagement plan and demonized Sharon as they had, with his support, once demonized Rabin and Peres. There were counter-demonstrations in favor of the disengagement plan.

The day before Arafat had been flown by air ambulance to a Paris hospital gravely ill. Arafat died on November 11 in Paris of undisclosed causes. Palestinians claimed that he had been poisoned by Israel and Israelis countered that he had died of AIDS as a known bisexual. Mahmoud Abbas asked for permission to bury Arafat in Jerusalem, but this was refused. Israel allowed him to be buried in the Mukata in Ramallah where he had spent the last years of his life. After an emotional and raucous funeral procession in which the shrouded body was carried by the crowd he was interred there.[29]

When defending the withdrawal, Sharon, Peres, and Shinui leader Tommy Lapid all argued demography. "In western Palestine today there are 5.2 million Jews and 4.8 million non–Jews," said Peres. "In another five years there will be 5.8 million Jews and 6.5 million non–Jews. We will lose the majority. We will destroy Herzl's vision of a Jewish state."[30]

The settlers took Arafat's death as a sign of divine intervention. Sharon, a shellfish-eating agnostic, just laughed at this theory. A budget was based with funding for compensation payments for evacuated settlers. On January 10 Labor entered the government in order to help it carry out the disengagement and were given seven ministries. Three weeks later the government voted 17 to 5 to approve the government's final disengagement plan. This was after a dispute with Shinui over the proposed budget led Sharon to side with the ultra–Orthodox parties and Shinui to quit the government in November. Labor leader Shimon Peres announced that Labor's presence was purely ad hoc in order to carry out the disengagement. Sharon was essentially left with a choice of a coalition composed of the Likud, Labor and Shinui, or one composed of the Likud, Labor and the religious parties. Sharon opted for the latter as he would be in the center of the coalition and have more flexibility than if he were the most conservative party in the coalition. He fired the five Shinui ministers immediately after the vote. Peres waived any claim to the finance ministry and was content to serve as deputy prime minister. But because the law

Prime Minister Ariel Sharon addresses the nation on the day of the implementation of the disengagement plan from Gaza Strip and North Samaria, August 15, 2005. Photograph by Avi Ohayon.

only allowed for one deputy prime minister and Olmert was already serving in that position, Peres had to settle for minister without portfolio.[31]

The level of terror attacks dropped sharply from January 2004 to August 2005. The only places suicide attacks were still taking place were in Jerusalem and in Beersheba where the separation barrier had not yet been completed. The lower levels were due to both better tactical intelligence and the barrier.[32]

On January 15, 2005, Mahmoud Abbas was sworn in as the new Palestinian Authority chairman and president of the PLO. His only opposition in the election was Mustafa Barghouti, a cousin of imprisoned Fatah leader Marwan Barghouti. Abbas, also known as Abu Mazen, was opposed to the armed struggle as a failed strategy but still publicly supported the right of return for Palestinian refugees. Abbas, the Bush administration and Meretz all pleaded with Sharon to coordinate his disengagement with the Palestinians but Sharon refused to do this. His advisor, Dov Weissglas, said, "The Palestinians are not a partner, they're a problem to be dealt with." This had the net result of allowing Hamas to take credit for the disen-

Nine. "You will get him as prime minister": Sharon

gagement rather than Abbas with banners that read, "Four years of resistance beat ten years of negotiations." Sharon and Abbas met at a summit at Sharm al–Sheikh on February 8 hosted by President Mubarak of Egypt and King Abdallah of Jordan.[33]

In February Defense Minister Shaul Mofaz announced that Chief of Staff Moshe "Boogie" Ya'alon's term would not be extended for the customary fourth year. Ya'alon was known as both a bit of a loose cannon and as mistrustful of the Palestinians. Sharon did not want him in charge when the disengagement took place. Sharon pulled strings behind the scenes to pick Dan Halutz as the IDF's next chief of staff and the first to come up through the IAF instead of the ground forces. He also ended Shabak director Avi Dichter's term in May and replaced him with Yuval Diskin. Sharon thought highly of Dichter as a professional, but Dichter was not in complete agreement with the disengagement.[34]

At midnight on August 15, 2005, the IDF closed the borders of Gaza and began the evacuation of settlers from the Gush Katif settlement bloc in southern Gaza. The entire evacuation from the seventeen settlements took a total of six days and was really only met with violence on one day at a single settlement, Kfar Darom, on August 15. Most of the resistance came from West Bank settlers who wanted to make the evacuation as difficult as possible in order to forestall a future possible evacuation of settlements in the main blocs of the West Bank. Hundreds of settlers gathered on the roof of the synagogue of the settlement and threw light bulbs filled with blue paint at the soldiers and pushed off their ladders. Finally the IDF had a shipping container filled with police put on the roof of the synagogue by crane and the settlers were forced off. Despite settler rabbis having issued religious opinions (pskei din—the Jewish equivalent of Muslim fatwas) for months forbidding the evacuation and urging soldiers not to obey their orders, problems were avoided by simply giving the job to secular units and allowing anyone who felt strongly opposed to the disengagement to opt out of the evacuation operation.[35]

James Wolfensohn, the former head of the World Bank, raised private funds to buy out the settlement greenhouses so that they could be used by the Palestinians. But they were soon vandalized by Palestinian mobs when the settlement bloc was turned over to the Palestinian Authority.[36]

Ever since Sharon publicly announced the disengagement, Labor MK Haim Ramon had been pushing the idea—it was not really developed enough to be called a theory—of the "big bang." The "big bang" was a shakeup of Israeli party politics by the creation of a new party from centrists from the existing three major parties: the Likud, Labor, and Shinui. His idea was to promote a centrist ideology composed of privatization of state enterprises, a mixed economy, the abandonment of both the Oslo process and the idea of Greater Israel (*Eretz Israel haShlema*) in favor of unilateralism on Israel's part in order to safeguard its future by withdrawing to safer, more defensible borders. Ramon talked about his idea with both Sharon and Shinui leader Tommy Lapid.[37]

Two months after the disengagement Sharon suddenly decided that he would implement the "big bang" by quitting the Likud with his followers and forming a new party, Kadima. Likud rebels loyal to Netanyahu had scheduled a party primary for April 2006. Sharon had big plans to implement an agenda of domestic reforms: electoral reform, reform of the education system, and several others. He needed a party that would back him in order to forge ahead with these. He had taken discrete soundings within the Likud and found thirteen Knesset members who were prepared to follow him into a new party. This was enough to have the new party officially recognized in the Knesset.[38] He knew that in Labor at least Haim Ramon and Shimon Peres would follow him—Ramon because it was his idea and Peres because he wanted the presidency to end his long political career.

On Saturday November 12, the ranch forum or septet (*sheviya* in Hebrew), Sharon's closest political advisors, met at the Sycamores Ranch for a marathon session to discuss whether or not Sharon should quit the Likud. Nearly all of them were in favor. Only Uri Dan, Sharon's longtime reporter friend, was opposed to the plan. Three days later Omry Sharon pleaded guilty to an amended indictment for keeping false financial records, perjury, and violating campaign finance laws. Sharon knew that his son's political career was over with. On November 19 Sharon met with Amir Peretz, the new leader of the Labor Party, who had just beaten Peres in the leadership contest. The two agreed to hold new elections on March 28, 2006. The next day Sharon thought about his decision all day. The day after that he woke up with his mind made up and called a press conference for that evening. That evening Sharon announced to the nation that he was leaving the party that he had formed 32 years earlier along with thirteen MKs in order to form a new party.[39]

Polls quickly predicted thirty to forty seats for the new party. Peres, Ramon and Telecommunications Minister Dalia Itzik announced in the next few days that they were quitting Labor to join the new party. Defense Minister Shaul Mofaz announced that he was staying with his political home, the Likud. The next day after a plea from Sharon, he changed his mind and followed Sharon into the political wilderness. A few mayors also announced that they were joining the new party.[40]

On the evening of December 18, 2005, Sharon suffered a mild stroke that left his mental faculties unimpaired. The doctors gave him a clean bill of health but gave him a blood-thinner medicine and told him to work no more than four hours per day. For a man used to fifteen-hour workdays this was impossible to follow. He was also put on a whole grain, nuts and fruit diet in order to deal with his obesity. But it was far too late in his life for this. Less than three weeks later, on the evening of January 3, 2006—the evening before he was to go into the hospital for heart surgery, Sharon felt a severe chest pain and his personal physician recommended immediate hospitalization. On the ambulance ride to the hospital Sharon suffered a severe stroke. He went into a coma from which he had yet to emerge over seven years later. His political career was over.[41]

In January 2006 Palestinian elections that Washington had pushed for resulted in a Hamas victory. On March 28, Kadima emerged as the largest party with 29 seats under the leadership of Ehud Olmert, who had started his career in the Free Center Party. Olmert formed a coalition with the Labor Party, Shas, and the Pensioneers' Party. In late 2008 Olmert was forced to resign due to corruption charges. Foreign Minister Tzipi Livni became the new party leader and prime minister but was forced to call new elections when she was unable to form a new coalition. In 2013 Kadima emerged with only two seats under the leadership of Mofaz. Sharon's final party only survived him by a few years.[42]

Sharon died of massive organ failure on January 11, 2014, just over eight years after having gone into a coma. He never revived from the coma.[43] Even if he would have, his political career was effectively over once he went into a coma due to the combination of his advanced age and worry about his cognitive abilities. It would have taken him months to recover basic functions after such a massive stroke—if he were not a vegetable beyond recovery.

Sharon's stroke was largely caused by his obesity and overwork. The former was caused by a lifetime of gluttony. Sharon would eat all day long consuming two or three separate breakfasts followed by lunch and dinner with falafel in between as snacks. Sharon ate slowly chewing each mouthful as he had been taught as a child. His overeating probably increased dramatically when he was prime minister due to both his loneliness following Lily's death and the increased stress due to the job. His major sources of stress relief seemed to have been chatting with his military aide Kaplinsky and listening to classical music.[44]

What is Sharon's legacy for Israel and the Israeli Right? His legacy for the nation was the disaster in Lebanon and the settlement of the West Bank and Gaza. He also demonstrated that settlements could be removed with determination, something that should have been clear from post-colonial history in Africa. Sharon also demonstrated that the leader most likely to withdraw from the West Bank is someone from the Right but who was educated and socialized on the Left. Unlike Begin, Shamir, and Netanyahu, Sharon was never a disciple of Jabotinsky and never belonged to Betar. Thus he may be a model for future military politicians who grow up in Labor homes but join the Likud for career reasons after finishing the IDF.

Sharon is like John Quincy Adams or Andrew Jackson—the last of the independence generation. When Adams died in 1848 as the Mexican War was coming to an end, he was celebrated as the last of the founders. As a teenager he served as an American diplomat abroad helping his father during the Revolution. Jackson served as a courier for the local militia in South Carolina during the Revolution. Sharon was a junior officer during the 1948 war. Peres is the only real politician of that generation who survives him. When Peres dies in a few years that generation of founders will be gone.

His legacy for the Right is much more complex because so much of it is now unacknowledged because he is now considered a traitor by the settlers. He demonstrated that unilateralism does not really work without coordination with the Palestinian Authority. And due to the aftermath of both the Lebanon withdrawal in 2000 and the Gaza disengagement it is not likely to be tried agreed for some time if ever. Sharon's biggest legacy for the Right is the creation of the Likud in 1973. The fact that he largely failed in two attempts to repeat this magic with Shlomzion and Kadima demonstrates that the preexisting material that one works with is more important than the architect. Because of Sharon the settlers may also be more wary of trusting generals—or at least those from the Center-Left, no matter what their positions are later in life.

Ten

Bibi Melekh Israel (King of Israel)

After his disastrous first term, Bibi decided to take a break from politics and make some money. For over two years he did speaking engagements, consulted and took advantage of his resume to expand his personal wealth. He did stay active in Likud politics and saw to the running of his camp within the party. In early November 2002 Sharon made him his foreign minister, returning the favor from four years before. When elections were held for the Knesset in 2003, for the first time in seven years under the old system of a single vote per voter, Sharon was at the top of the ticket. In the Likud leadership contest on November 28, 2002, Netanyahu lost to Sharon by 16 points: 40 to 56 percent. But this still gave him a claim on a major ministry in the new Likud government. Sharon made Netanyahu his finance minister. Netanyahu's supporters did much better than did Sharon's supporters in the formation of the Likud Knesset list.[1]

As finance minister, Netanyahu oversaw a major reform of the Israeli economy. This reform had begun in 1984–85 under Prime Minister Shimon Peres who ended many of the socialist subsidies in order to bring inflation under control. Netanyahu then instituted a number of neoliberal, or in American terms conservative, reforms such as taking what is known in Israel as the Wisconsin Plan, or in Wisconsin as the Work for Welfare plan. In Wisconsin in the 1990s Governor Tommy Thompson, a popular governor with broad bipartisan support, instituted a plan to end welfare dependency by forcing welfare recipients to apply for jobs or job training. The idea was to get as many as possible off of welfare and into the economy. This and a number of other Thompson reforms such as the school voucher program became standard Republican Party reform programs in the 2000s as Thompson became Secretary of Health and Human Services under President George W. Bush. Netanyahu brought the program with him back from Washington and introduced it into Israel. This was aimed mostly at forcing Haredi men and Arab women into the work force. The second part of his economic reform was trimming the fat from the public sector by both reducing salaries and reducing the number of jobs. The third part of his reform was tax reform—lowering the tax rates and privatization. And the fourth part was attacking monopolies and cartels that reduced competition in the economy. Netanyahu faced major backlash and resistance from special interests tied to the Histadrut (Labor Federation) and the Labor Party. As a result of this and other economic reforms the Israeli economy began performing better in the early 21st century and Netanyahu was credited with having performed an economic miracle by the time he left office in the second half of 2005: unemployment went down, salaries increased and the Tel Aviv Stock Exchange soared.[2]

Sharon's disengagement plan presented a special challenge to Netanyahu. If it proved successful and Netanyahu opposed it, it could finish his political career. Plus, if he defied Sharon openly too early he could lose his job before he was a real success as finance minister. But if it proved to be a disaster and he supported it he could be hurt just as badly. As usual in such situations, Netanyahu waffled. In the Likud referendum on disengagement, Netanyahu supported Sharon. Netanyahu led a three-minister Likud revolt within the government in early 2004 before Sharon's government shakeup. Tzipi Livni played Kissinger and shuttled back and forth between the two Likud camps in an attempt to mediate the dispute. This helped to force Sharon to cancel a vote on the disengagement plan on May 30, 2004. Instead he fired the National Union ministers and reformed his government.[3]

Netanyahu proposed to Sharon that he keep the funding for the disengagement out of the budget bill. He argued that this way Sharon could pass the budget and then later with the support of Labor pass the funding for disengagement in a separate bill. But Netanyahu refused to commit to voting for the funding and Sharon demurred. Netanyahu and the other three Likud rebels demanded a national referendum on the disengagement plan but voted for it in the Knesset vote. Netanyahu then used the death of Arafat in November 2004 as an excuse to remain within the government.[4]

Netanyahu's period as undisputed head of the Likud began on November 21–22, 2005 when Sharon left the party to form Kadima and Shaul Mofaz followed him a day later. Since 1998 Sharon had been Netanyahu's only real credible rival for the leadership within the Likud. Following Sharon's exit from the Likud and then from politics two months later,

Netanyahu's biggest opposition has come from outside the party on the Right. Ironically, the two who so far have emerged as possible successors to Netanyahu both served as his office manager, Avigdor Lieberman and Naftali Bennet. Lieberman took over from Eyal Arad once Bibi returned to Israel in the late 1980s. He then served Bibi for about a decade before leaving the Likud to form his own Russian immigrant party, *Israel Beitenu* (Israel is Our Home). He had since emerged as the one credible alternative to Lieberman on the Right, until Netanyahu co-opted him in 2013 by forming a joint Likud/Israel Beitenu list known as Likud Beitenu.

After Netanyahu emerged as the leader of the Likud following Sharon's departure, he told reporters repeatedly that he had learned his lesson from the late 1990s. Most reporters interpreted this to mean that he would never depend on the Right again. No, the real lesson that Netanyahu learned was that he must stay with the Right, but curtail its power by balancing it with a centrist party. This is what Sharon did in 2003 by bringing in Shinui as his largest coalition partner. It is also what Begin did in his first government by bringing in the Democratic Movement for Change to give himself support in making peace with Egypt against the hardliners in his own party.

In 2006 Netanyahu presided over the smallest Likud parliamentary party in history and the smallest main Revisionist party since Herut in the early 1950s. Likud won only twelve seats in March 2006 to make it the fourth largest party in the Knesset after Kadima with 29 seats, Labor with 19, and Shas with twelve but with over 17,000 more votes or half a percentage point more than the Likud.[5] As Ehud Olmert formed a coalition out of both Kadima and Labor, this made the head of Shas, a non–Zionist party, the leader of the opposition.

All Bibi could really afford to do in these circumstances was to repeat his strategy from 1996 of waiting for the other side to make the mistakes. He supported the government in its Second Lebanon War in the summer of 2006. The war went relatively poorly for Israel and Prime Minister Ehud Olmert emerged from it as a lame duck. The Winograd Reports on the conduct of the war were published on April 30, 2007 (preliminary) and January 18, 2008 (final). But Ehud Barak was strengthened by the performance of Amir Peretz as defense minister and returned to lead both Labor and take over Peretz's job. In 2008 Ehud Olmert was indicted on corruption charges and forced by his party to step down as party leader in favor of Foreign Minister Tzipi Livni, the last of the Likud princes to emerge. Livni won a fairly narrow victory over former Defense Minister Shaul Mofaz and Kadima began dividing into two rival camps. At the end of 2008 Livni was unable to form a governing coalition without a major bribe to Shas, which she refused to pay on principle. So elections were called for early

2009. Before these took place Israel invaded Gaza in December 2008 just before the inauguration of a new president in Washington and two days after the start of the Likud's election campaign.[6] The war proved to be both one-sided in the body count and inconclusive. The ground invasion was rather limited and late (January 3—a week after the war began) in coming. Total dead were between 1,166 and 1,417 for the Palestinians and 13 for Israel.[7]

In the 2009 campaign the Likud's platform had five main economic planks: a free market orientation with social sensitivity; disciplined budget, tax cuts, efficient financial markets, and private sector growth; the government should create economic opportunities for all; all those who are able should work; and investment in education and national infrastructure. The party had three main defense planks: Iran's nuclear potential was at the top of the agenda; Israel should make concessions for peace similar to those made by Begin in 1979; and Israel should focus on improving the daily lives of Palestinians rather than attempting to negotiate peace with them.[8]

The party attempted to attract voters with a combination of new and old stars running on its list. Benny Begin returned to run in fifth place and Dan Meridor in seventeenth place. Former Chief of Staff Moshe "Boogie" Ya'alon was in eighth place and Major General Yossi Peled in fifteenth place. Ze'ev Elkin, a Kadima defector, was in twentieth place. And the list even featured a Dayan: former Deputy Chief of Staff and National Security Advisor Uzi Dayan, in 44th place.[9]

The war served to raise militarism among the Israeli population during the election campaign. As a result the two parties of the Israeli Left, Labor and Meretz, lost voters across the socio-economic spectrum while the Likud gained them across the same spectrum. The Left ended up with a combined total of sixteen seats—thirteen for Labor and only three for Meretz compared with 44 and 12 respectively in 1992. Kadima was the benefactor that managed to nearly retain its 2006 total by cannibalizing the Left of voters as many 2006 Kadima voters, about a third, returned to the Likud and were replaced by former Labor, Meretz, and Pensioner Party voters. Kadima ended up with 28 seats.[10] The election resulted in three main things: the demise of the bipolar system that ruled Israel from 1977 to 2003, the near-total collapse of the Left, and the relative success of Kadima. Netanyahu targeted Tzipi Livni as his real opponent in the election and ran a sexist campaign that portrayed her as inexperienced, naïve, and indecisive. Livni was the first woman candidate for prime minister since Golda Meir in 1973 and like Meir had never been active as a feminist. The media personalized the election as a choice between Tzipi and Bibi.[11]

Ten. Bibi Melekh Israel (King of Israel)

After the polls closed and the votes were counted, both Livni and Netanyahu claimed victory. On the advice of most of the party leaders, President Peres decided to invite Netanyahu to attempt to form a coalition first. Netanyahu was able to form a coalition with Israel Beitenu, Labor and Shas, although he needed an extension of his mandate from Peres to sign the coalition agreements with the latter two parties. By the end of March he was able to present a coalition with 69 mandates to the Knesset and the next day United Torah Judaism with five mandates joined as well. Individually he had one of the most qualified cabinets in Israeli history, but it was paralyzed by political rivalries between the figures within the Likud and the other parties as well. Israel's low entry barrier to the Knesset had produced another dysfunctional government.[12]

Operation Cast Lead ended just days before President Obama was sworn into office and Israeli troops finished withdrawing from Gaza the day after he became president. Obama got his view of Israel from liberal Jews back in Chicago and both because of promises that he made to his early backers and because of Operation Cast Lead he was determined to revive the Israeli-Palestinian peace process that had briefly shown hope during President George W. Bush's last year in office. Obama told one private group in 2008 during his presidential campaign, "I think there is a strain within the pro–Israel community that says unless you adopt an unwavering pro–Likud approach to Israel that you are anti–Israel, and that cannot be the measure of our friendship with Israel." Netanyahu had clearly preferred a McCain victory in the 2008 presidential election to the actual outcome.[13]

In May Obama traveled to Cairo and make a speech on Middle East policy that offended Israelis because it seemed to tie Israel's right to exist to the Holocaust rather than their historic presence in Eretz Israel/Palestine over three millennia and the right of self-determination. The following month, Netanyahu traveled to Bar Ilan University, the main Orthodox Jewish university in Israel, to give a reply to Obama. Although he paid lip service to a two-state solution, he conditioned it on Palestinian recognition of Israel as a Jewish state. Netanyahu had arrived at the tactic of raising preconditions that he knew sounded reasonable to outsiders but were unacceptable to his peace "partners" as a means of avoiding negotiations. The idea was to create an endless set of loops that the other side would have to jump through in order to win independence. He also refuted the notion that Israel's right to exist was rooted in the Holocaust.[14]

Naftali Bennett, who was Netanyahu's chief of staff from 2006 to 2008 and later his rival as leader of the Jewish Home Party, said, "All the events that happened subsequent to his first premiership only reaffirmed

Prime Minister Benjamin Netanyahu meets American President Barak Obama at the Oval Office in the White House, May 18, 2009. Photograph by Moshe Milner.

and strengthened his beliefs." Bibi told his advisors that Obama knew little about the Middle East and might take Israel for granted while he reached out for support in the Arab world. During 2008 he had made clear that he believed that peace negotiations with the Palestinians were a waste of time.[15]

Obama and his advisors had decided that a settlement-construction freeze, like that which the George H.W. Bush administration had tried to get the Shamir government to enact in the early 1990s was the secret to reviving the peace process. This was supported both by many junior foreign policy advisors and by the Palestinian Authority who saw the lack of such a freeze as one of the prime causes for the failure of the 1990s Oslo process. Sharon agreed to a freeze as part of the Road Map agreement, but he never implemented it. After much pressure a ten-month settlement freeze was enacted in 2009–2010 but it was so full of exceptions that it looked like Swiss cheese: it did not apply to East Jerusalem, it did not apply to buildings already under construction, and it did not apply to buildings considered essential to the communal life of a settlement such as synagogues, schools, and nurseries. President Mahmoud Abbas did not think that the freeze went far enough as the U.S. government did not officially

Ten. Bibi Melekh Israel (King of Israel)

recognize the Israeli annexation of East Jerusalem he wanted it to apply to East Jerusalem as well. He finally agreed to sit down and negotiate during the final month of the freeze. During that month the Israeli team refused to discuss refugees, the status of Jerusalem or even borders with the Palestinians—they only discussed Israeli security needs. The Palestinians calculated that meeting these security "needs" would take up 40 percent of the West Bank. The Israelis even refused to accept from the Palestinian team a summary of Ehud Olmert's 2008 offer to them.

When the freeze expired in the run-up to midterm elections, Obama tried to bribe Netanyahu into extending the freeze with a generous offer of F-35 fighter jets, the latest in the American arsenal. But Netanyahu did not want to risk the stability of his coalition and refused. Israel-U.S. relations reached a nadir not seen since 1956 during this controversy. There were more new homes built during the period of the freeze than in 2008 and only slightly fewer than in 2009. After Netanyahu and Abbas finally met in September 2010 the talks quickly broke down. Netanyahu insisted that the IDF would have to remain in the Jordan Valley "for decades, many decades," which meant occupying a quarter of the West Bank indefinitely.[16]

Actual housing-unit starts in the occupied territories for the years 2008–10 are as follows: 2008 1,518; 2009 1,920; 2010 1,712. So the 2010 figure was 208 houses less than in 2009, but 194 more than in 2008 or just slightly closer to the 2008 figure but essentially midway between the two. Saeb Erekat, the chief Palestinian negotiator, predicted, "This will mean more settlement construction in 2010 than in 2008. You made a great effort to get a settlement freeze and you did not succeed.... Therefore, no settlement freeze at all, not for one hour. More construction in 2010 than in 2009. You know this."[17]

In the 2010 U.S. Senate race in Pennsylvania Democratic candidate Arlen Spector, a former long-term Republican who defected to avoid a tough primary challenge, won 76 percent of the Jewish vote—down only two percent from Obama's strong 78 percent showing among Jews in the 2008 election. Yet despite this when in December 2010 the Palestinian Authority sponsored a UN Security Council resolution demanding that Israel cease all settlement activity and several top Obama advisors including Secretary of State Clinton, Defense Secretary Robert Gates, and UN Ambassador Susan Rice all argued against an American veto, Obama had Rice veto at the last possible moment. As a result the Palestinians then turned to the Security Council for recognition as a state.[18]

In a speech on May 19, 2011, at the State Department, Obama said a peace agreement "should be based on the 1967 lines with mutually agreed [territorial] swaps." Bibi made a big fuss about Obama's mention of the

1967 lines, without mentioning land swaps, which Obama had mentioned. Netanyahu received a hero's welcome both at the America Israel Public Affairs Committee (AIPAC) and in the House of Representatives where he was cheered by both parties. Obama was furious at Netanyahu, but he was starting to lose support among Jewish Democrats in Congress. Obama treated Netanyahu icily and did not allow any photo ops of Bibi at the White House. Israeli officials announced the start of new construction two weeks before when Vice President Joe Biden was in Israel preparing for the Netanyahu visit. It almost appeared to be a deliberate provocation. Soon after this Obama abandoned his attempt to resolve the Israeli-Palestinian conflict and instead moved to the default American position of favoring Israel over the Palestinians. John Judis compares this as similar to what President Truman went through in 1948.[19]

American Jewish billionaire Haim Saban, who is both a major donor to the Democratic Party and the financer of a center for Middle East study at the Brookings Institution and has dual American-Israeli citizenship, announced that he would not contribute to President Obama's reelection campaign because Obama was not pro–Israel enough. Obama's speech to the United Nations in September 2011 signaled a full abandonment of evenhandedness in favor of pro–Israel partiality by Obama. Saban then came out in favor of Obama's reelection after the speech and a private meeting with the president. Saban donated $1 million to a Democratic super PAC and wrote an op-ed piece for the *New York Times* endorsing Obama's reelection.[20]

As Obama was making his pro–Israel speech at the UN, Abbas was attending to win recognition for Palestinian independence from the UN Security Council over American objections. Even the liberal pro–Israel, pro-peace lobby J Street opposed a strategy of granting conditional support for Palestinian statehood at the UN.[21]

Former Senate Majority Leader George Mitchell, who was appointed Middle East envoy on Obama's second day in office resigned at the start of 2011. He claimed that when he agreed to serve it was only for two years because he had a young son, whom he had been away from when he was the American mediator in Belfast from 1996 to 1999. At the end of 2011, Dennis Ross, who had been Middle East envoy under Clinton and was serving Obama in policy formulation related to Iran, resigned. "Ultimately there will be no peace without negotiations," wrote Ross in early 2012. "But there should also be no illusions about the prospects of a breakthrough any time soon."[22] Three high level veteran peacemakers from the Clinton administration served under Obama: Ross, Mitchell, and Richard Holbrooke. None had anywhere near comparable success under Obama.

Ten. Bibi Melekh Israel (King of Israel) 193

They failed to deliver in 2009–2012 because the United States was not nearly as strong and dominant as it had been under Clinton in the 1990s.[23]

When Mitchell was hired as Middle East envoy in 2009, National Security Advisor General James Jones promised him that former Middle East envoy Dennis Ross would not interfere with him and would only be working on Iran policy. Ross was skeptical about the wisdom of a settlement freeze. Ross managed to undercut Mitchell in policy discussions because Ross worked in the White House whereas Mitchell was usually either in the Middle East or at home with his family in New York. By the fall of 2010 Ross was firmly in control of Israel policy. "Dennis is very good at telling politicians why they don't have to do what they don't want to do anyway," said one outside expert. Ross was arguing throughout for "preemptive capitulations" to Netanyahu's coalition guidelines.[24]

Following the disengagement from Gaza and the subsequent launching of rockets by Hamas and other organizations at Israel, the Israeli government became determined to cause the overthrow of the Hamas government, which took power in a short civil war with Fatah in the summer of 2007. This led leftist sympathizers in Europe and Muslims in other countries, especially Turkey, to organize relief convoys to break the Israeli siege of Gaza. Israel allowed enough food and medicine to get through to ensure that the Palestinian population was not starving but that it suffered considerably. All supplies arriving from abroad were subject to search and confiscation if they were on a list of prohibited items. Residents in Gaza dug many underground tunnels into Egypt so that supplies could be smuggled into Gaza. Entrepreneurs would allow Hamas to use the tunnels to smuggle weapons as long as they could smuggle in scarce supplies at a tidy profit. Egypt cooperated with the Israeli siege except when a Muslim Brotherhood government was in power in Cairo in 2011–2012.

In the early morning hours of May 31, 2010, Israeli commandos boarded the Turkish built but Comoros registered ferry ship MV *Mavi Marmara*, which had been purchased by a Turkish charity organization, the IHH, which is considered by Israel and the Netherlands to be a terrorist organization due to its links with Hamas and al–Qaeda but is considered to be a charity organization by most other countries. The Israeli Navy had intercepted the flotilla of blockade runners sailing from Turkey and ordered them to go to Ashdod to be searched for contraband. But as this would have been contrary to the whole purpose of the flotilla they did not comply. The passengers of the ship resisted the boarding and ten Turkish citizens were killed and ten Israeli soldiers wounded, one seriously. The incident led to a rupture in relations between Turkey and Israel. In 2013 Netanyahu finally backed down and issued an apology to Turkey and agreed to pay compensation for the dead. Before the incident Deputy Foreign Minister Danny Ayalon, a professional diplomat who was elected on the Israel Beitenu list in 2008, had made a point of dressing down the Turkish ambassador over a Turkish television series that some in Israel considered anti–Semitic. During the discussion he had the ambassador sit on a seat that was lower than his own so that he looked down on him.[25]

The other major item that occupied the attention and energies of various members of Netanyahu's coalition and the Right in general was the attempt to turn the Middle East's "only democracy" into a very illiberal democracy, possibly to make for a better fit for its environment. Avigdor Lieberman had championed the idea of making Israel's Arab citizens take an oath of loyalty to the country. There were also measures to cut off foreign funding for non-governmental organizations in Israel that were critical of the government or were favorable to the Palestinians. And there was a bill introduced to prohibit boycotts of Israeli companies or products even if these boycotts were confined only to goods produced in the occupied territories. Under the bill anyone who advocated or supported a boycott would be liable for damages without the company necessarily having to prove causation. These bills were favorites of Israel Beitenu, the National Religious Party/Jewish Home, and the Likud.[26]

In November 2012 the Netanyahu government carried out another mini-war in Gaza: Operation Pillar of Smoke. This one was limited solely to aerial bombardment of the strip without a ground invasion. The eight-day operation was in response to the launch of over a hundred rockets in a 24-hour period, and attacks on Israeli forces patrolling near Gaza. The Palestinians launched some 1,456 rockets into Israel from Gaza and another 142 that fell short into Gaza. Israeli casualties were six dead, 240 wounded and another 200 treated for anxiety disorders. The Palestinians suffered 133 killed and some 840 wounded from over 1500 Israeli airstrikes into Gaza. Israel's right of defense was recognized by most Western democracies.[27]

Throughout 2011 and 2012 Bibi kept up pressure on Western governments to put economic pressure on Iran through economic sanctions over its alleged development of nuclear weapons. It did this through an elaborate game of chicken in which stories were continuously fed to the Western media, particularly in Britain, Canada, and the United States that speculated on Israel's willingness to engage in a unilateral series of conventional air strikes designed to destroy Iran's nuclear infrastructure. Such an effort served three separate purposes for Netanyahu. First, it eventually led to Iran's Western trading partners enacting tough economic sanctions against Iran. This had the effect of limiting the amount of money that Iran could devote to its nuclear effort and the amount of discretionary income it had to spend on aid to organizations like Palestinian Islamic Jihad, Hamas, and Hezbollah. Second, these stories combined with those on events related to developments in Egypt, Syria and elsewhere in the Arab world tied to the Arab spring soaked up much of the printer's ink devoted to the Middle East so that much less was available to focus on Israel's settlement efforts in the West Bank. Third, this effort and the speeches that Bibi devoted to the Middle East led to him being perceived within Israel as the leading advocate of stopping Iran's nuclear effort. Iran has been perceived as Israel's main potential threat since the 1991 Gulf War destroyed much of Saddam Hussein's military infrastructure.

When President Obama began his second term it was with a new secretary of state. Hillary Clinton resigned in order to rest up before deciding whether or not to run for president in 2016. Obama's first choice, Ambassador to the UN Susan Rice, was eliminated as a victim of the scandal of the Benghazi affair and had to settle for becoming national security advisor. Senator John Kerry, the 2004 Democratic presidential nominee, was chosen as second choice. Kerry came into office focused on the "old politics" of the Middle East, rather than on the "new politics" of East Asia following Obama's 2011 tilt towards Asia. Kerry's top three items on his agenda were all focused on the Middle East: negotiating a "grand bargain" with Iran that would end its nuclear weapons development in exchange for a lifting of Western economic sanctions; mediating an end to Syria's civil war; and mediating a final settlement of the Israeli-Palestinian conflict. Kerry had actually known Netanyahu since the latter was living in Boston and as a senator he regularly shared a meal with Bibi when he was visiting Israel.

In July 2013 Kerry got the Israelis and Palestinians to start talks on a final settlement. On the eve of negotiations the Netanyahu government announced plans for 1,187 new housing units in East Jerusalem and the West Bank including in the city of Ariel deep within the West Bank. Netanyahu pledged that he would never divide Jerusalem as he formed his new government. Abbas agreed to participate in the talks largely in order to obtain $4 billion that Kerry promised to the Palestinian Authority. Hamas denounced the talks. Kerry at age 77 had, unlike his predecessor, no further electoral political ambitions and thus was free to take risks in a quest for peace. President Obama, told President Peres in March 2013, "I want to focus on the peace process and no one understands it better than you." This meant that Obama could have Kerry expend the time, effort, and political capital in this risky venture and then disown it if, as seemed likely to be the case, it went sour. When the talks started, head Palestinian negotiator Saeb

Erekat was opposed to entering into the talks and told Abbas this. "I just think that Netanyahu will take you, Kerry, and everyone for a ride," he said.[28]

In early October 2012 Netanyahu called new elections for January 22, 2013, after he failed to reach agreement within his coalition on the budget for the next year. In order to neutralize his greatest potential rival on the Right, Netanyahu formed an electoral alliance with the Israel Beitenu party of Avigdor Lieberman. The two parties ran as Likud Beitenu and obtained 31 seats, which was eleven seats less than the combined total for the two parties running separately in 2009 but still made it the largest party. Coming in second with 19 seats was the Yesh Atid (There is a Future) party, which was a centrist reform party similar to the Democratic Movement for Change in 1977, the Center Party in 1999, Shinui in 2001 and 2003, etc. This party appealed to the floating voter who tends to be intrigued by whatever is new but who stays in the center. Former journalist Shelly Yakhimovich led the Labor Party, purged of most of its generals after Barak split from the party in 2011, to win fifteen seats, while the Jewish Home (the old NRP under a new name) won 12 seats and Shas received eleven. Netanyahu proceeded to form a government based on Likud Beitenu (31), Tzipi Livni's Hatnua (6) Yesh Atid (19), and Jewish Home (12) by March 14, 2013. During the bargaining phase Yesh Atid and Jewish Home made a pact that neither would join the government without the other. Former Chief of Staff Moshe "Boogie" Ya'alon was made defense minister and Yair Lapid, the leader of Yesh Atid and son of Shinui leader Tommy Lapid, was made finance minister. His party's emphasis was on economic reform and ending financial aid to the ultra–Orthodox.[29] Jewish Home was willing to tolerate some religious reforms aimed at the ultra–Orthodox as long as support for the settlement effort in the West Bank continued.

Tzipi Livni was made justice minister in the new government and put in charge of negotiations with the Palestinians. Thus she was taking up a role that she handled as foreign minister under Ehud Olmert's government in 2007–08 and by Shimon Peres and Shlomo Ben-Ami during the Oslo process. Despite Livni's best efforts the negotiations came to an end in the spring of 2014 after Netanyahu went back on his word to release a group of 104 pre–Oslo era security prisoners. The process was near collapse by the winter of 2014, partly because Netanyahu had a coalition of parties full of people opposed to a two-state solution and for domestic American political reasons Kerry tended to appease Netanyahu when problems arose by siding with Israel.[30] In order to create confidence building measures at the start of negotiations the Israelis can either enact a settlement freeze, which Netanyahu was unwilling to do again, or release security prisoners. Netanyahu had already released a huge load of prisoners to obtain the release of Gilad Shalit from Hamas. He had been close to closing the deal on Shalit with Hamas in 2009 for the release of 460 prisoners but he got cold feet and backed down only to release many more—1,027—when he made the deal two years later.[31] He seemed willing to release a smaller group to appease Washington. In the end he was only willing to release about 80 of the 104, keeping the worst offenders locked up to salvage his political base.[32]

Two-thousand thirteen was a record year for new construction in the territories. In a meeting of young Likud supporters in the spring of 2014, Bibi boasted of having defied the Obama administration over settlement construction. "What matters is that we continue to head straight towards our goal even if at one time we walk left and another time we walk right," Netanyahu told the group. When a member of the group asked about negotiations with the Palestinians, Bibi replied, "About the what?" to general laughter.[33]

There had long been predictions of the outbreak of a Third Intifada, starting with the outbreak of the Arab Spring in the winter of 2011. Interestingly, the Arab Spring probably prevented a Third Intifada by keeping the Arab and international media focused on what was going on in Arab countries like Egypt, Tunisia, Bahrein, Yemen, Libya, Syria, and Iraq. But when three youths from a West Bank settlement were kidnapped while hitchhiking on June 12, the Israeli security forces were mobilized to search for the three and hundreds of Hamas activists in the West Bank were rounded up and detained. Then a racist group of Jerusalem Betar football fans kidnapped and burned to death a Palestinian youth.[34] Netanyahu publicly blamed Hamas for the kidnapping of the three settler youths, but could produce no evidence to back up this accusation. His real purpose seemed to be to bring about the collapse of a Palestinian unity agreement between Hamas and the Palestinian Authority. The agreement had largely taken place on terms favorable to the PA. Such unity threatened Netanyahu's excuse for failing to engage in serious peace negotiations—that because the Palestinians were not united under a single leadership negotiations were impossible.

Finally, Hamas felt compelled to start firing rockets at Israel in response to the arrests of its activists on the West Bank and Netanyahu had the excuse he needed to carry out a war in the Gaza Strip. Initially, as in 2008, the war began with a series of air strikes against known Hamas military sites in Gaza and suspected rocket launching positions. This produced an ever-growing total of Palestinian dead, mostly civilians, while the Iron Dome anti-missile system protected Israeli cities from Hamas rockets fired from Gaza. Finally the IDF mounted a ground invasion and

Israeli casualties began to mount as soldiers were killed by improvised explosive devices or attacked while exploring the maze of tunnels that lay under Gaza. Once the extensive tunnels were featured in the Israeli media along with the news that "kidnap kits" of handcuffs had been found so that Hamas terrorists could emerge from the tunnels inside Israel near a settlement and kidnap hostages, support for the war effort increased. Instead of seventy percent of the population supporting the war, the figure soared to about 90 percent.[35] The war finally came to an end with a ceasefire after fifty days of warfare that largely restored the situation to the status quo ante bellum. The final butcher's bill was more than 2200 dead, of which Israel suffered only 69 dead—64 soldiers and five civilians. But as in Operation Cast Led in 2008–09, the war did not boost the popularity of those who prosecuted it once it was over. The Israeli public did not feel that they were safe from another round breaking out anytime in the future.[36] It would seem that Netanyahu is quite content to return to Gaza every few years in order "to mow the grass." This will likely increasingly erode the image of Israel as a responsible law-abiding nation within Europe and help to lead to the resurgence of anti–Semitism and anti–Semitic attitudes within European politics.[37]

Benjamin Netanyahu's long-term goal seems to be to break David Ben-Gurion's record for longevity as prime minister. He has already broken Yitzhak Shamir's runner-up status of over six years in 1983–84 and 1987–92. Netanyahu is at eight years and counting. Ben-Gurion served for a bit more than thirteen years between May 1948 and June 1963. As Netanyahu manages to last for about three years between elections, he will need to fight and win two more elections in order to beat Ben-Gurion's record. Netanyahu seems to be more focused on being prime minister than on doing anything as prime minister. Because he is leader of the Likud, a former paramilitary party turned settler party, he will likely have to avoid concluding a peace settlement with the Palestinians and continue building settlements in order to keep his electorate happy. Israeli academic Ze'ev Sternhell said, "I consider AIPAC's role to have been absolutely disastrous, because it prevents any possibility to move with the Palestinians. We cannot move without American intervention—but we are more or less free of American intervention. This is AIPAC's job. So the present coalition has this sentiment of impunity."[38]

Based on his sponsorship of Ron Lauder's mediation mission in 1998, Netanyahu would probably be amenable to giving back the Golan to Syria in exchange for peace provided that a credible Syrian government existed that wanted to and could politically afford to make peace with Israel. Such a government appears a long time off.

Ten. Bibi Melekh Israel (King of Israel)

What is Benjamin Netanyahu's legacy for Israel and the Likud? First, along with Sharon, Netanyahu played a role in sanctioning the atmosphere of incitement that led to the murder of Yitzhak Rabin in 1995. Netanyahu then took a peace process that was struggling but still healthy, and turned it over in a very sick condition to Ehud Barak who let it die. In his second and third terms, Bibi has concentrated on settling the West Bank, fending off demands for negotiations, and focusing the attention of the West on Iran's nuclear effort. If Kerry is able to negotiate a deal with Iran that results in Iran not developing a bomb, then much of the credit should go to Netanyahu. But if Mahmoud Abbas retires from office without ever having become prime minister of an independent Palestine, much of the credit or blame can also go to Netanyahu, who is carrying on in the tradition of Sharon.

Netanyahu's legacy for the Likud is probably the ties that he constructed between the Likud and the Republican Party in the United States. By building this relationship in the early 1990s when he was opposition leader, Netanyahu laid the foundation for Sharon's very close relationship with George W. Bush. However, the cost for this is the destruction of the bipartisan support enjoyed by Israel in the United States from the Nixon administration to the George W. Bush administration. Obama strongly supports the security of Israel, but the relationship between Obama and Netanyahu was very cold—colder than that between Eisenhower and Ben-Gurion.

His other legacy for the Likud is that by supporting the voter reform law in 1992 along with Labor, he led to a situation that destroyed the two-party dominant system that lasted in Israel from 1974 to 1996. The Likud Party now has a caucus of MKs that numbers in the high 20s to low 30s rather than one that numbers in the low 40s to mid–40s, i.e., a quarter of the Knesset rather than a third. This has created a situation where it is much more difficult for a prime minister to govern because the major compromises he makes are no longer within his ruling party but between the ruling party and its many coalition partners. This makes a two-state solution even more difficult to conceive of.

Eleven

The Future of the Likud

Predictions, especially about the future, are a hazardous business. What one has to go on is the past and present and the conclusions that come from an analysis of this, and a comparison with similar phenomena elsewhere.

The closest equivalent to the Likud in the West is probably the Fianna Fail party in Ireland. Fianna Fail was founded in the spring of 1926—a year after the Revisionist Party was founded—and like Herut was a continuity paramilitary party. Eamon de Valera, was, like both Ze'ev Jabotinsky and Menahem Begin, a charismatic ideologue. He participated in the Easter Rising in Dublin in April 1916 as the commander of Boland's Mill, one of the outposts that held out until the end of the rebellion. Thus, like Jabotinsky in the Jewish Legion in the Jordan Valley of Palestine in 1918 or Begin and Shamir in Tel Aviv in the 1940s, he had the basis of a myth in his background. During the Irish War of Independence of 1919–21 he served as president of the Republic. Then during the Irish Civil War of 1922–23 he served as the political leader of the rebel anti-treaty forces. Like Begin and Shamir, he was a simple man of modest material means and desires, and he served as leader of the party for its first four decades first as Taoiseach (prime minister) and then as president of the Republic.

Fianna Fail was a paramilitary party based on those who fought first in the War of Independence and then on the anti–Treaty side in the Irish Civil War. It emphasized a conservative brand of nationalism based economically on autarky and an agricultural economy and politically on irredentism and hostility towards the United Kingdom. It lost its last paramilitary trappings in 1973 with the retirement from politics of the last major participants in the Civil War fifty years before. This corresponds to the Likud losing its last paramilitary vestiges with the retirement of Shamir in 1993. The first two party leaders were Eamon de Valera and Sean Lemass who both participated in the Easter Rising, the War of Independence and the Civil War. Lemass retired as prime minister in 1966 and De Valera as president in 1973. Because Ireland lacked real external military threats and enemies, it had no need like Israel to develop a class of military politicians. Although in Richard Mulcahy, a former general during the Civil War era on the pro–Treaty side, Fine Gael did have a military politician as leader. As an alternative source of celebrity politicians athletes developed a role in Irish politics. Sportsmen who excelled in Gaelic football, soccer, and cricket had a future in Irish politics. Fianna Fail had its first athlete leader in Jack Lynch who became Taoiseach in November 1966 after emerging as a compromise party leader in 1966 following the retirement of Lemass. This is similar to what happened to Golda Meir in 1969.

Irish politics, particularly in the Republic, has a long tradition of family-controlled parliamentary seats where a seat is passed from father to son or daughter or from uncle to nephew or niece. Thus a group of princes emerged in both Fianna Fail and Fine Gael. Jack Lynch retired in December 1979 and was followed by Charles Haughey, who was the son-in-law of Lemass and thus a prince. He also turned out to be very corrupt and thus the equivalent of a Sharon or an Olmert.

Haughey was finally forced to retire from politics in 1992 and was followed by industrialist and self-made man Albert Reynolds. Reynolds as a successful dance hall and band promoter on the island in the 1950s and 1960s and then the owner of a pet food company is similar to Netanyahu as the businessman turned politician. Reynolds after only two years was forced out of office, but not before starting the ultimately successful Northern Ireland peace process. He was quickly followed by Bertie Ahern, a successful Dublin politician who was a protégé of Haughey's and a second-generation Fianna Fail supporter, if not exactly a prince. Ahern was also corrupt and a machine politician who knew how to take care of his constituents.[1]

The first big change for Fianna Fail was in the late 1980s when it was forced to enter into coalition governments with the Progressive Democrats and the Irish Labour Party. Previously the party had governed solo with either minority governments or support from independents in the Dail. This change made Irish politics much more comparable to Israeli politics. The next big change was when the property crash of 2010 led to Fianna Fail losing, at least temporarily, its status as Ireland's largest political party. Tired of decades of corruption voters abandoned it by the thousands and tens of thousands in the 2011 election.

In the post–Ahern era Fianna Fail has had two party leaders, Brian Cowen, a lawyer who became a professional politician and Michael Martin, who qualified as a history teacher but only taught for a year before becoming a professional politician. Cowen as minister of foreign affairs played a major role in the post–1998 peace process in Northern Ireland.[2]

Fianna Fail started as a paramilitary party and developed into a populist nationalist party with key support from certain economic sectors such as property developers, publicans, and others dependent on government largesse or favoritism. Under Albert Reynolds and Bertie Ahern it eventually dropped its irredentism as part of the Northern Ireland peace process in exchange for London giving up its legal claim to Northern Ireland. This proved possible because Ireland after joining the Common Market with Britain in 1973 became integrated economically and politically into Western Europe. It was also relatively easy because it never actually controlled Northern Ireland.[3] It also benefitted in this regard from the increasing secularity in Ireland during the 1990s as the Catholic Church in Ireland suffered from a number of embarrassing scandals involving both prominent clergy and the church as an institution and from the Celtic Tiger economy of the 1990s.[4] Thus, Dublin giving up its claim on Northern Ireland was similar to the Herut Party giving up its claim to Jordan during the 1960s and 1970s, although it took a while longer for the Likud to give up its claim on Jordan on behalf of the Palestinians.

So, if De Valera and Lemass can be seen as the equivalent of Begin and Shamir respectively, then it might be said that Jack Lynch is the equivalent of Ariel Sharon, and Netanyahu is the equivalent of a combination of Reynolds and Ahern. So, if the Likud follows the development of Fianna Fail further in its arc, its next leaders will be professional politicians who are not as flamboyant as someone like Netanyahu. Someone like Dan Meridor or Limor Livnat would fit the bill. But is this actually realistic considering the influence that the settlers now have in the party? Netanyahu's second ministry reflected the growing power of the settlers and the waning influence of the liberal strain in the Likud represented by Benny Begin and Dan Meridor.

What do most Likud leaders have in common? They seem to have three things in common: a fidelity to Revisionist ideology as developed by Jabotinsky and Begin, a prominent military or underground background, and a great facility with both the spoken and written word in several languages. These three things combined to create a sort of charisma around the leader: around Jabotinsky as Rosh Betar and Etzel commander, around Begin as haMefeked (the commander), and around Netanyahu and Sharon, the commandos. Shamir is the major exception. Shamir was a man of few

Eleven. The Future of the Likud

words who did not make major speeches on the stump. Although probably the most talented in military terms as a planner after Sharon he never served in the IDF.

Jabotinsky spoke ten languages, Begin seven, Shamir five, Sharon three or four,[5] and Netanyahu two. But all the leaders could speak in the languages that were necessary to communicate with their followers and to deal diplomatically with their foreign allies. The difference was that by the end of the twentieth century the vast majority of Jews spoke either Hebrew or English, or both. Jabotinsky, Begin and Shamir picked up several of their languages in the diaspora. In Poland most Zionist Jews would know at least Hebrew or Yiddish, if not both, and Polish. Both Jabotinsky and Begin had a talent for languages. Jabotinsky used them as professional tools as a journalist and Zionist activist and Begin imitated his mentor. Shamir worked in the Mossad during the era of the alliance with France and thus acquired the one language that he did not have a natural need for. Sharon spoke Russian and Hebrew at home and grew up during the mandate when knowing some English was a necessity. Netanyahu lived as a child in both countries of the two languages that he developed a native fluency in and he returned to the United States as an adult to work.

Jabotinsky and Begin both carefully practiced the art of oratory. Begin consciously copied the gestures of Jabotinsky, his mentor. Both were demagogues to a certain extent knowing the power of words and gestures and their combination for effect. Jabotinsky, Begin, Sharon, and Netanyahu were all from the professional class. Jabotinsky was a journalist and writer, Begin was a lawyer, and Netanyahu was an architect. Sharon was a professional officer and very talented—probably Israel's most talented field general since Yigal Allon. Shamir was a professional assassin and spy.

Jabotinsky, Begin, Sharon, and, to a lesser extent, Netanyahu were/are all charismatic politicians. Jabotinsky combined his literary talent, creation of the Jewish Legion and prison time to create a charismatic persona as the talented leader ready to suffer for his people. Begin did the same thing with his time in the Gulag and in the underground. Shamir, possibly because he had blood on his hands (to use the modern Israeli expression) and because he was naturally shier than either Jabotinsky or Begin was unable to create this same type of persona. It is hard to be opposed to terrorism when one is actually a former terrorist. Shamir's prison time though fits into this image of the Revisionist leader created by Jabotinsky and Begin. Among Labor politicians, few, with the exception of Dayan, spent much time in prison. But much of the support is based around taking a hard line against the Arabs. This has been the defining feature of Likud leaders. The only Likud leader to make a major withdrawal from an area of mandatory Palestine/Eretz Israel was the one leader who was not raised on Revisionist ideology. And his move now appears to his former followers to have been a major mistake.

When it comes to defense and foreign policy—the Arab question—which has been the focus of Revisionism, the party has supported a combination of military force and inside democratic pressure within the country that was the Zionists' main ally in order to obtain its goals. Jabotinsky's iron wall philosophy has become nearly universal within Israel, if not universally acknowledged. The Revisionists conflated the mandatory boundaries with the historic area of Israelite settlement to produce an irredentism and expansionism based first on the 1920 mandatory borders and then on the post–1922 boundaries, i.e., Western Palestine.[6]

This accommodation was only done under political pressure while the Herut Party was still in opposition and looking for political allies. That external pressure inside Israel is now totally lacking because of the relative collapse of the Left since 1977 and especially since 2001. It is possible that external pressure from abroad such as from Washington could serve as a substitute but that appears not to be feasible due to the degree of Republican Party-Likud coordination dating from Netanyahu's cultivation of this from the 1980s to the present and the structure of the American presidential system with its division of powers and checks and balances. The Likud has probably reached the end of its territorial flexibility. But it can still give up territory that is occupied by Israel and was not part of Eretz Israel or was peripheral to the Land of Israel such as Gaza and the Golan. But it must do so in a way that promises to enhance Israel's security rather than to degrade it.

Netanyahu is likely to approach negotiations with the Assad regime or a successor with caution the way he approached them in 1998 or the way Barak approached them in 1999–2000. In Gaza Israel's iron wall could increasingly face a Palestinian iron, concrete and flesh wall that through a combination of increasing casualties to Israeli soldiers and attrition to Israel's image in the West, could force Israel to eventually stop mowing the lawn and simply let the grass grow. This then will be when we see Hamas struggling with a parallel process of irredentism and accommodation. But Hamas's irredentism will find much more support in the region than Israel's irredentism finds in either the region or in Europe. Whether increasing European displays of anti–Semitism will encourage reflection in Israel or merely a further retreat into the mental ghetto—a Masada or Samson complex, only time will tell.

Likud leaders can be divided ideologically into two broad groups: the rigid ideologues and the more flexible pragmatists or opportunists. In the former group I would place Jabotinsky, Begin, Shamir and Netanyahu. In the latter group I would put Sharon. But there are degrees. Begin was flexible about going after peace with Egypt and refusing to annex the West Bank in order to keep Dayan in his government. Netanyahu seems to be rigid ideologically in terms of territorial issues, but flexible in his presentation so that he seems much more flexible than he actually is. Netanyahu is willing to say that he will accept a Palestinian state, but then place so many conditions on it so as to keep it from arising. Sharon was probably similar in regard to the West Bank but was willing to withdraw from Gaza. And he was willing to adopt some of the language of the Left: "occupation of another people," etc.

Shamir was in a class by himself: rigid in both practice and rhetoric. Shamir refused to support Begin's peace policy with Egypt, but muted his opposition for the sake of his career. He wanted to stay with Begin, whom he respected, rather than join Geula Cohen, whom he did not. Because of a lack of a moderate Syrian leader comparable to either Sadat in Egypt or Hussein in Jordan, there is little opportunity for the Likud's moderates to demonstrate their differences from the hard liners.

With the weakening of the two-party-dominant system thanks to Netanyahu siding with the Labor Party in support of electoral "reform," the action on the Israeli Right is in some of the Likud's nationalist rival parties such as Jewish Home and Israel Beitenu. Yair Shamir, the last prince to enter the arena, with an impressive background in both the IAF and the private sector has the potential to be the most impressive prince after Bibi. Israel Beitenu provides a vehicle that Tehiya failed to provide for Geula Cohen or the second Herut Party/National Union failed to provide for Benny Begin. Israeli Beitenu leader Avigdor Lieberman is similar to Netanyahu in his combination of hard-line positions regarding Israel's Arab minority and flexibility in regard to a Palestinian state. This author does not know if Shamir follows his father in his rigidity. If he does, he may have problems with Lieberman's ideological flexibility. The other potential leader of the Right is Naftali Bennett, the leader of the Jewish Home Party.

Chapter Notes

Preface and Acknowledgments

1. Charles Enderlin, *Shamir* (Paris: O. Orban, 1991). The president who served only a month was William H. Harrison; He died in 1841 after catching pneumonia during his inauguration and possibly suffered from a bacterial infection due to the bad hygienic conditions in Washington, D.C., around the White House. With such luck he should have been Jewish!

Chapter One

1. Jabotinsky's latest biographer, literary author Hillel Halkin, claims that Jabotinsky's family was not acculturated except by comparison with shtetl Jews. His mother spoke with a Yiddish accent and hired a prominent Hebrew scholar to teach Jabotinsky Hebrew for his bar mitzvah and that in fact he read Hebrew well enough to be able to translate between Russian and Hebrew as a teenager.
2. On Jabotinsky's early life see Michael Stanislawski, *Zionism and the Fin de Siecle* (Berkeley: University of California Press, 2001), pp. 121–35.
3. Ibid., pp. 149, 153–60. On Herzl's conversion see Ibid., pp. 3–16; on Nordau see Ibid., pp. 61–72.
4. Jehuda Reinharz, *Chaim Weizmann: The Making of a Zionist Leader* (New York: Oxford University Press, 1985), pp. 291, 326, 334.
5. Stanislawski, pp. 183–84, 187, 190, 202. Several Slavic languages have had a grammatic influence among Yiddish including Ukrainian.
6. Denis Brian, *The Seven Lives of Colonel Patterson* (Syracuse: Syracuse University Press, 2008), pp. 83–85.
7. Ibid., pp. 103–07.
8. Ibid., pp. 106–07, 114.
9. Ibid., pp. 109–110.
10. Ibid., pp. 115, 117, 121.
11. Ibid., pp. 127–28, 133, 137.
12. Ibid., pp. 142, 145, 147–48, 149.
13. Ibid., pp. 150–53; Zev Golan, *Free Jerusalem* (Jerusalem: Devora, 2003), pp. 28–29, 31.
14. Brian, p. 157.
15. Gideon Shimoni, *The Zionist Ideology* (Hanover, NH: Brandeis University Press, 1995), p. 237.
16. Golan, *Free Jerusalem*, pp. 19–20.
17. Shimoni, p. 245; Colin Shindler, *The Land Beyond Promise: Israel, Likud and the Zionist Dream* (London: I.B. Tauris, 2002), pp. 14–15, Stanislawski, pp. 220–21.
18. Avi Shlaim, *The Iron Wall: Israel and the Arab World* (New York: W.W. Norton, 2001), pp. 12–16; Jacob Shavit, *Jabotinsky and the Revisionist Movement 1925–1948* (London: Frank Cass, 1988), pp. 253, 255.
19. Mitchell Cohen, *Zion & State* (New York: Basil Blackwell, 1987), pp. 138, 141.
20. Shavit, pp. 26, 33.
21. Ibid., p. 86.
22. Shindler, *The Land Beyond Promise*, p. 19; Shimhoni, pp. 245–46; Shavit, p. 55.
23. Stanislawski, pp. 239–42.
24. Cohen, p. 143.
25. Shavit, pp. 64, 182, 209,220; Colin Shindler, *The Triumph of Military Zionism* (New York: I. B. Tauris, 2010), p. 184.
26. Shavit, pp. 46–47.

27. Shimon Peres (with David Landau), *Ben-Gurion: A Political Life* (New York: Schocken, 2011), pp. 44–45.
28. Ibid., pp. 45–46.
29. Cohen, p. 151; Peres, p. 47.
30. On the maximalists see Shindler, *Military Zionism*; Shavit, pp. 68–71; Shimoni, pp. 249–52.
31. Shabtai Teveth, *Ben-Gurion: The Burning Ground 1886–1948* (Boston: Houghton Mifflin, 1987), pp. 412, 414, 415; Peres, p. 52.
32. Teveth, pp. 422–23; Brian, p. 173; Peres, p. 53.
33. Ned Temko, *To Win or To Die* (New York: William Morrow, 1987), pp. 40–41.
34. Ibid., pp. 170–74.
35. Ibid., p. 174; Golan, *Free Jerusalem*, p. 184. The two were Abdul Magid and Issa al-Abras.
36. Teveth, pp. 481–88; Peres, pp. 54, 55.
37. Shavit, pp. 187, 213, 215–16.
38. Ibid., p. 217; Yaacov Eliav, *Wanted* (New York: Shengold, 1984), pp. 34, 38; Golan, pp. 97–134 for an account of early Etzel reprisal actions.
39. Stanislawski, pp. 223–36.
40. Ibid., pp. 229–38. This author has read *The Five* but not *Samson*.
41. Shimoni, pp. 373–76; Kati Marton, *A Death in Jerusalem* (New York: Pantheon, 1994), p. 49; Eliav, p. 26; Golan, p. 196.
42. Zev Golan, *Stern: The Man and His Gang* (Tel Aviv: Yair, 2011), pp. 15, 18, 20, 22–24.
43. Shavit, pp. 97–98; J. Bowyer Bell, *Terror Out of Zion* (New York: Discus, 1978), pp. 30, 44–45, 56–57; Eliav, pp 59, 61–65; Golan, pp. 108, 110–12.
44. Temko, pp. 46–48.
45. Shavit, p. 221.
46. Ibid., pp. 228–29; Golan, pp. 167–69.
47. Golan, p. 175.
48. Ibid., pp. 171, 174.
49. The other two were that the Palestine mandatory authorities would be pro-Arab and that the Arabs would not be ready to make peace with the Zionists for at least a generation of two.
50. Benzion Netanyahu, *The Founding Fathers of Zionism* (Noble, OK: Balfour Books, 2012), p. 228.
51. Ibid., p. 229.
52. Golan, pp. 154–55, 166.
53. Rafael Medoff, *Militant Zionism in America: The Rise and Impact of the Jabotinsky Movement in the United States, 1926–1948* (Tuscaloosa: University of Alabama Press, 2002), pp. 47–48.
54. Ibid., pp. 49–50; Golan, pp. 166–67.
55. Medoff, pp. 53, 58–60, 62.
56. Ibid., p. 63; Brian, p. 193; Peres, p. 55.
57. Netanyahu, *Founding Fathers*, pp. 223–27.

Chapter Two

1. Avi Shilon, *Menachem Begin: A Life* (New Haven: Yale University Press, 2012), pp. 1–4, 7.
2. Ibid., pp. 6, 11.
3. Ibid., p. 13; Ned Temko, *To Win or To Die: A Personal Portrait of Menachem Begin* (New York: William Morrow, 1987), p. 33; Eitan Haber, *Menachem Begin: The Man and the Legend* (New York: Dell, 1978), p. 39.
4. Shilon, p. 13.
5. Temko, p. 39; Shilon, p. 11.
6. Shilon, pp. 13, 16; Haim Misgav, *Conversations with Yitzhak Shamir* (New York: Talpiot, 2000), p. 15; Zev Golan, *Free Jerusalem* (Jerusalem: Devora, 2003), p. 18.
7. Shilon, pp. 12–13.
8. Temko, pp. 44–45.
9. Shilon, pp. 19–20; Temko, pp. 46–48; Haber, pp. 81–84.
10. Temko, pp. 49, 52–53.
11. Shilon, pp. 25–29; Haber, pp. 86–94; Golan, p. 163.
12. Haber, pp. 94–113; Shilon, pp. 29–34.
13. Shilon, p. 34.
14. Menahem Begin, *White Nights: The Story of a Prisoner in Russia* (New York: Harper & Row, 1977), pp. 138, 140, 141–48.
15. Ibid., pp. 150–54, 177–79, 183.
16. Ibid., pp. 191, 194.
17. Ibid., pp. 204, 208.
18. Temko, pp. 64–65.
19. Begin, pp. 212, 215–18.
20. Ibid., pp. 135–36; Shilon, p. 30.
21. Shilon, pp. 39–40, 42.
22. J. Bowyer Bell, *Terror out of Zion: The Shock Troops of Israeli Independence* (New York: Avon, 1978), pp. 80, 86.
23. Nicholas Bethell, *The Palestine Triangle: The Struggle for the Holy Land 1935–1948* (New York: G. P. Putnam's Sons, 1979), p. 129.
24. Yaacov Eliav, *Wanted* (New York: Shengold, 1984), pp. 171–72.
25. Bell, pp. 89–90; Shilon, p. 42; Haber, p. 148.
26. Temko, p. 54; Shilon, p. 44.
27. Bell, pp. 72–73; Shilon, p. 43.
28. Shilon, p. 44.
29. Ibid., pp. 46–47.
30. Ibid., pp. 49–50; Bell, pp. 139–41.
31. Bell, pp. 133–34.
32. Bethell, pp. 175, 178–79.
33. Bell, pp. 159–60.

34. Ibid., p. 166; Bethell, pp. 188–91;
35. Bell, pp. 162–66; Bethell, p. 193.
36. Bell, p. 169.
37. Ibid., pp. 156–57; Haber, pp. 227–30
38. Bethell, p. 180.
39. Ibid., pp. 193, 209.
40. Ibid., pp. 211, 214–15, 246.
41. Temko, p. 88; Bethell, pp. 249, 253.
42. Bethell, pp. 254, 260–61.
43. Ibid., pp. 249, 253–54, 257, 263, 266.
44. Ibid., p. 267.
45. Bell, pp. 284–85, 295–99; Amos Perlmutter, *The Life and Times of Menachem Begin* (Garden City, NY: Doubleday, 1987), p. 156.
46. Bell, pp. 298–99.
47. Ibid., pp. 366–72; Larry Collins and Dominique Lapierre, *O Jerusalem* (New York: Touchstone, 1972), pp. 256, 273–76, 280–81, 287;Perlmutter, p. 214. See Benny Morris, *1948* (New Haven: Yale University Press, 2008), pp. 127–28 for the lower figures.
48. Perlmutter, pp. 218–34 for a pro–Hagana account and Bow, pp. 218–34 for a pro–Hagana account and Bell, pp. 400–11 for a pro–Etzel account.
49. Perlmutter, pp. 186–91; Bethell, p. 358.
50. On Lehi's politics and foreign policy see Joseph Heller, *LEHI: Ideology and Politics: 1940–49* (Jerusalem:Keter, 1989).

Chapter Three

1. There are three countries in the West with a long history of paramilitary parties: Israel, Ireland and Northern Ireland. Northern Ireland has mainly political-wing parties that were tied to a still-operating military wing such as the IRA, UDA, or UVF. Ireland continued to have paramiltary parties after the two mentioned as various leaders separated from the IRA and formed their own parties like Cumann naPoblachta in the 1940s and Sinn Fein: the Workers' Party in the 1980s, which eventually became the Democratic Left before merging into the Irish Labour Party. .
2. Ned Temko, *To Win or To Die: A Personal Portrait of Menachem Begin* (New York: William Morrow, 1987), pp. 128–30; Amos Perlmutter, *The Life and Times of Menachem Begin* (Garden City, NY: Doubleday, 1987), pp. 241–46.
3. Temko, pp. 131–33, 140.
4. Ibid., pp. 134–36; Avi Shilon, *Menachem Begin: A Life* (New Haven: Yale University Press, 2012), pp. 162–64, 167.
5. Temko, pp. 136–40.
6. Ibid., p. 131.
7. Ibid., pp. 164–68; Shilon, pp. 195–99; Perlmutter, pp. 269–71.
8. Temko, pp. 144, 172; Peter Y. Medding, *The Founding of Israeli Democracy 1948–1967* (New York: Oxford University Press, 1990), pp. 65–70, 197; Perlmutter, p. 277.
9. Temko, pp. 169–70; Perlmutter, pp. 281–87.
10. Medding, pp. 192–93, 199, 226–28; Amos Perlmutter, *Israel: The Partitioned State, A Political History Since 1900* (New York: Charles Scribner's Sons, 1985), pp. 191–95; Asher Arian, *The Second Republic: Politics in Israel* (Chatham, NJ: Chatham House, 1998), pp. 1–18. The 1974 data is my own entry based on the combination of the emergence of the Likud and Yitzhak Rabin emerging as the first non–Mapai prime minister and the coming to power of the 1948 generation (Allon, Begin, Dayan, Rabin, Shamir, et al.).
11. Shilon, p. 210; Perlmutter, pp. 289–90.
12. Shilon, pp. 210, 217–18.
13. Ibid., p. 220.
14. Ibid., pp. 221–22.
15. Ibid., pp. 225, 229, 231; Temko, pp. 180–83.
16. Perlmutter, pp. 295–97, 307–11; Ariel Sharon, *Warrior* (New York: Simon & Schuster, 2001), pp. 280–86; Uzi Benziman, *Shaon: An Israeli Caeser* (New York: Adama, 1985), pp. 130–34; David Landau, *Arik: The Life of Ariel Sharon* (New York: Alfred Knopf, 2013), pp. 90–92.
17. Shilon, pp. 207, 229, 239–40.
18. Ibid., p. 253.
19. Ibid., pp. 241–43.
20. Ibid., pp. 244–45; Colin Shindler, *The Land Beyond Promise: Israel, Likud and the Zionist Dream* (London: I.B. Tauris, 2002), p. 78.
21. Shilon, pp. 245–46.
22. Dan Kurzman, *Soldier of Peace: The Life of Yitzhak Rabin* (New York: HarperCollins, 1998), p. 374. Ben-Gurion dismissed Allon prematurely from the IDF following the War of Independence and promoted Dayan before his time on the basis of their respective party memberships. This helped to exacerbate an already existing personal feud. Then in 1967 Dayan beat out Allon to become defense minister. When Rabin beat Peres in the Labor leadership contest in 1974 and became prime minister it was a kind of surrogate victory for Allon, although he probably felt that he should have been prime minister rather than Rabin.
23. Shindler, *The Land Beyond Promise*, pp. 77–82.

24. Ibid., pp. 343–46, 362; Robert Slater, *Rabin of Israel* (New York: St. Martin's Press, 1993), pp. 260–97; Shindler, *The Land Beyond Promise*, pp. 77–82.
25. Temko, pp. 195–96, Shilon, p. 252.
26. The reference here is to the American conservative movement that William F. Buckley and William Rusher founded in the mid–1950s.
27. Shilon, p. 258.

Chapter Four

1. Amos Perlmutter, *The Life and Times of Menachem Begin* (Garden City, NY: Doubleday, 1987), pp. 324, 331, 334.
2. Moshe Dayan, *Breakthrough* (New York: Alfred Knopf, 1981), pp. 1–2, 4, 7; Yehuda Avner, *The Prime Ministers* (London: The Toby Press, 2010), p. 356.
3. Daniel Gordis, *Menachem Begin: The Battle for Israel's Soul* (New York: Schocken, 2014), pp. 141, 142, 144, 146–48.
4. Ibid., p. 150; Gal Beckerman, *When They Come for Us, We'll Be Gone: The Epic Struggle to Save Soviet Jewry* (Boston: Mariner, 2010), p. 506.
5. Dayan was not noted for his work ethic, but for his brilliance and intuitive grasp of a situation. He had few real friends and if something did not interest him he did not work on it.
6. Dayan, pp. 38–54.
7. Avner, pp. 359, 369, 459.
8. Gordis, pp. 152–53.
9. Dayan, pp. 55–74; Moredecai Bar-On, *Moshe Dayan: Israel's Controversial Hero* (New Haven: Yale University Press, 2012), p. 196.
10. Dayan, pp. 75–76.
11. Ibid., pp. 77, 82–83; Gordis, p. 161.
12. Dayan, pp. 91–97, 109.
13. Ibid., pp. 102–05; Slater, p. 407.
14. Dayan, pp. 110–14.
15. Ned Temko, *To Win or To Die: A Personal Portrait of Menachem Begin* (New York: Wlliam Morrow, 1987), pp. 198, 209; Gordis, p. 163, 165.
16. Anita Miller et al., *Sharon: Israel's Warrior Politician* (Chicago: Academy Chicago, 2002), pp. 136–38; Nir Hefez and Gadi Bloom, *Ariel Sharon* (New York: Random House, 2006), pp. 192–93.
17. Avner, p. 482; Gordis, p. 167.
18. William Quandt, *Camp David: Peacemaking and Politics* (Washington, D.C.: The Brooking's Institution Press, 1986), pp. 197–203
19. Gordis, pp. 161, 168, 171. See Sa'adia Touval, *The Peace Brokers* (Princeton: Princeton University Press, 1982), pp. 10–16, 327–29.
20. Dayan, pp. 259–84; Anita Shapira, *A History of Israel* (Waltham, MA: Brandeis University Press, 2012), p. 373; Avner, pp. 535–39; Gordis, pp. 165–66, 175, 176.
21. Gordis, pp. 177–78, 183.
22. Dayan, pp. 312–14.
23. On Weizman's decision to leave see his memoir, *The Battle for Peace* (New York: Bantam, 1981), pp. 383–85.
24. Avner, p. 535.
25. Uzi Benziman, *Sharon: An Israeli Caeser* (New York: Adama, 1985), p. 212; Ariel Sharon, *Warrior* (New York: Simon & Schuster, 2001), pp. 400–01; Hefez and Bloom, pp. 199–200.
26. Benziman, pp. 221, 224–25; Miller et al., p. 150.
27. Shapira, pp. 373, 375; Perlmutter, p. 361.
28. Sharon, pp. 382–83; Perlmutter, pp. 362–66.
29. Shapira, pp. 376–77; Avi Shilon, *Menachem Begin: A Life* (New Haven: Yale University Press, 2012), p. 442; Avner, pp. 553–57. Rabin signed a letter along with over a hundred MKs in 1991 thanking Begin for the decision to bomb Iraq.
30. Perlmutter, pp. 378–79.
31. Avner, pp. 580–82.
32. Gordis, pp. 199- 200; David Landau, *Arik: The Life of Ariel Sharon* (New York: Alfred Knopf, 2013), pp. 177–81.
33. Shapira, p. 380.
34. Hefez and Bloom, pp. 216–18; Miller et al., p. 162.
35. Miller et al., p. 162.
36. Benziman, pp. 242–44.
37. Gordis, pp. 202–05.
38. Howard M. Sachar, *A History of Israel From the Rise of Zionism to Our Time* (New York: Alfred Knopf, 1996), pp. 908–09.
39. Temko, p. 276.
40. Sachar, pp. 909–11; Hefez and Bloom, p. 235; Gilad Sharon, *Sharon: The Life of a Leader* (New York: HarperCollins, 2011), p. 275.
41. Sachar, pp. 911, 913. The mercenary was Eli Hobeika who defected to the Syrians after the Sabra and Shatila massacre.
42. Ibid., p. 914.
43. Ibid., pp. 914–15. The author was active in Peace Now when it was first formed until he left the country in August 1980.
44. Ibid., p. 915; Sharon, p. 509; Gordis, p. 215.
45. Avner, pp. 629, 632–33.
46. Temko, p. 287; Avner, pp. 658, 664.
47. Avner, pp. 669–75.
48. Hefez and Bloom, pp. 246–51; Sharon,

p. 522; Avner Falk, *Fratricide in the Holy Land* (Madison: University of Wisconsin Press, 2004), pp. 65–66.
49. Shapira, pp. 383, 386; Gordis, p. 214.
50. Temko, pp. 289–93; Shilon, pp. 427–31; Yitzhak Shamir, *Summing Up* (Boston: Little, Brown, 1994), p. 140; Avner, p. 678.
51. Shilon, pp. 443–46.
52. Avner, p. 371.
53. Ibid., pp. 364, 372.
54. Ibid., pp. 460, 464, 470, 471.
55. Ibid., pp. 541, 544–45.
56. Ibid., pp. 545–46.
57. Ibid., pp. 523–25.
58. Gordis, p. 154.
59. Zev Golan, *Stern: The Man and His Gang* (Tel Aviv: Yair, 2011), p. 226.

Chapter Five

1. Yitzhak Shamir, *Summing Up* (Boston: Little, Brown, 1994), pp. 1–4, 6; "Yitzhak Shamir, *Wikipedia*, accessed July 21, 2014, for birthdate.
2. Ibid., p. 11.
3. Ibid., pp. 7–8, 86.
4. Ibid., pp. 15–16.
5. Ibid., p. 23. This is probably an inelegant phrasing in one particular sentence as elsewhere in the memoir he said he participated in actions against the Arabs, which in the Etzel first took place in 1938.
6. Haim Misgav, *Conversations with Yitzhak Shamir* (New York: Talpiot, 2000), pp. 17, 24; Charles Enderlin, *Shamir* (Paris: Orban, 1991), p. 40.
7. Shamir, pp. 21–22; Zev Golan, *Free Jerusalem* (Jerusalem: Devora, 2003), p. 132.
8. Enderlin, *Shamir*, p. 80; Shamir, p. 31.
9. Golan, *Stern*, pp. 28, 30, 32.
10. Golan, *Stern*, pp. 25–26; Golan, *Jerusalem*, p. 211.
11. Golan, *Stern*, p. 33.
12. Ibid., p. 37.
13. Golan, *Jerusalem*, pp. 218, 222, 224–25.
14. Shamir, p. 35; Golan, *Stern*, p. 143.
15. Golan, *Jerusalem*, pp. 217, 226–27; Golan, *Stern*, p. 34.
16. Misgav, p. 32.
17. Golan, *Jerusalem*, pp. 160, 242; Golan, *Stern*, p. 156; Geula Cohen, *Woman of Violence* (New York: Holt, Rinehart and Winston, 1966), pp. 80–84; Ya'acov Eliav, *Wanted* (New York: Shengold, 1984), pp. 195, 219.
18. Gerold Frank, *The Deed* (New York: Simon & Schuster, 1963), pp. 124–26; Golan, *Jerusalem*, p. 238; Golan, *Stern*, p. 94.
19. Frank, pp. 129, 134–35, 140; Golan, *Jerusalem*, pp. 241–42.
20. Golan, *Stern*, pp. 36, 159–60.
21. Frank, pp. 147, 151–52, 153; Golan, *Jerusalem*, p. 209; Golan, *Stern*, p. 153.
22. Golan, *Jerusalem* p. 151; Nicholas Bethell, *The Palestine Triange: The Struggle for the Holy Land, 1935–1948* (New York: G. P. Putnam's Sons, 1979), p. 173.
23. Golan, *Jerusalem*, p. 155; Shamir, pp. 35, 61; Frank, p. 213.
24. Frank, pp. 181–84; Golan, *Jerusalem*, pp. 236–37; Golan, *Stern*, pp. 162–65.
25. J. Bowyer Bell, *Terror Out of Zion* (New York: Avon, 1978), pp. 111–15; Golan, *Stern*, p. 109. Bell claimed the number of attempts was five and Golan claimed that it was seven, both relied on the memories of participants decades after the events.
26. Frank, pp. 190–91,; Bethell, pp. 167–69, 181.
27. Shamir, pp. 52–53; Ned Temko, *To Win or To Die* (New York: William Morrow, 1987), p. 88.
28. Shamir, pp. 53–55.
29. Golan, *Stern*, pp. 102–09.
30. Bethell, pp. 180–87.
31. Ibid., p. 215; Kati Marton, *A Death in Jerusalem* (New York: Pantheon, 1994), p. 104.
32. Eliav, pp. 207–9, 212.
33. Ibid., pp. 214–15, 231.
34. Shamir, pp. 49–50; Marton, p. 92.
35. Golan, *Stern*, pp. 116–17.
36. Eliav, pp. 230–33, 236, 262.
37. Golan, *Jerusalem*, pp. 261–70 for a detailed description of the action; also Bell, p. 206; Golan, *Stern*, p. 253.
38. Shamir, p. 61; Bethell, pp. 270–71.
39. Shamir, pp. 63–65.
40. Ibid., pp. 65–67; Golan, *Stern*, p. 122.
41. Shamir, pp. 67–68, 71–73; Golan, *Jerusalem*, p. 284; Golan, *Stern*, p. 145.
42. Misgav, p. 48.
43. Marton, p. 182.
44. Ibid., pp. 183, 186, 191.
45. Ibid., pp. 191–93.
46. Bell, pp. 422–28.
47. Shamir, pp. 75–76; Golan, *Stern*, p. 140.
48. Marton, pp. 252, 255–57; Enderlin, *Shamir*, p. 246.
49. Shamir, pp. 47, 77; Bell, pp. 32, 437; Golan, *Stern*, p. 253 listed its size as 950 members, which is probably the number of people that ever belonged to it and from this can be subtracted the 127 killed either in action against the British or in the War of Independence.
50. Israel, unlike the U.S., has always had a fixed number of representatives (120) in its unicameral parliament, the Knesset. So as

the population increased the number of persons that each representative increased as well.

51. Shamir, pp. 77–78; Golan, *Stern*, p. 146.
52. Golan, *Stern*, p. 146; Dan Raviv and Yossi Melman, *Every Spy a Prince* (Boston: Houghton Mifflin, 1990), p. 52. Ben-Ellisar was in the Etzel instead of in Lehi.
53. Enderlin, *Shamir*, pp. 274, 277.
54. Misgav, p. 42 Shamir says he was in the Mossad for ten years. But Golan, *Stern*, p. 147 has him leaving in 1963—after only eight year.
55. Golan, *Stern*, pp. 143–46.
56. Dennis Eisenberg, Uri Dan and Eli Landau, *The Mossad—Inside Stories* (New York: Paddington Press, 1978), pp. 133–41.
57. Enderlin, *Shamir*, p. 279.
58. Eisenberg, et al., pp. 143, 180, 183, 184. Lotz ended up being arrested in a routine sweep arrest of German citizens in Egypt meant to pressure Bonn. He panicked and confessed in order to protect his undercover wife, a German intelligence agent. He spent several years in prison from mid–1965 to 1968 when he was traded as part of a prisoner swap following the 1967 war.
59. Ibid., pp. 185–86.
60. Ibid., p. 186; Raviv and Melman, p. 129; Golan, *Stern*, p. 147.
61. Golan, *Stern*, p. 147.
62. Gal Beckerman, *When They Come for Us, We'll Be Gone: The Epic Struggle to Save Soviet Jewry* (Boston: Mariner, 2010), pp. 164–65, 168.
63. Ibid., pp. 285, 292.
64. Golan, *Stern*, p. 148.
65. Enderlin, *Shamir*, p. 319.
66. Daniel Gordis, *Menachem Begin: The Battle for Israel's Soul* (New York: Schocken, 2014), pp. 190–91.
67. See Misgav for a confirmation of this.
68. Golan, *Stern*, p. 148.

Chapter Six

1. Yitzhak Shamir, *Summing Up* (Boston: Little, Brown, 1984), pp. 154–57.
2. Howard M. Sachar, *A History of Israel from the Rise of Zionism to Our Time* (New York: Alfred Knopf, 1996), pp. 895–96; Chaim Hertzog, *Living History* (New York: Pantheon, 1996), pp. 352–53; Shamir, pp. 151–52.
3. Nir Hefez and Gadi Bloom, *Ariel Sharon* (New York: Random House, 2006), p. 258; Ariel Sharon, *Warrior* (New York: Simon & Schuster, 2001), p. 529.
4. Shamir, pp. 166–70, 174; Sachar, pp. 957–58; Michael Bar-Zohar, *Shimon Peres: The Biography* (New York: Random House, 2007).
5. Colin Shindler, *The Land Beyond Promise* (New York: I. B. Tauris, 2002), p. 206; Asher Arian, *The Second Republic: Politics in Israel* (Chatham, NJ: Chatham House Publishers, 1998), pp. 118, 126; "Zalman Shoval," *Wikipedia*, accessed July 25, 2014.
6. Shamir, pp. 170–72l Bar-Zohar, *Shimon Peres*, pp. 388–89, 396; Michael Bar-Zohar, *Facing a Cruel Mirror* (New York: Charles Scribner's Sons, 1990), p. 151.
7. Bar-Zohar, *Cruel Mirror*, pp. 1–3.
8. Ibid., pp. 190–91; Glenn Frankel, *Beyond the Promised Land* (New York: Touchstone, 1996), pp. 251–55.
9. Hefez and Bloom, p. 280.; Bar-Zohar, *Cruel Mirror*, pp. 150–55, 203–6.
10. Bar-Zohar, *Cruel Mirror*, pp. 200, 212–16.
11. Frankel, pp. 124–25.
12. Hefez and Bloom, pp. 281–82; David Landau, *Arik: The Life of Ariel Sharon* (New York: Alfred Knopf, 2013), p. 254.
13. Robert Slater, *Rabin of Israel* (New York: St. Martin's Press, 1993), pp. 354–55; Shamir, p. 213. Shamir writes of the PLO rather than Amman, probably a reference to Weizman, but this was not true of the party as a whole in 1990.
14. Slater, pp. 356–57.
15. Shamir, p. 214.
16. Ibid., p. 219.
17. Ibid., pp. 221–22.
18. Moshe Arens, *Broken Covenant* (New York: Simon & Schuster, 1995)), p. 201.
19. Shamir, p. 223.
20. Ibid., p. 189.
21. Ibid., pp. 189–90.
22. Ibid., p. 225.
23. Arens, pp. 218, 220.
24. Ibid., p. 223.
25. Shamir, pp. 226–29.
26. Arens, pp. 227, 235–36, 238.
27. Shamir, p. 233.
28. Arens, p. 255; Shamir, pp. 236–37 for a list; Landau, p. 255.
29. Arens, p. 257; Frankel, pp. 309–10; Shamir, pp. 241–42.
30. Frankel, pp. 311–12; Shamir, pp. 244–46; Connie Bruck, "Friends of Israel," *The New Yorker* Sept. 1, 2014.
31. Frankel, p. 318; Shamir, pp. 249–51.
32. Slater, p. 376.
33. Frankel, pp. 317–18; Arens, pp. 264–69.
34. Frankel, p. 318; Arens, p. 272; Landau, p. 254.
35. Frankel, pp. 318–19; Arens, pp. 284, 287.

36. Slater, p. 380.
37. On Lincoln see any standard Lincoln biography. Clay ran for president five times and only came close to being elected once, in 1844. Peres ran for prime minister seven times, and was only elected once.
38. Slater, pp 389–92.
39. Arens, p. 296.
40. Hefez and Bloom, pp. 302–02.
41. Haim Misgav, *Conversations with Yitzhak Shamir* (New York: Talpiot, 2000), pp. 163–76.
42. Frankel, p. 28.
43. "Yitzhak Shamir," *Wikipedia*, accessed July 24, 2014.
44. Golan, *Stern*, pp. 206–15, 222.

Chapter Seven

1. Ariel Sharon, *Warrior* (New York: Simon & Schuster, 2001), pp. 12–13; Uzi Benziman, *Sharon: An Israeli Caesar* (New York: Adama, 1985), pp. 11–12; Anita Miller, Jordan Miller and Sigalit Zetouni, *Sharon: Israel's Warrior Politician* (Chicago: Academy Chicago, 2002), p. 3.
2. Ted Schwarz, *Walking with the Damned* (New York: Paragon House, 1992), pp. 90–92.
3. David Landau, *Arik: The Life of Ariel Sharon* (New York: Alfred Knopf, 2013), p. 4.
4. Sharon, pp. 15–16, 25, 35–36; Benziman, pp. 21–22.
5. Landau, p. 7.
6. Nir Hefez and Gadi Bloom, *Ariel Sharon* (New York: Random House, 2006), pp. 31–32; Sharon, pp. 15, 30–31, 36.
7. Landau, pp. 3, 5, 410; Sharon, pp. 36, 50.
8. Landau, pp. 13–18, 22–28.
9. Ibid., pp. 40–46.
10. The battle was later taught at a number of military staff colleges in NATO countries during the late Cold War period of the 1970s and 1980s.
11. Hefez and Bloom, pp. 86–89; Benziman, pp. 91–92.
12. Benziman, pp. 108–09.
13. This is an abridged version of my chapter on Sharon's military career found in Thomas G. Mitchell, *Israeli Military Politicians from Dayan to Barak* (Jefferson, NC: McFarland, 2015) and the sources used are the biographies mentioned in this chapter.
14. Miller et al., pp. 121–22.
15. Sharon, pp. 346–47; Nir Hefez and Gadi Bloom, *Ariel Sharon* (New York: Random House, 2006), pp. 181–84; Benziman, p. 186.
16. Benziman, pp. 187–200; Hefez and Bloom, pp. 185–88.

17. These were: Pinchas Lavon, Levy Eshkol, and Dayan. Sharon, p. 354; Benziman, p. 202.
18. Miller et al., pp. 136–38; Hefez and Bloom, pp. 192–93.
19. Benziman, p. 212; Sharon, pp. 400–01; Hefez and Bloom, pp. 199–200.
20. Sharon, pp. 432–35.
21. Miller et al., p. 129; Howard M. Sachar, *A History of Israel from the Rise of Zionism to Our Time*, 2d ed. (New York: Alfred Knopf, 1996), pp. 902–03; Landau, p. 248.
22. Landau, pp. 247–48. On these negotiations see Avi Shlaim, *Lion of Jordan: The Life of King Hussein in War and Peace* (New York: Alfred Knopf, 2008).
23. On this relationship and Sharon's plans see John Boykin, *Cursed Is the Peacemaker: The American Diplomat Versus the Israeli General, Beirut 1982* (Belmont, CA: Applegate Press, 2002); Ben Caspit and Ilan Kfir, *Netanyahu: The Road to Power* (Secaucus, NJ: Carol, 1998), p. 101.
24. "Ministry of Foreign Affairs (Israel)," and "Defense Ministry (Israel)," *Wikipedia*, accessed July 25, 2014.
25. Sharon, p. 530; Hefez and Bloom, pp. 258–59.
26. Uri Dan, *Ariel Sharon: An Intimate Portrait* (New York: Palgrave Macmillan, 2006), pp. 124–25; Miller et al., pp. 174–77.
27. Moshe Maoz, *Asad: The Sphinx of Damascus* (New York: Grove Weidenfeld, 1988), p. 168.
28. Hefez and Bloom, pp. 263, 275.
29. Ibid., pp. 264–65, 267.
30. Ibid., pp. 275–76; Dan, p. 77.
31. Hefez and Bloom, pp. 278–79.
32. Landau, pp. 252, 253.
33. Ibid., pp. 257–58.
34. Hefez and Bloom, pp. 290–91; Gilad Sharon, *Sharon: The Life of a Leader* (New York: HarperCollins, 2011), p. 303; Landau, p. 260.
35. Landau, p. 262.
36. Ibid., pp. 273–74.
37. Ibid., p. 275.
38. Hefez and Bloom, pp. 301–2.
39. Ibid., pp. 304–06, 309; Dan, pp. 135–37.
40. Landau, pp. 277–79.
41. Ibid., pp. 280–81.
42. Ibid., pp. 282–84.
43. Ibid., pp. 286–88. See previous Sharon chapter for info on 1947.
44. Ibid., pp. 293, 295.
45. Hefez and Bloom, pp. 317–18; Landau, p. 298.
46. G. Sharon, *pp.* 310–11.
47. Landau, pp. 304–7.

48. Hefez and Bloom, pp. 324–27; Landau, p. 298.
49. Landau, pp. 301, 303.
50. Freddy Eytan, *Ariel Sharon* (Paris: Studio 9, 2006), pp. 98–100; Hefez and Bloom, p. 327.
51. Landau, pp. 310, 313.
52. Anita Miller, Jordan Miller and Sigalit Zetouni, *Sharon: Israel's Warrior-Politician* (Chicago: Academy Chicago, 2002), pp. 241–44, 247–49.
53. Ibid., pp. 257–58; Landau, p. 316.
54. Landau, p. 318.
55. Ibid., pp. 321–25.
56. pp. 340–43.; Landau, p. 332.
57. Hefez and Bloom, p. 341; Landau, p. 338.
58. Ahron Bregman, *Elusive Peace: How the Holy Land Defeated America* (New York: Penguin, 2005), pp. 123–24, 125.
59. Bernard Wasserstein, *Divided Jerusalem* (London: Profile Books, 2002), p. 318.
60. Charles Enderlin, *Shattered Dreams: The Failure of the Peace Process in the Middle East, 1995–2002* (New York: Other Press, 2003), p. 303.
61. Hefez and Bloom, pp. 344–46; Miller et al pp. 300–02; G. Sharon, p. 346; Dennis Ross, *The Missing Peace* (New York: Farrar, Straus and Giroux, 2004), p. 728; Landau, p. 346.
62. Hefez and Bloom, pp. 348–49.
63. Ibid., pp. 350–55; Landau, p. 357.

Chapter Eight

1. Peter Beinart, *The Crisis of Zionism* (New York: Times Books, 2012), pp. 106–08; for a detailed discussion of Benzion Netanyahu in the 1940s in America see Rafael Medoff, *Militant Zionism in America: The Rise and Impact of the Jabotinsky Movement in the United States, 1926–1948* (Tuscaloosa: University of Alabama Press, 2002), pp. 53–218, passim.
2. Ben Caspit and Ilan Kfir, *Netanyahu: The Road to Power* (Secaucus, NJ: Carol, 1998), pp. 13–20. Unless otherwise indicated this will be the sole source for information on Netanyahu's career until 1993.
3. Ibid., pp. 33, 35, 37–38.
4. Ibid., pp. 41–43, 46, 48, 49, 53, 58.
5. Ibid., pp. 58, 60–61.
6. Ibid., pp. 63, 65, 67.
7. Ibid., pp. 24, 70, 72.
8. Ibid., pp. 73–76.
9. Ibid., pp. 82–84, 87–88.
10. Ibid., p. 22; Beinart, p. 106.
11. Beinart, pp. 109, 133.
12. Caspit and Kfir, pp. 90–92, 95–96, 112.
13. Ibid., pp. 98–99.
14. Ibid., pp. 102, 104, 106–07.
15. Ibid., pp. 113–14, 116.
16. Ibid., pp. 117, 123–25.
17. Ibid., pp. 126–27, 130–31, 133.
18. Ibid., pp. 135, 144, 148, 152–53.
19. Ibid., p. 153. This list could also include Yair Shamir, who has entered right-wing politics but not in the Likud and not in the 1990s.
20. Ibid., pp. 154, 160–62.
21. Ibid., p. 157.
22. Ibid., pp. 164, 168–70.
23. Ibid., pp. 170, 172–74.
24. Ibid., pp. 174–80.
25. Ibid., p. 181; David Landau, *Arik: The Life of Ariel Sharon* (New York: Alfred Knopf, 2013), p. 275.
26. Caspit and Kfir, pp. 182–85.
27. Ilan Peleg, "The Likud under Rabin II," in Robert O. Freedman, *Israel Under Rabin* (Boulder: Westview Press, 1995), pp. 158, 160.
28. This author had a good friend who was an American Likud supporter and so has a good feel for the bookshelf based on his.
29. Caspit and Kfir, pp. 186–87.
30. Ibid., pp. 208, 210–11, 212–13.
31. Ibid., pp. 215–19.
32. Ibid., pp. 222–23, 227.
33. Nif Hefez and Gadi Bloom, *Ariel Sharon* (New York: Random House, 2006), p. 315.
34. Itamar Rabinovich, *Waging Peace* (Princeton: Princeton University Press, 2004), p. 85; Caspit and Kfir, p. 225.
35. Caspit and Kfir, pp. 226, 228–29.
36. Ibid., pp. 231–35.
37. Ibid., pp. 242–44.; Michael Bar-Zohar, *Shimon Peres: The Biography* (New York: Random House, 2007), p. 467; Hirsh Goodman, *The Anatomy of Israel's Survival* (New York: Public Affairs, 2011), pp. 65–67.
38. Caspit and Kfir, pp. 247–50.
39. Ibid., pp. 257–59.
40. Ibid., pp. 260–61; Dennis Ross, *The Missing Peace* (New York: Farrar, Straus and Giroux, 2004), pp. 264–65.
41. Caspit and Kfir, pp. 262–64.
42. Ibid., p. 265; Ross, pp. 356–58; Efraim Halevy, *Man in the Shadows* (New York: St. Martin's Press, 2006), pp. 164–80.
43. Caspit and Kfir, pp. 265–66.
44. Ross, p. 298.
45. Ibid., pp. 301–22; "Protocol Concerning the Redeployment in Hebron," *Wikipedia*, accessed July 28, 2014.
46. Haim Misgav, *Conversations with Yitzhak Shamir* (New York: Talpiot, 2000), pp. 171, 204.
47. Rabinovich, pp. 106–07.

48. "Har Homa," *Wikipedia*, accessed July 31, 2014.
49. Ross, p. 333.
50. Rabinovich, p. 86. The interviews were with David Makovsky of the *Jerusalem Post* and Shimon Schiffer of *Yediot Ahronot* on May 10 and May 23, respectively.
51. Ibid., pp. 116–19; Landau, p. 318; Ross, pp. 328, 330.
52. Ross, pp. 362–63.
53. Ibid., p. 361.
54. Ibid.,, pp. 390–97, 339, 415, 420.
55. Charles Enderlin, *Shattered Dreams* (New York: Other Press, 2002), pp. 84–86.
56. Ross, p. 448.
57. Enderlin, *Shattered Dreams*, pp. 86, 88.
58. Ibid., p. 94.
59. Ross, pp. 455–57.
60. Enderlin, *Shattered Dreams*, pp. 95–96; Ross, p. 468. Ross gives the figures as 8 in favor, 4 against, and 5 abstentions.
61. Enderlin, *Shattered Dreams*, pp. 97–99; Ross, pp. 482, 487, 489.
62. Ross, pp. 462, 474.
63. Enderlin, *Shattered Dreams*, p. 102.
64. Ross, pp. 492–93.
65. Neill Lochery, *The Difficult Road to Peace: Netanyahu, Israel and the Middle East Peace Process* (Reading, UK: Ithaca, 1999) and Lochery, *Why Blame Israel* (London: Icon, 2006), p. 190 where he compares Netanyahu to Dayan and Sharon to Ben-Gurion.
66. Goodman, pp. 70–72.

Chapter Nine

1. Anita Miller, Jordan Miller and Sigalit Zetouni, *Sharon: Israel's Warrior-Politician* (Chicago: Academy Chicago, 2002), pp. 357, 363–64; Nir Hefez and Gadi Bloom, *Ariel Sharon* (New York: Random House, 2006), p. 358.
2. Mark Matthews, *Lost Years: Bush, Sharon and Failure in the Middle East* (New York: Nation Books, 2007),pp. 11–14, 18–23.
3. Landau, p. 366.
4. Freddy Eytan, *Ariel Sharon* (Paris: Studio 9, 2006), pp. 112–14; Hefez and Bloom, pp. 366–69.
5. Landau, pp. 370–71.
6. Hefez and Bloom, p. 371.
7. Uri Dan, *Ariel Sharon: An Intimate Portrait* (New York: Palgrave Macmillan, 2006), pp. 209–11.
8. Hefez and Bloom, pp. 392–4.
9. Eytan, p. 115; Hefez and Bloom, pp. 374–77; Dan, pp. 203–04; G. Sharon, p. 474.
10. Landau, pp. 398–99.
11. Hefez and Bloom, pp. 413–15; Landau, pp. 415, 417–18, 425.
12. Colin Shindler, *A History of Modern Israel* (New York: Cambridge University Press, 2008), pp. 326–32; Bernard Reich, *A Brief History of Israel* (New York: Checkmark Books, 2008), pp. 235–37; Landau, pp. 401, 437.
13. Landau, pp. 373–74.
14. On the Road Map see Aaron D. Miller, *The Much Too Promised Land* (New York: Bantam, 2008), pp. 73–74, 350–53; William B. Quandt, *Peace Process*, 3d ed. (Washington, D.C.: The Brookings Institution, 2005) Chapter 13, pp. 385–414; Hefez and Bloom, pp. 351–58; Eytan, pp. 135–43; G. Sharon, p. 563; Landau, pp. 443, 445, 447, 453.
15. Dan, pp. 206–08, 246–47; Landau, p. 402.
16. The author saw so many parallels between the two leaders that he wrote a double biography of the two leaders. He later decided not to get it published, but there was enough material for the biography. Sharon founded three political parties; Jackson was the main founder of the Democratic Party in the late 1820s along with Martin Van Buren. Jackson fought Indians around Nashville as a young attorney and militia member in the late 1780s. He later fought them in a second round during the Creek War of 1813–14, within the War of 1812. The third round was the First Seminole War of 1818. The fourth and final round was the Indian removal of the 1830s, which led to the Black Hawk War of 1832 when he was president and the Second Seminole War of 1835–42. Both started their military careers while teenagers.
17. Hefez and Bloom, pp. 425, 430.
18. The author wrote his doctoral dissertation partially on the Indaba.
19. Charles Enderlin, *The Lost Years: Radical Islam, Intifada, and Wars in the Middle East 2001–2006* (New York: Other Press, 2007), pp. 152–53.
20. Landau, pp. 483–84.
21. Dan, p. 216.
22. For a summary of the various affairs see Hefez and Bloom, pp. 400–12; Eytan, pp. 124–31; Landau, pp. 473–79.
23. G. Sharon, pp. 542–43.
24. Hefez and Bloom, pp. 435, 438–40; Eytan, p. 158.
25. Hefez and Bloom, pp. 441, 443; G. Sharon, pp. 556–57; Landau, p. 464.
26. G. Sharon, p. 551.
27. Hefez and Bloom, pp. 446, 449–50; Landau, pp. 485, 487–88.
28. Hefez and Bloom, pp. 451, 453.
29. Ibid., pp. 457, 459–61; Landau, pp. 503, 508.
30. Landau, p. 504.
31. Eating shellfish is against Jewish dietary

law. Ibid., pp. 461–62; Eytan, p. 163; Landau, p. 512.
32. Landaup. 490.
33. Hefez and Bloom, p. 463; Sylvain Cypel, *Walled: Israeli Society at an Impasse* (New York: Other Press, 2005), pp. 450–53; Enderlin, *The Lost Years*, p. 266; Mark Matthews, *Lost Years: Bush, Sharon and Failure in the Middle East* (New York: Nation Books, 2007), p. 388.
34. Hefez and Bloom, pp. 463–64.
35. Ibid., pp. 466–67; Enderlin, *The Lost Years* pp. 263–65.
36. Enderlin, *The Lost Years*, p. 264.
37. Hefez and Bloom, p. 469. Ramon's reward was to be appointed minister of justice in the new Kadima government in April 2006.
38. Ibid., pp. 471–72.
39. Ibid., pp. 472–73; Dan, pp. 275–76.
40. Hefez and Bloom, pp. 474, 476.
41. Ibid., pp. 478, 481–82; Eytan, pp. 218, 234–35. Sharon was 77—nearly 78, when he had the stroke. Only a handful of politicians in Israel have had political careers beyond age 80 among them Ben-Gurion and Peres. Sharon was probably severely cognitively impaired as a result of the stroke if not brain dead. Voters will not take a chance on a leader who had been in a coma for years before recovering. And now the party that he created barely exists anymore.
42. Hefez and Bloomp. 485; Livni founded her own party, which won six seats.
43. Karl Vick, "Ariel Sharon: Israel's Soldier and Strongman, 1928–2014," *Time* Jan. 11, 2014.
44. Landau, pp. 404–07.

Chapter Ten

1. Nir Hefez and Gadi Bloom, *Ariel Sharon* (New York: Random House, 2006), pp. 393–94; David Landau, *Arik: The Life of Ariel Sharon* (New York: Alfred Knopf, 2013), p. 423.
2. Hefez and Bloom, p. 458; Landau, p. 438; Ofira Seliktar, "The Israeli Economy," in Robert O. Freedman, ed., *Contemporary Israel* (Boulder: Westview, 2009), pp. 164–67, 170. This author is from Wisconsin and hence familiar with the Wisconsin Plan and with Gov. Tommy Thompson.
3. Hefez and Bloom, pp. 452–53; Landau, p. 491.
4. Landau, p. 511; Hefez and Bloom, p. 457.
5. "Israeli Legislative Election, 2006," *Wikipedia*, accessed Aug. 1, 2014. Shas had 299,054 votes to the Likud's 281, 996.
6. Ofir Abu, Fany Yuval and Guy Ben-Porat, "'All That is Left': The Demise of the Zionist Left Parties, 1992–2009," in Asher Arian and Michal Shamir, eds., *The Elections in Israel 2009* (New Brunswick, NJ: Transaction, 2011), pp. 41–68.
7. "Gaza War," *Wikipedia*, accessed Aug. 1, 2014.
8. Abraham Diskin, "The Likud: The Struggle for the Centre," in Sandler et al., pp. 51–68.
9. Ibid., p. 59.
10. Giora Goldberg, "Kadima Goes Back: The Limited Power of vagueness," in Shmuel Sandler, Manfred Gerstenfeld, and Hillel Frisch, eds., *Israel at the Polls, 2009* (New York: Routledge, 2011), pp. 31–50.
11. Einat Gadalya, Hanna Hertzog and Michal Shamir, "Tzipping Through the Elections: Gender in the 2009 Elections," in Arian and Shamir, eds., pp. 165–89.
12. "Israel legislative elections, 2009," *Wikipedia*, accessed Aug. 1, 2014; Hirsh Goodman, *The Anatomy of Israel's Survival* (New York: Public Affairs, 2011), pp. 208–09.
13. John B. Judis, *Genesis: Truman, American Jews and the Origins of the Arab-Israeli Conflict* (New York: Farrar, Straus and Giroux, 2014), pp. 364–65; Goodman, p. 174.
14. Judis, pp. 65–66; James Mann, *The Obamians* (New York: Viking, 2012), p. 324.
15. Beinart, pp. 123, 125, 127.
16. Judis, p. 367; Mann, p. 324; Josef Federman, "Netanyahu: No Settlement Freeze," *Huffington Post* Sept. 27, 2011; Goodman, pp. 178–81; Beinart, pp. 128–29, 132, 142.
17. Beinart, p. 139.
18. Ibid., pp. 143, 146, 147.
19. Judis, p. 368; Mann, p. 324.
20. Judis, pp. 370–71.
21. Mann, p. 325.
22. Idem. The quote is from Dennis Ross, "How to Break a Middle East Stalemate," *Washington Post* Jan. 8, 2012 p. B-3.
23. Mann, p. 325.
24. Beinart, pp. 137–38, 141, 143.
25. "Mavi Marmara," *Wikipedia*, accessed Aug. 1, 2014; Herb Kenon, "Netanyahu Apologizes to Turkey over Gaza flotilla," *Jerusalem Post* Mar. 22, 2013, online; "Danny Ayalon," *Wikipedia*, accessed Aug. 1, 2014.
26. Goodman, p. 170.
27. "Operation Pillar of Defense," *Wikipedia*, accessed Aug. 1, 2014.
28. Judis, pp. 372–73; Ben Birnbaum and Amir Tibon, "The Explosive Inside Story of How John Kerry Built an Israeli-Palestinian Peace Plan and Watched it Crumble," *The New Republic* July 20, 2014.
29. "Israel Legislative Elections 2013," *Wikipedia*, accessed Aug. 2, 2014.

30. Birnbaum and Tibon.
31. Goodman, pp. 207–08.; Ruth Margalit, "Hadar Goldin and the Hannibal Directive," *The New Yorker* Aug. 6, 2014.
32. Birnbaum and Tibon.
33. Connie Bruck, "Friends of Israel," *The New Yorker* Sept. 1, 2014.
34. Liel Leibovitz, "Soccer Thugs Burned Alive a Palestinian Boy in Jerusalem," *Tablet Magazine* July 7, 2014.
35. This is based on a daily reading of the Israeli media provided by the *News Nosh* service of journalist Orly Hfalperin for Americans for Peace Now and a daily watching of the international newscast of the BBC and PBS Newhour.
36. Ruth Eglash, "After Gaza Ceasefire, Israeli Prime Minister Netanyahu in Tough Spot at Home," *Washington Post* Aug. 28, 2014, online.
37. Jonathan Spyer, "Netanyahu's Long War Doctrine," *PJ Media* Aug. 5, 2014; David Rothkopf, "On Israel's Defeat in Gaza," *Foreign Policy* Aug. 7, 2014, online.
38. Bruck.

Chapter Eleven

1. For background on these various Fianna Fail politicians and the party itself see Stephen Collins, *The Power Game* (Dublin: The O'Brien Press, 2001) and Donal O'Shea, *80 Years of Fianna Fail* (Manlo: Castlebar, Co. Mayo, 2006).
2. "Micheal Martin" and "Brian Cowen," *Wikipedia*, accessed Aug. 2, 2014, for details. I used the English version of Martin's first name so as to not confuse my spell checker.
3. Under the Treaty of 1921 Northern Ireland could opt out of the Irish Free State if it exercised this right within a month. It did so and so the Dublin government never ruled over Northern Ireland.
4. On this see Thomas G. Mitchell, *Israel/Palestine and the Politics of a Two-State Solution* (Jefferson, NC: McFarland, 2013), pp. 128–30.
5. Sharon's memoirs seem to indicate that he at least understood French if he did not speak it. His other languages were Hebrew, Russian and English.
6. See Nadav G. Shelef, *Evolving Nationalism: Homeland, Identity, and Religion in Israel, 1925–2005* (Ithac: Cornell University Press, 2010), pp. 81–106 for details on this transformation of territorial goals in the Revisionist Movement.

Bibliography

Arens, Moshe. *Broken Covenant.* New York: Simon & Schuster, 1995.

Avner, Yehuda. *The Prime Ministers.* London: The Toby Press, 2010.

Bar-On, Mordecai. *Moshe Dayan: Israel's Controversial Hero.* New Haven: Yale University Press, 2012.

Bar-Zohar, Michael. *Facing a Cruel Mirror.* New York: Charles Scribner's Sons, 1990.

———. *Shimon Peres.* New York: Random House, 2007.

Bauer, Yehuda. *From Diplomacy to Resistance: A History of Jewish Palestine 1939–1945.* New York: Atheneum, 1973.

Beckerman, Gal. *When They Come for Us, We'll Be Gone: The Epic Struggle to Save Soviet Jewry.* Boston: Mariner, 2010.

Begin, Menachem. *White Nights: The Story of a Prisoner in Russia.* New York: Harper & Row, 1977.

Beinart, Peter. *The Crisis of Zionism.* New York: Times Books, 2012.

Bell, J. Bowyer. *Terror Out of Zion.* New York: Discus, 1978.

Benziman, Uzi. *Sharon: An Israeli Caesar.* New York: Adama, 1985.

Bethell, Nicholas. *The Palestine Triangle: The Struggle for the Holy Land, 1935–1948.* New York: G. P. Putnam's Sons, 1979.

Boykin, John. *Cursed Is the Peacemaker: The American Diplomat Versus the Israeli General, Beirut 1982.* Belmont, CA: Applegate Press, 2002.

Brian, Denis. *The Seven Lives of Colonel Patterson.* Syracuse: Syracuse University Press, 2008.

Caspit, Ben and Ilan Kfir. *Netanyahu: The Road to Power.* Secaucus, NJ: Carol, 1998.

Cesarani, David. *Major Farran's Hat.* Cambridge, MA: Da Capo Press, 2009.

Clarke, Thurston. *By Blood and Fire: The Attack on the King David Hotel.* New York: G.P. Putnam's Sons, 1981.

Cohen, Geula. *Woman of Violence.* New York: Holt, Rinehart and Winston, 1966.

Collins, Larry, and Dominique Lapierre. *O Jerusalem.* New York: Touchstone, 1972.

Dan, Uri. *Ariel Sharon: An Intimate Portrait.* New York: Palgrave Macmillan, 2006.

Dayan, Moshe. *Breakthrough.* New York: Alfred Knopf, 1981.

Eisenberg, Dennis, Uri Dan, and Eli Landau. *The Mossad—Inside Stories.* New York: Paddington Press, 1978.

Eliav, Yaacov. *Wanted.* New York: Shengold, 1984.

Enderlin, Charles. *The Lost Years: Radical Islam, Intifada, and Wars in the Middle East 2001–2006.* New York: Other Press, 2007.

———. *Shattered Dreams Dreams: The Failure of the Peace Process in the Middle East, 1995–2002* New York: Other Press, 2003.

_____. *Shamir*. Paris: O. Orban, 1991.
Eytan, Freddy. *Ariel Sharon*. Paris: Studio 9, 2006.
Frank, Gerold. *The Deed*. New York: Simon & Schuster, 1963.
Frankel, Glenn. *Beyond the Promised Land*. New York: Touchstone, 1996.
Freedman, Robert O., ed. *Contemporary Israel*. Boulder: Westview Press, 2009.
Golan, Zev. *Free Jerusalem*. Jerusalem: Devora, 2003.
_____. *Stern: The Man and His Gang*. Tel Aviv: Yair, 2011.
Goodman, Hirsh. *The Anatomy of Israel's Survival*. New York: Public Affairs, 2011.
Gordis, Daniel. *Menachem Begin: The Struggle for Israel's Soul*. New York: Schocken, 2014.
Haber, Eitan. *Menachem Begin: The Man and the Legend*. New York: Dell, 1978.
Efraim Halevy, *Man in the Shadows*. New York: St. Martin's Press, 2006.
Hefez, Nir. and Gadi Bloom. *Ariel Sharon: A Life*. New York: Random House, 2006.
Judis, John B. *Genesis: Truman, American Jews and the Origins of the Arab-Israeli Conflict*. New York: Farrar, Straus and Giroux, 2014.
Landau, David. *Arik: The Life of Ariel Sharon*. New York: Alfred Knopf, 2013.
Lochery, Neill. *The Difficult Road to Peace: Netanyahu, Israel and the Middle East Peace Process*. Reading, UK: Ithaca, 1999.
_____. *Why Blame Israel*. London: Icon, 2006.
Mann, James. *The Obamians*. New York: Viking, 2012.
Marton, Kati. *A Death in Jerusalem*. New York: Pantheon, 1994.
Matthews, Mark. *Lost Years: Bush, Sharon and Failure in the Middle East*. New York: Nation Books, 2007.
Medding, Peter Y. *The Founding of Israeli Democracy 1948–1967*. New York: Oxford University Press, 1990.
Medoff, Rafael. *Militant Zionism in America: The Rise and Impact of the Jabotinsky Movement in the United States, 1926–1948*. Tuscaloosa: University of Alabama Press, 2002.
Miller, Anita, Jordan Miller, and Sigalit Zetouni. *Sharon: Israel's Warrior Politician*. Chicago: Academy Chicago, 2002.
Misgav, Haim. *Conversations with Yitzhak Shamir*. New York Talpiot, 2000.
Netanyahu, Benjamin. *A Durable Peace: Israel and Its Place Among the Nations*. New York: Warner Books, 2000.
_____. *Fighting Terrorism: How Democracies Can Defeat Domestic and International Terrorism*. New York: Farrar, Straus and Giroux, 1996.
_____, ed. *Terrorism: How the West Can Win*. New York: Farrar, Straus and Giroux, 1986.
Netanyahu, Benzion. *The Founding Fathers of Zionism*. Noble, OK: Balfour Books, 2012.
Perlmutter, Amos. *The Life and Times of Menachem Begin*. Garden City, NY: Doubleday, 1987.
Peres, Shimon. *Ben-Gurion: A Political Life*. New York: Schocken, 2011.
Rabinovich, Itamar. *Waging Peace: Israel and the Arabs, 1948–2003*. Princeton: Princeton University Press, 2004.
Reinharz, Jehuda. *Chaim Weizmann: The Making of a Zionist Leader*. New York: Oxford University Press, 1985.
Ross, Dennis. *The Missing Peace*. New York: Farrar, Straus and Giroux, 2004.
Sachar, Howard M. *A History of Israel From the Rise of Zionism to Our Time*. New York: Alfred Knopf, 1996.
Shamir, Yitzhak. *Summing Up*. Boston: Little, Brown, 1994.
Shapira, Anita. *Israel: A History*. Waltham, MA: Brandeis University Press, 2012.
Sharon, Ariel. *Warrior*. New York: Simon & Schuster, 2001.
Sharon, Gilad. *Sharon: The Life of a Leader*. New York: HarperCollins, 2011.
Shavit, Yaacov (Jacob). *Jabotinsky and the Revisionist Movement, 1925–1948*. London: Frank Cass, 1988.
Shilon, Avi. *Menachem Begin: A Life*. New Haven: Yale University Press, 2012.
Shimoni, Gideon. *The Zionist Ideology*. Hanover, NH: Brandeis University Press, 1995.
Shindler, Colin. *The Land Beyond Promise: Israel, Likud and the Zionist Dream*. New York: I.B. Tauris, 2002.
_____. *The Triumph of Military Zionism: Nationalism and the Origins of the Israeli Right*. New York: I.B. Tauris, 2009.
Slater, Robert. *Rabin of Israel*. New York: St. Martin's Press, 1993.

Spiegel, Philip. *Triumph Over Tyranny.* New York: Devora, 2008.

Stanislawski, Michael. *Zionism and the Fin de Siecle.* Berkeley: University of California Press, 2001.

Temko, Ned. *To Win or to Die: A Personal Portrait of Menachem Begin.* New York: William Morrow, 1987.

Teveth, Shabtai. *Ben-Gurion: The Burning Ground, 1886–1948.* Boston: Houghton Mifflin, 1987.

Index

Abbas, Mahmoud (Abu Mazen) 139, 174, 179–81, 190–92, 195, 196, 199
Ahdut ha'Avoda 20, 48, 52, 53, 55, 81
Al-Aksa Intifada 145
Allon, Yigal 13, 46, 48, 52–53, 56, 58, 82, 130, 135, 167, 203, 209n10, 209n22
Altalena 40, 44–46, 59, 67
Arafat, Yasir 47, 108–9, 111, 142, 160, 179; and Begin 73, 75; and Netanyahu 153, 159, 161–63, 166, 170, 186; and Shamir 114, 175, 177; and Sharon 133, 138, 140, 141, 144–45, 168, 171–74
Arens, Moshe 72, 78, 104, 107, 116, 120–22, 131–32
Arlosoroff, Haim 17, 18

Barak, Ehud 13, 82, 132–33, 143–46, 149–50, 161–62, 167–68, 170, 173, 187, 190, 196, 199, 204
Begin, Aliza 30, 33, 40, 77–78, 80
Begin, Benjamin "Benny" 137, 153
Begin, Menahem: Altalena 44–46; arrested by NKVD 31; bombing of Iraqi reactor 71, 72; at Camp David 1978 66; character 80–81; childhood 26–27; comparison with Jabotinsky 55–56; death 80; declares Revolt 35–36; Deir Yassin 39, 43–44; elected prime minister 56–59; flees Warsaw to Vilna 30; forms Gahal 51–52; forms Herut Party 48; forms Likud 55, 56; German reparations 51; hanging of British sergeants 39, 43; as head of Herut 48–51; head of Polish Betar 30; invades Lebanon 1982 73–77; joins Anders army 33; joins Betar 26–27; joins the Etzel as commander 35; King David Hotel bombing 39, 41–42; legacy 81–83; marries 30; in National Unity Government 52–54; negotiations with Lehi and Hagana 38, 39; 1979–81 Interregnum 68–71; in Palestine 33–34; peace negotiations with Egypt 60–67; post-political life 78–80; reelected prime minister 1981 71–72; resigns as prime minister 77–78; rise in Betar 28–30; Saison 36–37, 38; settlement of West Bank 60, 61, 65, 69; in Soviet Gulag 31–33
Begin, Ze'ev Dov 26, 27
Ben-Gurion, David 2, 11, 16, 20, 38, 39, 44, 83, 88, 92, 97–99, 101, 108, 167, 198–99, 208n22, 215n65, 216n41; and Begin 44–46, 50–53, 55, 57, 66, 70, 81; and Jabotinsky 13, 17, 18–19, 25
Betar 12–15, 18, 21–26, 28–30, 33–35, 38
Bush, George H.W. 111, 114, 115, 117, 118, 119, 154, 190
Bush, George W. 168, 171–72, 174, 177, 180, 186, 189, 199

Carter, Jimmy 49, 62, 63, 65–68, 84, 86, 102, 117, 162, 184, 197, 202
Clinton, Bill 140–41, 162, 165–66, 191–93
Cohen, Geula 59, 67, 69, 88, 90, 101, 102, 119, 151, 153, 205
Cohen, Yehoshua 88, 89, 90, 96–97, 98

Dayan, Moshe 13, 45, 52–53, 57–59, 82, 96–97, 103, 107, 125–26, 129–31, 155,

167, 203, 209*n*22, 210*n*5; as foreign minister 60–67, 68–69, 70, 72, 103, 205
Democratic Movement for Change (Dash) 58, 61, 69, 71, 128, 187, 196

Egypt 9, 52, 54, 60–67, 68, 70–71, 77, 82, 92–93, 98, 99–101, 103, 108–9, 112, 114, 117, 126–28, 130, 138, 150, 181, 187, 193, 195, 197, 205, 212*n*58
elections (Israeli) 49–52, 97–98, 120; (1965) 52; (1969) 52, 53, 56; (1973) 55, 56; (1977) 54, 58–59, 60, 69, 83, 129; (1981) 70–72, 107; (1984) 79, 106–7; (1988) 107, 110, 134, 135, 153; (1992) 119, 120–21, 137, 155; (1996) 139, 158–60; (1999) 142–43, 167; (2001) 145–46; (2003) 172, 185; (2006) 178, 182, 183, 216*n*5; (2009) 183, 187–88; (2013) 183, 196
Eliav, Ya'acov 88, 92–94, 98
Eshkol, Levi 25, 52, 53, 57, 70, 132, 213*n*17
Etzel (Irgun Zvai Leumi) 7, 13–15, 19–23, 25, 28, 33–40, 42–47, 48–49, 51–52, 56, 60, 67, 75, 79, 80, 82, 85–92, 93–97, 102, 104, 122–25, 137, 153, 202, 208*n*38, 209*n*48, 211*n*5, 212*n*52

Fianna Fail (Ireland) 200–2
Friedman-Yellin, Natan 21, 22, 30, 33, 34, 37–39, 44, 47, 87–91, 97, 98, 122

Gahal (Gush Herut Liberalim) 51–52, 53, 54, 56, 81, 82, 107
Gaza 52, 60, 63–65, 82, 105, 108–9, 111, 114, 126–27, 129, 131, 138, 153, 166, 171, 173, 175, 176–81, 183–84, 188, 189
Golan Heights 73, 99, 106, 114, 118, 143, 159, 160, 163–64, 167, 198, 204
Golomb, Eliahu 11, 36, 88, 89, 93
Gush Emunim 64, 65, 106, 128

Hagana 7, 11–12, 20–21, 25, 36–40, 42–44, 48, 58, 78, 82, 85, 88–89, 92–93, 96, 124–25, 209*n*48
Harel, Isser 98–101
Herut Party 1, 24–25, 48–57, 59, 67, 71–72, 81–82, 97, 102–4, 107, 122–23, 129, 137, 143, 148, 150, 153, 187, 200, 202, 204, 205
Herzl, Theodor 2, 7–8, 13, 14, 25–26, 83, 147, 179, 207*n*3
Hussein, King 107, 108, 110, 114, 117, 130–31, 141–42, 162, 165, 205
Hussein, Saddam 71, 114, 133, 166, 195

Intifada 109–110
Iran 71, 81, 143, 171, 188, 192, 193, 194–95, 199
Iraq 34, 65, 71–73, 103, 114–16, 126, 129, 137, 166, 174, 197, 210*n*29

Jabotinsky, Vladimir "Ze'ev" 2, 26, 28, 34, 48, 49, 67, 83, 84, 100, 108, 147–48, 152–53, 156, 161, 184, 200, 203–5, 207*n*1, 207*n*2; becomes Zionist 7–8; and Begin 18, 22, 27, 28–30, 31, 38, 51, 55, 56, 59, 63, 68, 80, 82, 104, 202, 203; and Ben-Gurion 17, 18, 19, 39, 81; challenges facing 15–16; childhood 5–6; death 24–25; diplomacy of 14, 15, 16; founds Betar 12–13; founds Etzel 20–21; founds Hagana 7; founds Jewish Legion 9–11; founds Revisionist Party 13–14; and Holocaust 23; ideology of revisionists 13; imprisoned by British 12; legacy 25; literary career 7, 8–9, 20; and Peel Plan 19–20; and Stern 21–22; in United States 24–25
Jordan 11, 12, 16, 19, 25, 44, 50, 52, 60, 65, 73, 75, 76, 77, 82, 107–8, 111, 113–14, 117–18, 129

Kerry, John 195, 196, 199, 216*n*28
Kissinger, Henry 62, 116, 128, 162, 186

Labor Zionists 15, 17, 20, 25, 38, 53
Lebanon 73–76, 78, 80, 82, 103, 108–9, 118, 122, 130–31, 133, 138–39, 151, 153, 160, 175, 183, 184, 187
Lehi (Lohemei Herut Israel) 13, 18, 22, 25, 30, 34, 35, 36–38, 39, 42, 43, 46–48, 56, 75, 80, 82, 84–85, 86–98, 101, 102, 104, 122–24, 153, 209*n*50
Levy, David 59, 71, 104, 107, 111–12, 115–17, 120
Liberal Party 51, 52, 54–56, 71, 107, 135
Lieberman, Avigdor 155, 160–62, 170, 178, 187, 194, 196, 205
Likud 2, 202–4, 204–5; Princes 104, 120, 121, 150, 153, 155–56, 187, 201
Livni, Eitan 47, 51, 75, 82, 153
Livni, Tzipi 153, 183, 186–89, 196, 216*n*42
Lotz, Wolfgang 99–100

Mapai 16–18, 20, 37–39, 48, 52, 53, 72, 81, 99, 101, 124, 148
Maximalists (Brit haBiryonim) 16
Meir, Golda 17, 53–55, 57–58, 61, 63, 82, 101–2, 188

Index

Meretz 121, 141, 143, 145, 167, 173, 175, 180, 188
Meridor, Dan 78, 79, 115–16, 139, 153, 156, 158, 160, 163, 188
Meridor, Ya'akov 34, 35, 37, 40, 47, 52, 54, 75, 79, 94–95
Moledet 113, 117, 119
Mossad 61, 62, 71, 98–101, 102, 122–23, 141, 161–62, 203, 212n54

National Religious Party 52, 58–59, 61, 65, 68, 72, 146, 160, 168, 173, 194, 196
Netanyahu, Benjamin "Bibi" 1, 2, 25, 78, 81, 120–22, 142–43, 146; elected Likud leader 121, 137, 155; elected prime minister 158–60; elected prime minister (2009) 188–89; enters politics 1988 153; family and childhood 147–48; graduate studies 149–50; and Iran issue 194–95; leader of opposition 2006 182, 186–88; legacy 199; at Madrid conference 117, 155; marriages 150–51, 153–54; and Mavi Marmara 193–94; and Obama 189–93, 195–96; Operation Pillar of Smoke 195; Operation Protective Edge 197–98; opposition to Oslo 156–58; as prime minister (1996–99) 140–43, 160–67; reelected 2013–15 197–98; in Sayeret Matkal 148–49; and Shamir 121–22, 152, 155; and Sharon 131, 137, 138–41, 143, 158, 173, 174; in Sharon government 172, 177, 178, 185–86; 2000 decision not to run 144–45; at UN 152–53
Netanyahu, Benzion 23, 24, 147–48, 150–51
New Zionist Organization 14, 19, 147
Nixon, Richard 132, 199

Obama, Barack 189–92, 195, 197, 199

Paglin, Gideon "Giddy" 40, 42, 43, 47, 51, 65, 75, 82, 92
Palestine Liberation Organization (PLO) 71, 73–74, 75–76, 108, 110–14, 133, 135, 154, 180, 212n13
Patterson, John 9–12, 18, 24, 25, 148
Peres, Shimon 58, 59, 72–73, 79, 82, 103, 106–8, 110, 112, 113, 117, 120–21, 128, 131–33, 136, 137, 139, 152, 154, 158–61, 163–64, 168, 171–72, 179–80, 182, 184–85, 213n37, 216n41

Rabin, Yitzhak 13, 46, 48, 57, 58–59, 61, 65, 72–73, 80–82, 106–7, 110–13, 120–21, 125, 128–30, 132–33, 135, 137–39, 143, 156–59, 162, 164, 166, 173, 179, 199, 209n10, 209n22
Rafi 48, 52, 55, 99
Raziel, David 21, 34, 86
Reagan, Ronald 59, 72, 73, 75, 77, 78, 103, 108, 133, 135
Rice, Condoleeza 177, 191

Sadat, Muhammad Anwar as- 62–68, 70, 76–77, 80, 82, 130, 163, 205
Scheib, Israel (Eldad) 21, 22, 30, 31, 33, 34, 39, 44, 46–47, 86–91, 96, 97, 101, 102, 122–23
Shamir, Yitzhak 1, 2, 28, 56, 59, 61, 69, 72, 81; after Lehi 97–98; arrested (1946) 94; becomes prime minister 79, 104, 105–6; and Begin 85, 102–4, 116, 122; and Bernadotte murder 95–97; childhood 84; in Eritrea 94; escapes from detention 88; escapes from prison 94–95; in Etzel 1937–40 85; as foreign minister 70, 71, 76, 78, 103–4, 108; and George Bush 118, 119; Gulf War 114–16; joins Herut 54, 102–3; joins Stern 85–86; as Knesset speaker 103; legacy 122–23; as Lehi operations chief 89–94; and Levy 116–17, 120; Madrid Conference 116–18; Mossad activities 98–101; and Netanyahu 121–22; in Palestine 85; and Peres 107–8; as Prime Minister (1986–92) 79, 82, 108–21; Rabin-Shamir plan 111–13; reforms Lehi 88–89; in retirement 122; in rotation 106–7; and Sharon 106, 111–12, 115, 117, 120; Soviet Jewry activist 101–2; at university 85
Sharon, Ariel "Arik": as agricultural minister 129–30; childhood 124, 125; death 183; as defense minister 71–77, 130–31, 133; elected prime minister 145–46, 168; elected to Knesset 127; fired by Begin 78; as foreign minister 141–43; forms Kadima 181–82; forms Shlomzion 128–29; and Gaza disengagement 175–81; joins Hagana 125; joins Herut 129; leaves IDF and forms Likud 55–56, 127; legacy 183–84; as lesser minister 133–41; and Levy 104, 107, 111–12, 120–21, 132, 134, 139, 140, 143, 153, 170; and Netanyahu 137, 139, 140, 143, 153, 155, 158, 165, 172–74, 177–78, 182, 184; in 1948 war 125–

26; in 1956 war 126; in 1967 war 126; in 1973 war 127; and Rabin 128, 133, 138–39; as Rabin advisor 128–29; and Shamir 106, 107, 111–12, 115, 117, 120, 121; stroke 182–83; suppresses intifada 168–73; and Temple Mount walk 144–45
Shas 146, 159, 160, 161, 167, 168, 173, 183, 187, 189
Shinui 173, 179, 181, 182, 187, 196
Shultz, George 107, 108, 111, 135
Stavsky, Avram 17, 18, 45
Stern, Avraham (Yair) 21–23, 28, 33–36, 56, 82, 85–87, 89–91, 93, 102
Syria 52, 61–63, 65, 71, 73–76, 78, 89, 99, 103, 114, 117–18, 126, 129, 143–44, 151, 154, 163–64, 195, 197–98, 205, 210n41

Tamir, Shmuel 51–52, 55
Tehiya 59, 67, 69, 88, 90, 101, 102, 119, 151, 153, 205

Weizman, Ezer 54–56, 59–60, 64, 66, 67, 69–72, 102, 129, 130, 133, 142, 210n23, 212n13
Weizmann, Haim 2, 8, 9, 11, 13–17, 20, 38–39, 83, 92
Wye River Summit (1998) 141, 164, 166–67

Yellin-Mor, Natan *see* Friedman-Yellin

Zionism, Zionist Congresses 2, 8, 12, 13, 20, 22, 25–26, 31, 59, 61, 84, 91–92

www.ingramcontent.com/pod-product-compliance
Ingram Content Group UK Ltd.
Pitfield, Milton Keynes, MK11 3LW, UK
UKHW041950140426
5217IPUK00014B/724